WOMEN PLAYWRIGHTS
The Best Plays of 1996

EDITOR'S NOTE

Women Playwrights: The Best Plays of 1996 is the fifth volume in the Best Plays by Women Playwrights series initiated by Smith and Kraus in 1992.

Each year we consider plays, written by American Women, that have premiered during that year's theatrical season. Submissions are made on a continuous basis by playwrights, agents, literary managers, and theatres.

Next year's book, *Women Playwrights: The Best Plays of 1997,* will include plays that premiered between September 1, 1996 and August 31, 1997.

—*Marisa Smith*

Marisa Smith has edited

Women Playwrights: The Best Plays of 1992
Women Playwrights: The Best Plays of 1993
Women Playwrights: The Best Plays of 1994
Women Playwrights: The Best Plays of 1995
Women Playwrights: The Best Plays of 1996
Women Playwrights: The Best Plays of 1997

Act One Festival '95: The One-Act Plays
Act One Festival '95: The One-Act Plays

EST Marathon '94: The One-Act Plays
EST Marathon '95: The One-Act Plays
EST Marathon '96: The One-Act Plays
EST Marathon '97: The One-Act Plays

Humana Festival '93: The Complete Plays
Humana Festival '94: The Complete Plays
Humana Festival '95: The Complete Plays

WOMEN PLAYWRIGHTS
The Best Plays of 1996

CONTEMPORARY PLAYWRIGHTS
SERIES

SK
A Smith and Kraus Book

A Smith and Kraus Book
Published by Smith and Kraus, Inc.
PO Box 127, Lyme, NH 03768

Copyright ©1998 by Smith and Kraus
All rights reserved
Manufactured in the United States of America
Cover and Text Design by Julia Hill

First Edition: July 1998
10 9 8 7 6 5 4 3 2 1

The Library of Congress Cataloging-In-Publication Data
Women Playwrights: the best plays of 1996 / edited by Marisa Smith
   p. cm. — (Contemporary playwrights series)
ISBN 1-57525-111-6
1. American drama—women authors. 2. American drama—20th century. 3. Women—drama.
I. Smith, Marisa. II. Series: Contemporary playwrights series.
PS628.W6W668   1994
812'.540809287—dc20
ISSN 1067-327X   94-10071
          CIP

CONTENTS

INTRODUCTION

You can find plays by and about women at theatres all over the country. But sometimes you have to look a little harder for them. It is still true that women's words are not spoken as often as men's words on our stages. The work of women playwrights is not produced as much.

So it's a pleasure to find a group of plays by women collected in one volume. The reader can enjoy the particular voice of each writer, and the eclectic array of characters, settings, and ideas these plays offer. One comes away from this book enriched by the variety of the plays and heartened by the power of these women's words. And that's important, while we're still working to open our stages to a greater diversity of work.

The plays represent a broad, stimulating range of concerns and storytelling techniques: Theresa Rebeck's wry social commentary; Leslie Ayvazian's spot-on, loving attention to details of language and behavior; Mary Gallagher's perception of the mythic proportions of small-town life. Some of these writers choose to represent the world on stage as we see it every day—down to the last meal cooked or cell phone whipped out of a briefcase. Others choose to give it a little satirical spin or to create a whole new reality.

Linda Manning captures the life of Charlotte Brontë by imagining her struggle for creative achievement and personal fulfillment in delightfully theatrical terms. Jeannie Zusy portrays a contemporary New Yorker who needs to conceive a child to release the pain and creativity she holds inside.

Leslie Ayvazian reveals the celebratory spirit and deep, turbulent emotions within an Armenian-American family as a new generation comes to terms with its legacy of suffering and endurance.

Theresa Rebeck spins a modern morality tale about an idealistic heroine's odyssey through the seat of American power.

Mary Gallagher conveys the essence of yearning in her story about tragic love and thwarted dreams.

And yet I can't help looking for a common thread in these plays—maybe because as a "The best of 1996," they spring from approximately the same moment in time and may reveal something about our collective experience of that moment. Or maybe just because it's a fun exercise.

It strikes me that the protagonists, from a female novelist in 19th century England to a teenage girl in the Catskill Mountains, are all striving to break through barriers. Some of the limitations they face are self-imposed, others are external. Some are a product of the time or place in which they live, others have to do with their relationships to loved ones, or their deepest fears and self-doubts.

The writing in this book is lively and soulful. These playwrights offer us paths to discovery and understanding by playfully poking at our preconceptions, or pushing us to the edge of darkest grief. Read, enjoy, and then imagine them fully realized on the stage.

Kate Loewald
Director of Play Development
Manhattan Theatre Club

DO SOMETHING WITH YOURSELF!
The Life of Charlotte Brontë

by Linda Manning

TO MICHAEL

THE AUTHOR

Linda Manning is a writer, actor, and producer. She cofounded The Invisible Theatre in New York City. Her plays that have premiered there, in which she has also performed, include *DO SOMETHING WITH YOURSELF! The Life of Charlotte Brontë*, and an adaptation of Edgar Allan Poe's *The Fall of the House of Usher*. She has performed regionally, most notably at Trinity Repertory Company in Providence, Rhode Island, and at Germinal Stage Denver and The Changing Scene in Denver, Colorado. *DO SOMETHING WITH YOURSELF!* won Third Prize in the 1994 Center Theatre International Playwriting Contest, Chicago, Illinois, and Third Prize in the 1994 Great Platte River Playwrights' Festival at the University of Nebraska. In 1991 Linda received the Jane Chambers Playwriting Graduate Student Award for a compilation of material entitled *Writings on the Wall*. Linda most recently completed a writing fellowship at Ledig House International Writers' Colony, and is currently working on a new play about the life and times of a used truck salesman, and a memoir based on the life of her disabled sister. She is a member of The Dramatists Guild, AEA, and SAG.

This play contains excerpts from the novels, journal entries, and letters of Charlotte Brontë and others. They are footnoted where they appear in the script.

AUTHOR'S NOTE

I began writing this play as a vehicle for myself to perform in, and then it became much more. Charlotte's perseverance against the obstacles in her life (death of her mother and five siblings, persistent rejection by publishers, attractions to impossible men, serious doubts about her own ability) grabbed my interest in the first place, continually spurred me forward, and kept me involved with this play for four years. She was so very wonderfully human and not the expected cliché of the Victorian novelist. Yes, she toiled endlessly and alone on those bleak romantic English moors, but she also went after what she wanted, stumbled, made a fool of herself, got arrogant and righteous with her publisher, and kept writing those amazing novels where the character of individuals and their choices collided with the unpredictability of life's circumstances ending in a full, messy, honest portrait of life. She spoke her mind.

My goal with this play was to bring to life all her contradictions and complexities. I chose to write the play for one man to perform all the men because I love the magical transformation possible in live theatre where everything can change from one moment to the next. Men were a powerful force in Charlotte's life. From reading her novels it is clear she understood them, from reading the record she left of her life through her letters it is also clear she was thwarted, frustrated, and enthralled by them. Her desire to know a man intimately in the way that is only possible with a long, romantic relationship motivated much of what she did. It made sense to me that for an audience experiencing this play, and for Charlotte coming to life in the world of this particular play, her father is her brother is her teacher is her hero is her nemesis is her husband.

"Unless I have something of my own to say, and a way of my own to say it in, I have no business to publish. Unless I can look beyond the greatest Masters, and study Nature herself, I have no right to paint. Unless I can have the courage to use the language of Truth in preference to the jargon of Conventionality, I ought to be silent." Charlotte Brontë, 1848.

ORIGINAL PRODUCTION
DO SOMETHING WITH YOURSELF! The Life of Charlotte Brontë was first produced in a workshop production by The Invisible Theatre in August, 1993, at Studio Theatre in New York City with the following cast, and was again mounted with a full production in April, 1996, by The Invisible Theatre at the Miranda Theatre in New York City:

Charlotte Brontë. . . . . Linda Manning
All the men. . . . . Michael Pinney

Directed by Douglas Wagner. Original Music by Douglas Wagner with additional music from Steve Reich and The Art of Noise.

In the fall of 1994 this production toured the New England area, and in 1997 the production was toured in Colorado.

CHARACTERS

CHARLOTTE BRONTË: During the course of the play she ages from 22 to 38. She has a Northern English dialect. She is a brilliant, passionate, fiercely honest woman living in the restricted world of Victorian England. Her ambition and desire are in constant conflict with her powerful sense of responsibility and duty. (It is important when playing this character that she never see herself as a victim.)

The following characters are all played by one male actor:

PATRICK BRONTË: Charlotte's father. In his 60s and 70s during the course of the play. His dialect is Irish, tempered with a proper English education. He is a very private, sharp, opinionated man, but at the same time needy of Charlotte.

HENRY NUSSEY: Brother of Charlotte's good friend, Ellen. He is young, British and quite confident.

MONSIEUR HEGER: Charlotte's instructor in Brussels. He is 35 and Belgian, provoking, intellectual, and sexy.

ROBERT SOUTHEY: Poet Laureate, uptight, aristocratic, very British, and self-important.

ARTHUR NICHOLLS: The town curate and Charlotte's husband. He is in his 30s and is Irish. He is a kind, gentle, straightforward man. He is intelligent and perceptive and cares deeply for Charlotte from the moment he first sees her.

EDWARD ROCHESTER: The hero of Charlotte's novel *Jane Eyre*. He has a proper English dialect and is in his early 40s. He is a brooding, powerful, stunning, sensual man—the embodiment of the Victorian romantic hero.

REVIEWERS: Five different people, all British.

BRANWELL BRONTË: Charlotte's younger brother. He is in his late twenties and has the same dialect as Charlotte. He is smart, sarcastic and extremely depressed and angry as he has not become the famous artist he had hoped to be. He is a drunk and an opium addict coming to the end of his life and therefore falling apart psychologically and emotionally.

GEORGE SMITH: Charlotte's publisher. He is 25 years old and has a very proper upper-class, educated English dialect. He is an ambitious, successful, outgoing businessman. He cares for Charlotte, but he cares mostly about the success of her novels.

JAMES TAYLOR: A member of Charlotte's publishing firm. He is Scottish, middle-aged and dumpy. He is enthralled with Charlotte.

DO SOMETHING WITH YOURSELF!

The Life of Charlotte Brontë

ACT I

This play is to be performed by a man and a woman, the man will play all the male characters. In some moments the male actor transforms instantaneously from one character to another, therefore the differentiation of his characters should be done physically and vocally rather than with costumes. (Minor costume pieces can be used to differentiate characters if the use of them does not interrupt the action.) The style of DO SOMETHING WITH YOURSELF! is episodic and expressionistic. Although the true story of Charlotte Brontë's life is at the center of this work, the play is not a historical documentary.

The actress playing Charlotte wears traditional Victorian underwear, camisole and bloomers, and a long burgundy skirt. She should be barefoot with her hair hanging loosely down. The male actor wears heavy work pants, boots and a long knotted cravat around his neck. He is bare-chested. As stated above he may quickly put on a shirt or jacket to differentiate character.

The set consists of a large desk that will stand on its end and become a huge book, a plain wooden chair, a wooden pushcart on wheels that also functions as a writing desk, a rolling office chair (used by Mr. Brontë somewhat like a wheelchair), a very tall stack of miniature-size journals suspended from the ceiling on a rope, a large clear glass washbasin on the floor with a little water and a rag in it, and a small brightly colored platform that has a standing microphone on it (to be used by George Smith and all the suitors who propose to Charlotte). Upstage hangs a long black riding cloak. There are prop tables for small hand props stage right and left so they are easily accessible to the actors, and noticeable to the audience. The actress playing Charlotte wears a body microphone so her most internal speeches/letters will have the amplified sound of intimate speech on a microphone. Both actors remain on stage during the entire play.

The action begins in the year 1838 when Charlotte is twenty-two years old.

CHARLOTTE: *(She speaks to the audience.)* All this day I have been in a dream half-miserable and half-ecstatic miserable because it showed in the vivid light of reality the ongoings of the infernal world. I have been toiling for nearly an hour with Miss Lister, Miss Marriott, and Ellen Cook striving to teach them the distinction between an article and a substantive. The parsing lesson was completed, a dead silence had succeeded it in the schoolroom and I sat sinking from irritation and weariness into a kind of lethargy. The thought came over me am I to spend all the best part of my life in this wretched bondage, forcibly suppressing my rage at the idleness the apathy and the hyperbolical and most asinine stupidity of those fat-headed oafs and on compulsion assuming an air of kindness, patience, and assiduity? Must I from day to day sit chained to this chair prisoned within these four bare walls, while these glorious summer suns are burning in heaven and the year is revolving in its richest glow and declaring at the close of every summer's day the time I am losing will never come again? Stung to the heart with these reflections I started up and mechanically walked to the window... I shut the window and went back to my seat. Then came on me rushing impetuously, all the mighty phantasms that Branwell and I had conjured from nothing to a system strong as some religious creed. I felt as if I could have written gloriously—I longed to write. If I had time to indulge it I felt that the vague sensations of that moment would have settled down into some narrative better at least than anything I ever produced before. But just then a Dolt came up with a lesson. I thought I should have vomited.[1]

(Mr. Brontë enters rolling on in his office chair. He is carrying a large pistol. He periodically aims and fires the pistol into the air. It makes no sound, but he says "Bang" every time he fires and seems to be shooting at something.)

MR. BRONTË: Charlotte! What are you doing home?

CHARLOTTE: I'm home for the holiday Father, I missed you.

MR. BRONTË: Did Miss Wooler allow you to go?

CHARLOTTE: Where are Emily and Anne?

MR. BRONTË: They are out with the dogs. Did Miss Wooler allow you to go or did you quit like Emily?

CHARLOTTE: Miss Wooler felt it was important that I come home.

MR. BRONTË: Why?

CHARLOTTE: I haven't felt well. I've been quite sick actually. I didn't want to worry you, so I didn't mention it in my letters. I caught a cold and it went into my chest, I was coughing and coughing this horrendous cough, my chest got very tight, you know how it does...

MR. BRONTË: You're not going back are you?

CHARLOTTE: Papa...

MR. BRONTË: Charlotte.

CHARLOTTE: I hate teaching. I'm suffocating there.

MR. BRONTË: Charlotte, your brother is home.

CHARLOTTE: What?

MR. BRONTË: He came home a week after he left for London.

CHARLOTTE: What happened?

MR. BRONTË: Branwell showed his paintings, his drawings to the Director at the Royal Academy, and they didn't let him in.

CHARLOTTE: Oh, Father.

MR. BRONTË: But he stayed in London for a week and spent all the money we gave him.

CHARLOTTE: On what!?

MR. BRONTË: He said the only reason he came home was because he ran out of money.

CHARLOTTE: How could he spend all of that in a week?

MR. BRONTË: Whiskey is expensive.

CHARLOTTE: He couldn't drink that much whiskey in a week.

MR. BRONTË: In London taverns my dear there are other things to spend money on besides drink. Charlotte...what are you going to do with yourself?

CHARLOTTE: What do you mean?

MR. BRONTË: With your life?

CHARLOTTE: Live here with you, take care of you, make myself useful, of course.

MR. BRONTË: Prepare yourself Charlotte, prepare yourself for the worst. *(He aims and fires the gun.)* Bang! It's going to come, you can be ready or you can be slapped down by it.

CHARLOTTE: Well being a governess is the worst, I've arrived. I want...

MR. BRONTË: Bang! We all have a duty in this life, a sacred duty, to achieve our potential. Anything less than our absolute best is not acceptable.

CHARLOTTE: I know...that's why I want...I want to do the right thing with my life. I don't want to waste it.

MR. BRONTË: Only God knows what the right thing is my dear. You must teach.

That's how you'll earn a living. Go back to Miss Wooler's and learn to be a great teacher! Bang!

(The male actor discards Mr. Brontë's pistol, and becomes Henry Nussey. He holds a sign which says "Proposal Number One. Henry Nussey, brother of Charlotte's close friend, Ellen Nussey". He plays the following proposal on the small platform that has a standing microphone and proclaims himself to the audience very presentationally.)

MR. NUSSEY: Dear Miss Brontë, it was a pleasure to have you as a guest in our home. I'm sorry your experience at Miss Wooler's school was not more satisfying, but I know my beloved sister Ellen enjoyed the opportunity to nurse you back to good spirits. I trust your return trip to Haworth went safely. I am writing to you as I have recently become curate of Donnington in Sussex. Within a month I will be comfortably settled there, my health is much improved from the last time you saw me, and it is my intention to take pupils on very soon. I shall need a wife to help in the education of these pupils, and I cordially ask you to fill that position. Quite sincerely, Henry Nussey.

CHARLOTTE: *(Charlotte also faces out.)* Dear Mr. Nussey, thank you very much for your kind words as to my visit to Brookroyd. In terms of the other matter, I cannot marry you as I have not, and could not have, that intense attachment which would make me willing to die for you, and, if I ever marry, it must be in that light of adoration that I will regard my husband. Cordially, Charlotte Brontë.[2]

(The male actor dejectedly drops Nussey's sign and steps down from the platform. The lights change and Charlotte is suddenly thrown into a strange new room. She awaits her first meeting with Heger. He is very French, and he interrogates her by holding a spotlight on her face and moving it across various parts of her body.)

HEGER: Miss Brontë? Monsieur Constantin Heger. You call me Monsieur. Your place…before…was with a Miss Wooler?

CHARLOTTE: Yes.

HEGER: At an institution…Roe Head?

CHARLOTTE: Yes.

HEGER: Why did you quit it?

CHARLOTTE: My sisters and I are…

HEGER: You come here to Brussels to strengthen your education, so that you and your sisters can open your own school in Haworth, in England. You are from Haworth?

CHARLOTTE: Yes.

HEGER: It is only for this that you continue to study, Miss Brontë?

CHARLOTTE: Well, yes.

HEGER: So you want to be a...governess?

CHARLOTTE: I'm afraid I don't understand.

HEGER: Of course you do not understand. You do as all the English girls with
　　no wealth and no beauty do, you become a governess, like sheep you
　　become governess. You are not thinking for yourself. If you seek an
　　authentic education, you must learn to think.

CHARLOTTE: Yes, sir. Monsieur.

HEGER: For the moment, since you are older than most students here, and you
　　know English well, I will make you teach the, uh, the nuances to the
　　younger girls. Reassure yourself. You will still have plenty of time for your
　　own studies, and you will be paid for your work. There it is.

　　(Charlotte begins to leave.)

HEGER: Again, one thing, you will join my wife and me and our children this
　　evening for dinner. You may go.

　　*(Charlotte crosses to the pushcart that has a large open book attached to it that
　　enables it to double as a writing desk. During the next monologue she moves
　　the cart/writing desk across the stage as she writes in the book. The push-
　　cart/writing desk throughout the play is a literal symbol of the effort Charlotte
　　expends writing.)*

CHARLOTTE: Something of daylight still lingered, and the moon was waxing
　　bright: I could see him plainly. His figure was enveloped in a riding cloak,
　　fur collared, and steel clasped; its details were not apparent, but I traced the
　　general points of middle height, and considerable breadth of chest. He had
　　a dark face, with stern features and a heavy brow; his eyes and gathered eye-
　　brows looked ireful and thwarted just now; he was past youth, but had not
　　reached middle age; perhaps he might be thirty-five. I felt no fear of him,
　　and but little shyness. Had he been a handsome, heroic-looking young
　　gentleman, I should not have dared to stand thus questioning him against
　　his will, and offering my services unasked. I had hardly ever seen a hand-
　　some youth; never in my life spoken to one. I had a theoretical reverence
　　and homage for beauty, elegance, gallantry, fascination; but had I met
　　those qualities incarnate in masculine shape, I should have known instinc-
　　tively that they neither had nor could have sympathy with anything in me,
　　and should have shunned them as one would fire, lightning, or anything
　　else that is bright but antipathetic.[3]

　　(She is interrupted by Heger who carries his light.)

HEGER: Have you made a walk, Miss Brontë?

CHARLOTTE: No, Monsieur.

HEGER: The garden is resplendent. Will you accompany me?

(*They stroll across the stage as in a garden, in unison, using very specific chore-ographed steps.*)

CHARLOTTE: Do you want to speak to me about something?

HEGER: I want, very much, that you give me particular English lessons.

CHARLOTTE: Sir?

HEGER: I know the language, but not as well as you.

CHARLOTTE: As you wish.

HEGER: We will start tomorrow, in the afternoon, after classes.

CHARLOTTE: Is that all then?

HEGER: Yes. No. There is something else. Your work, not schoolwork, but the work of the tales that you started with your brother…ah…

CHARLOTTE: Branwell.

HEGER: Yes, that is it, Branwell. The tales that you have begun together years ago…the tale that you gave to me is the most recent?

CHARLOTTE: Yes.

HEGER: You have written it without your brother?

CHARLOTTE: Yes. Branwell and I started these stories together, but we actually haven't written together for about ten years. I continued on in my vein, and I'm not really sure if he's kept up with his.

HEGER: I do not know how too much to say this Charlotte… I want to be very honest. I debate whether to say anything. But in the measure that my opinion would be useful for you…

CHARLOTTE: It is worth a great deal to me Monsieur.

HEGER: In this measure…You are extraordinary girl. I regard this simple, plain face and I…I am full.

CHARLOTTE: Monsieur?

HEGER: Since so many, many Springs I sit in this garden, amazed by the power of God that is in every tree and every…luscious flower, but on this day of Spring in this garden where I am sitting since so many, many times, I am again amazed by the power of God. I do not see the flowers, I see you. God has given me a gift. He has brought you to me. You do not know yet what you have done, or what you will do. He is mysterious, I do not understand. He has chosen this young girl and rendered her so powerful, like a man. While you are my student, I want you to write. I want you to write day and night, every moment you are free, I want you to write.

CHARLOTTE: Yes. Monsieur.

HEGER: Do not speak. Put yourself to your work. I want to read everything.

(Charlotte crosses to her partially completed canvas on the back wall and paints. Heger enters, his English is much better.)

HEGER: Am I interrupting? *(He is holding a manuscript and his light.)*

CHARLOTTE: No. Monsieur Heger.

HEGER: How is your writing going?

CHARLOTTE: Poorly.

HEGER: What are you working on?

CHARLOTTE: A portrait…

HEGER: May I look?

CHARLOTTE: No!

HEGER: I know you have not enjoyed teaching Charlotte, but it is this that has made it possible for you to afford staying here…

CHARLOTTE: I don't mind teaching.

HEGER: …for two years…for two years I have tried to help you. I have watched over you. I have known you for two years Charlotte.

CHARLOTTE: I don't mind teaching. I particularly enjoyed our English lessons.

HEGER: Why did you give my wife your letter of resignation?

CHARLOTTE: She showed it to you?

HEGER: Of course.

CHARLOTTE: Already?

HEGER: Answer me!

CHARLOTTE: When I first came here I felt welcome.

HEGER: What are you saying?

CHARLOTTE: My family…I should be getting back.

HEGER: That is why you are leaving?

CHARLOTTE: The time period we agreed to is over.

HEGER: That is why you are leaving? *(Silence.)* I have finished reading your man-uscript. *(He drops it.)* You are not expressing yourself. The language is artful, but much too controlled.

CHARLOTTE: I don't know what has happened to me, I feel distracted and when I write, what I want to say is not there.

HEGER: And you think you can no longer benefit from my instruction?

CHARLOTTE: No.

HEGER: You think you have achieved your potential as a writer?

CHARLOTTE: You have given me a great deal Monsieur.

HEGER: Then tell me the truth.

CHARLOTTE: You've left me alone for six months. This is the first time you have come to my room and spoken to me face to face. You address me during lessons only when you have to. You read my compositions, write your notes, and leave them silently on my desk when I am not there. During the summer holiday you left me alone in this house, for two months, without a soul to talk to. I walked the streets just to be with people. I missed you.

HEGER: So you will return to Haworth. Live in the country. Perhaps teach.

CHARLOTTE: I came here to get the skills to teach.

HEGER: And is that still what you want?

CHARLOTTE: I want many things.

HEGER: You are a writer, Charlotte.

CHARLOTTE: I didn't know that until I met you. I don't know what I'm suppose to do now.

HEGER: May I have this? *(Referring to her canvas.)*

CHARLOTTE: It's not finished…

HEGER: You will stay through the holiday then?

CHARLOTTE: If you insist.

HEGER: It is up to you. You are a free woman.

CHARLOTTE: I am completely trapped.

HEGER: So am I.

CHARLOTTE: May I write to you?

HEGER: I cannot promise you anything Charlotte.
> *(He stands offstage right slowly tearing up large pieces of paper during the next speech. Charlotte writes at her cart/writing desk.)*

CHARLOTTE: Dear Monsieur. Mr. Taylor has returned from Brussels. I asked him if he had a letter for me.

HEGER: No; nothing.

CHARLOTTE: Patience, said I—his sister will be here soon. Miss Taylor has returned.

HEGER: I have nothing for you, neither letter nor message.

CHARLOTTE: It has been one year Monsieur since I left. Day and night I find neither rest nor peace. If I sleep I am disturbed by tormenting dreams in which I see you, always severe, always grave, always incensed against me. Forgive me then, Monsieur, if I adopt the course of writing to you again. How can I endure life if I make no effort to ease its sufferings? I know you will be irritated when you read this letter. All I know is, that I cannot, that I will not, resign myself to lose wholly the friendship of my master. I would rather suffer the greatest physical pain than always have my heart lacerated by smarting regrets. If my master withdraws his friendship from me entirely, I shall be altogether without hope; if he gives me a little—just a little—I shall be satisfied—happy; I shall have a reason for living on, for working. You showed me of yore a little interest, when I was your pupil in

Brussels, and I hold on to the maintenance of that little interest—I hold on to it as I would hold on to life. You will tell me perhaps—"I take not the slightest interest in you, Mademoiselle Charlotte. You are no longer an inmate of my house; I have forgotten you." Well, Monsieur, tell me so frankly. It will be a shock to me. It matters not. It would be less dreadful than uncertainty. I shall not reread this letter. I send it as I have written it. One suffers in silence so long as one has the strength so to do, and when that strength gives out one speaks without too carefully measuring one's words. I wish Monsieur happiness and prosperity! C.B.[4]

(Southey enters, wearing sunglasses, languidly applauding Charlotte's letter.)

SOUTHEY: My dear Miss Brontë?

CHARLOTTE: Mr. Southey!

SOUTHEY: In response to your letter and poems that you sent me, you evidently possess, and in no inconsiderable degree, what Wordsworth calls "the faculty of verse". You should not, however, be encouraged to high hopes as there are nowadays so many poets writing. Whoever, therefore, is ambitious of distinction in this way ought to be prepared for disappointment. Literature cannot be the business of a woman's life, and it ought not to be. The more she is engaged in her proper duties, the less leisure will she have for it, even as an accomplishment and a recreation. To those duties you have not yet been called, and when you are you will be less eager for celebrity. The daydreams in which you habitually indulge are likely to induce a distempered state of mind; and in proportion as all the ordinary uses of the world seem to you flat and unprofitable, you will be unfitted for them without becoming fitted for anything else. Write poetry for your own private use, and not with a view to celebrity...so written, it is wholesome both of the heart and soul; it may be made the surest means, next to religion, of soothing the mind, and elevating it. You may embody in it your best thoughts and your wisest feelings, and in so doing discipline and strengthen them.[5]

(Long quiet pause as Southey/the male actor recedes to the background. Charlotte speaks to the audience.)

CHARLOTTE: I shall be thirty-one next birthday. What have I done these last thirty years? Precious little.[6] I've been thinking a great deal lately about leaving Haworth, and finding another situation in Paris. Perhaps now is the time. After all, I am a trained governess, that is something. I mentioned it to both my sisters Anne and Emily and they are silent. I have no employment here, we were not able to find enough pupils to make our own school a reality. No one wants to send their children to this desolate place. My French is good enough, I could obtain a situation in Paris.

(Nicholls enters carrying an old, tattered traveling bag overflowing with everything he owns, i.e., clothes, pots and pans, his Bible, some tools, and so forth.)

CHARLOTTE: A stalwart form, a massive head,

> A firm determined face,
>
> Black Spanish locks, a sunburnt cheek,
>
> A brow high, broad and white...[7]

NICHOLLS: Excuse me? *(The contents of his bag clank when he sets it down.)*

CHARLOTTE: Who are you?

NICHOLLS: I'm sorry, I didn't mean to startle you. I'm Arthur Bell Nicholls, the new curate.

CHARLOTTE: Yes?

NICHOLLS: I was looking for your father.

CHARLOTTE: Do you often enter other people's homes unwelcomed and unannounced?

NICHOLLS: I beg your pardon. Your father instructed me to come and meet with him at this hour, he suggested I enter freely. I did knock.

CHARLOTTE: I didn't hear you. He is in his room across the hall.

NICHOLLS: Your name is Charlotte.

CHARLOTTE: Yes.

NICHOLLS: Are you a writer? I heard you reciting some verse when I came in.

> *(He looks at what is written on Charlotte's pushcart/writing desk.)*

CHARLOTTE: I suppose you find that amusing in a woman.

NICHOLLS: No. Not at all. *(Pause.)* Shall I collect your father?

CHARLOTTE: If that is what he asked you to do.

NICHOLLS: Good day.

CHARLOTTE: Good-bye.

> *(Charlotte seats herself behind the large desk that is covered with a plain tablecloth that goes to the floor, and speaks to the audience.)*

CHARLOTTE: My sister has written a novel. *(She throws off the tablecloth to expose the table that is a huge book. On the cover of the book that is also the top of the desk "Wuthering Heights by Ellis Bell" is printed.)* She calls it "Wuthering Heights". *(Charlotte throws open the cover of the book so that the hinged cover and pages fly open downstage toward the audience.)* My sister Emily (Ellis Bell, it is wise to be thought of as a man, I suppose), Emily doesn't seem to need people. In fact she prefers solitude. She expresses herself in her writing and is not troubled with the consequences. She has an original mind. She has allowed her natural impulses to guide her...and this book is frightening, shocking really, but wonderful. No woman that has ever lived has written such a book as this, and none ever will. *(Charlotte closes the cover of the book.)* I am a writer also.

(Charlotte crosses to the suspended miniature journals. The male actor cuts off the knot in the bottom of the rope and the books scatter on the floor.)

CHARLOTTE: These are my journals and books. *(Charlotte gathers a few up in her arms or skirt and shows them to the audience.)* I have been writing adamantly, diligently and tirelessly for over fifteen years now in the hopes of producing a great novel, the work of art that will change the literary world forever. People will read my book and gasp and sigh and wonder what kind of a person wrote it because it will contain the barest, simplest Truth. I will capture that in a novel, and it will be undeniable, and for the first time the world will know who I truly am.

(Black out. Next is a series of four separate tableaus of Charlotte and the big book. The lights come up on the following and black out between each one: 1) Charlotte lifting one end of the desk/book; 2) desk/book sitting on its end with Charlotte balancing on top of it; 3) desk/book cover is now facing directly down stage and Charlotte lies on the ground in front of it; 4) Charlotte rips off the Wuthering Heights cover to expose the real book cover that says "Jane Eyre by Currer Bell". She opens the book in triumph. Mr. Brontë rolls in on his office chair, aiming and firing his pistol. Charlotte jumps up and down in front of her creation.)

MR. BRONTË: Bang! Bang! Bang! Charlotte!

CHARLOTTE: Papa I've been writing a book.

MR. BRONTË: Charlotte, bring me my tea.

CHARLOTTE: Papa I've been writing a book.

MR. BRONTË: Have you my dear? Bang!

CHARLOTTE: But Papa I want you to look at it.

MR. BRONTË: I can't be troubled to read manuscripts.

CHARLOTTE: But it is printed. The title is Jane Eyre.

MR. BRONTË: I hope you have not been involving yourself in any silly expense.

CHARLOTTE: I think I shall gain some money by it.

MR. BRONTË: I'll be in my room.[8] *(He rolls away.)*

CHARLOTTE: *(Charlotte opens the front cover and steps inside the book to talk to the audience.)* Mr. Edward Rochester has fallen hopelessly in love with Miss Jane Eyre. *(She then sets down the desk/book so it can function again as a desk.)* Rochester has gotten himself into something that is bigger than he thought.

ROCHESTER: Jane!

(All the lights black out. There is a thunder clap and a quick burst of light [lightning] that illuminates Rochester's entrance. He is wearing the riding cloak that was hanging upstage. The moment is meant to be extremely theatrical and stereotypically romantic in the best sense. It will elicit laughter.)

CHARLOTTE: Mr. Rochester!

ROCHESTER: Miss Eyre.

CHARLOTTE: No. I'm sorry, you have me confused with…

ROCHESTER: Miss Eyre. Come to the fire.

(He puts her in a chair. Charlotte looks around. She has been transported to a beautiful drawing room.)

ROCHESTER: You have been a resident in my house three months?

CHARLOTTE: Yes, sir.

ROCHESTER: And you came from—?

CHARLOTTE: From Lowood school, in Colchester.

ROCHESTER: Ah! a charitable concern. How long were you there?

CHARLOTTE: Eight years.

ROCHESTER: Eight years! you must be tenacious of life. I thought half the time in such a place would have done up any constitution! No wonder you have rather the look of another world. I marveled where you had got that sort of face. Who are your parents?

CHARLOTTE: I have none.

ROCHESTER: Nor ever had, I suppose: Do you remember them?

CHARLOTTE: No.

ROCHESTER: I thought not. Well, if you disown parents you must have some sort of kinsfolk: uncles and aunts?

CHARLOTTE: No; none that I ever saw. *(She slips off her skirt and plays the rest of the scene as a coquettish girl in her camisole and bloomers. Not necessarily what Jane would do, but Charlotte feels the freedom of becoming her heroine.)*

ROCHESTER: And your home?

CHARLOTTE: I have none.

ROCHESTER: Where do your brothers and sisters live?

CHARLOTTE: I have no brothers and sisters.

ROCHESTER: Who recommended you to come here?

CHARLOTTE: I advertised and Mrs. Fairfax answered.

(Pause.)

ROCHESTER: Miss Eyre, have you ever lived in a town?

CHARLOTTE: No, sir.

ROCHESTER: Have you seen much society?

CHARLOTTE: None but the pupils and teachers at Lowood; and now the inmates of Thornfield.

ROCHESTER: Have you read much?

CHARLOTTE: Only such books as came in my way; and they have not been numerous or very learned.

ROCHESTER: You have lived the life of a nun: No doubt you are well drilled in religious forms; Brocklehurst, who I understand directs Lowood, is a parson, is he not?

CHARLOTTE: Yes, sir.

ROCHESTER: And you girls probably worshiped him, as a convent full of religieuses would worship their director?

CHARLOTTE: Oh, no.

ROCHESTER: You are very cool! No! What! A novice not worship her priest! That sounds blasphemous.

CHARLOTTE: I disliked Mr. Brocklehurst; and I was not alone in the feeling. He is a harsh man; at once pompous and meddling; he cut off our hair; and for economy's sake bought us bad needles and thread, with which we could hardly sew.

ROCHESTER: And was that the head and front of his offending?

CHARLOTTE: He starved us when he had the sole superintendence of the provision department, before the committee was appointed; and he bored us with long lectures once a week, and with evening readings from books of his own inditing, about sudden deaths and judgments, which made us afraid to go to bed.

ROCHESTER: What age were you when you went to Lowood?

CHARLOTTE: About ten.

ROCHESTER: And you stayed there eight years; you are now, then eighteen? *(She nods "yes".)*

ROCHESTER: Arithmetic, you see, is useful; without its aid I should hardly have been able to guess your age. It is a point difficult to fix where the features and countenance are so much at variance as in your case. And now what did you learn at Lowood? Can you play?

CHARLOTTE: A little.

ROCHESTER: Of course, that is the established answer. Adele showed me some sketches this morning, which she said were yours. I don't know whether they were entirely of your doing: Probably a master aided you?

CHARLOTTE: No, indeed!

ROCHESTER: Ah! that pricks pride. Well, fetch me your portfolio, if you can vouch for its contents being original; but don't pass your word unless you are certain: I can recognize patchwork.

CHARLOTTE: Then I will say nothing and you shall judge for yourself, sir.[9]

(Charlotte crosses upstage to her canvas. Meanwhile Rochester discards his cloak leaving it open to show the letter that is in the pocket. He walks away. Charlotte turns around and is propelled back to her own reality, she sees the letter, and reads it.)

MR. BRONTË: Charlotte…Charlotte, come in my room. It's time to read. Charlotte do you hear me?

CHARLOTTE: *(She quickly disposes of Rochester's cloak and puts her skirt back on.)* Yes…I…

MR. BRONTË: What have you got there?

CHARLOTTE: A letter from my publisher.

MR. BRONTË: Who?

CHARLOTTE: My publisher Father. Mr. George Smith of Smith, Elder & Co. As I told you before Father, I sent them my manuscript of *Jane Eyre* in August and they agreed to publish it.

MR. BRONTË: Yes. Bang!

CHARLOTTE: He sent me something.

MR. BRONTË: Well what for God's sake?

CHARLOTTE: Reviews of the book.

MR. BRONTË: Reviews?

CHARLOTTE: Yes.

MR. BRONTË: Magazine reviews and such.

CHARLOTTE: Yes.

MR. BRONTË: What do they say?

CHARLOTTE: I don't know yet.

MR. BRONTË: *(Grabbing them out of her hand.)* Give them here.

CHARLOTTE: No Father! Don't read them.

MR. BRONTË: Why not?

CHARLOTTE: I'm not ready.

MR. BRONTË: That's ridiculous.

CHARLOTTE: Father…

MR. BRONTË: What is it?

CHARLOTTE: I don't know. It suddenly occurs to me people might not like the book.

MR. BRONTË: No they might not. Bang! But what does that have to do with you?

CHARLOTTE: Everything.

MR. BRONTË: Take these. Read them.

CHARLOTTE: This is from the *Atlas*. "*Jane Eyre* is not merely a work of great promise, it is one of absolute performance. It is one of the most powerful domestic romances which has been published for many years. It has little or nothing of the old conventional stamp upon it; none of the jaded, exhausted attributes of a worn-out vein of imagination...but it is full of youthful vigour, of freshness and originality, of nervous diction and concentrated interest...It is a book to make the pulses gallop and the heart beat, and to fill the eyes with tears."

(Mr. Brontë kisses her on the forehead and leaves. She is aware he is walking out on her. The male actor then performs the following reviews, each one as a different character. During this Charlotte reads the reviews to herself.)

REVIEWER 1: *Jane Eyre* is a book of decided power, such power that although it is a woman's story, I cannot believe that it has been written by a woman.

REVIEWER 2: For a book more unfeminine, both in its excellences and defects, it would be hard to find in the annals of female authorship. Throughout there is masculine power, breadth and shrewdness, combined with masculine hardness, coarseness, and freedom of expression. The humour is frequently produced by a use of Scripture at which one is rather sorry to have smiled. The love scenes glow with a fire as fierce as that of Sappho, and somewhat more fuliginous.

REVIEWER 3: *Jane Eyre* is a remarkable book. It is the work of a person who with great mental powers combines a total ignorance of the habits of society, a great coarseness of taste, and a heathenish doctrine of religion. It is a dangerous picture of a natural heart, one where religion failed to reign over the passions. Jane is a mere heathen mind, dangerously masquerading as a woman of self-control and principle. It is by her own talents, virtues, and courage that she is made to attain the summit of human happiness, and, as far as Jane Eyre's own statement is concerned, no one would think that she owed anything either to God above or to man below. This is an anti-Christian composition.

REVIEWER 4: This is an extraordinary book. Although a work of fiction, it is no mere novel, for there is nothing but nature and truth about it. We have no high life glorified, caricatured or libeled; nor low life elevated to an enviable state of bliss...The tale is one of the heart, and the working out of a moral through the natural affections.

REVIEWER 5: The desire of the present generation is to be bold and fearless. Their boast is, that they dare to overstep 'conventional rules', and by conventional rules they mean all moral, religious and social laws...The writer evidently seeks throughout to show how impossible it is to reconcile religion with love of mankind… Religion is stabbed in the dark—our social distinctions attempted to be leveled, and all absurdly moral notions done away with. The authoress is unacquainted with the commonest rules of society, and affects to present us with specimens of fashionable life, within whose circles she has never entered.[10]

(Charlotte reads his letter as George says the following speech from the small platform with the microphone.)

GEORGE: Mr. Currer Bell, Haworth, Yorkshire. Dear Mr. Bell, As a publisher of many years experience, I don't remember the last time a book has caused such an uproar in our precious London literary circles. You're a smash! I know some of the reviews are harsh but that is only because they are frightened by you and your honesty. Besides, the fiery critical reviews sometimes sell more books than the good ones do. Take heart. You're a brilliant writer and all of us at Smith, Elder are terribly proud of our association with you. Enclosed is your first royalty check. Yours sincerely and faithfully, George Smith. P.S. Please think about coming to London so I can introduce you to everyone who is waiting to meet you.

(With this the male actor turns to leave the stage.)

CHARLOTTE: Papa, Mr. Smith wants me to come to London.

(The male actor turns back as Mr. Brontë.)

MR. BRONTË: That's ridiculous…he's just being polite.

(Branwell enters, falls forward, he is completely drunk, and has a terrible cough throughout this scene. His oversized shirt is tattered and torn. Charlotte runs to help him up. He is deadweight in her arms.)

BRANWELL: Charlotte! Shhhhhhh!

CHARLOTTE: Come on Branwell, get up before Father sees you.

BRANWELL: He sees me. He doesn't mind. What do you think, the old fart's never had a little sip or two himself.

CHARLOTTE: He most certainly has not. Come on.

BRANWELL: Where? Where shall we go?

CHARLOTTE: To your room.

BRANWELL: No. God no. Not to the dungeon. Please master don't lock me up again.

CHARLOTTE: Branwell…

BRANWELL: I'll be a very very good quiet boy. I'll sit right here quietly.

CHARLOTTE: Come upstairs now!

BRANWELL: No.

CHARLOTTE: Fine. I'm going to bed. *(She still holds her reviews.)*

BRANWELL: What's that letter?

CHARLOTTE: Nothing.

BRANWELL: Love letters? Oh, Charlotte loves only one particular fellow. Did he finally write you back?

CHARLOTTE: What are you talking about?

BRANWELL: Your "master." Monsieur Heger.

CHARLOTTE: You read my letters?

BRANWELL: I read your mind.

CHARLOTTE: When did you read my letters?

BRANWELL: When you weren't looking.

CHARLOTTE: Why?

BRANWELL: I was curious.

CHARLOTTE: You are pathetic.

BRANWELL: Because I drink? Or because I too…

CHARLOTTE: SHHHHHHH!

BRANWELL: … I am in love with Lydia Robinson, a married woman I can't have. I guess I'm as pathetic as you.

CHARLOTTE: You know nothing about me Branwell.

BRANWELL: I know you love Monsieur Heger, a married man with children.

CHARLOTTE: Be quiet.

BRANWELL: And I love Lydia Robinson, a married woman with a stupid husband and many stupid children. Quite a pickle we're both in, eh?

CHARLOTTE: Lydia Robinson is not the source of your problems.

BRANWELL: Tell me something Charlotte…where did you get that judgmental unforgiving heart.

CHARLOTTE: I am not judgmental.

BRANWELL: I couldn't possibly live up to your standards of perfection. You are unrelenting Charlotte, I feel sorry for you. You know why I feel sorry for you? Because if you are this hard on me you must be torturous to yourself.

CHARLOTTE: I wouldn't call simply wanting you to come home sober once and a while perfection.

BRANWELL: You need me to be an absolute perfect genius at everything I do, one tiny little hint of failure…

CHARLOTTE: Being dismissed for having an affair with your employer's wife is tiny…

BRANWELL: …one tiny little hint and there she goes with those huge screaming silences, parading through the house not speaking to me, and those glaring angry eyes doing a very poor job of hiding what she is really thinking. How dare I, her genius little brother fail!

CHARLOTTE: You are a genius.

BRANWELL: That's very funny.

CHARLOTTE: Fine. It happened, it's over, but now you continue to let your feelings for her completely destroy you and take you over.

BRANWELL: Oh, now we're getting somewhere.

CHARLOTTE: I keep my feelings for Monsieur Heger locked up. I don't sit up in my room drunk out of my mind, moaning at the top of my lungs for the disappointment and loss I feel, but that doesn't mean I don't feel it.

BRANWELL: Maybe you should moan a little Charlotte. It helps.

CHARLOTTE: It is very simple Branwell, you can spend your life worrying, or you can do something with yourself.

BRANWELL: Well, you ought to know Charlotte.

CHARLOTTE: You have everything.

BRANWELL: What everything?

CHARLOTTE: You are a man! Why don't you try behaving like one. Go out into the world and live your own independent life.

BRANWELL: We both suffer from a lack of courage Charlotte.

CHARLOTTE: I have all the courage I could ever need. If I was a man absolutely nothing would stop me.

BRANWELL: Well, good thing you're not. You don't honestly think this family is ever going to amount to anything do you? You little fool, standing there with your pitiful face. Come on Chief Genius Charry, sit down here and we'll write our stories like we used to and maybe some day we'll write a great novel! Come on, sit down! We'll pick up where we left off ten years ago.

CHARLOTTE: Go to bed.

BRANWELL: You go to bed little girl and dream your little dreams of Monsieur Heger and all your moving prose. Because that's all they will ever be Charlotte. We weren't meant for anything more.

CHARLOTTE: It's hard work making something out of yourself. That's it, plain and simple. There are no short cuts and no one is going to hand you anything. What do you think Branwell, the world owes you success?

(His cough becomes increasingly painful and severe.)

BRANWELL: Can I get some of your success Charlotte? Two years in Brussels studying with the fabulous Monsieur Heger so you can open your own school. You haven't opened your school, you haven't done anything but write ridiculous love letters. Maybe you could get those published, Charlotte. My big sister living her quiet little shut-in life is going to tell me about success. You don't know the first thing about it. There is a story in my head that could change the world. If I could just get the chance, the opportunity for someone to read my work I know, I know they would love it. I wrote to Wordsworth…and Southey, I sent them some poetry, and they never wrote back. No one will give me a chance. I don't know what else to do.

CHARLOTTE: Stop drinking.

BRANWELL: That doesn't have anything to do with it. Where are you going?

CHARLOTTE: To bed.

BRANWELL: To bed with your love notes?

CHARLOTTE: These are not love notes.

BRANWELL: What are they?

CHARLOTTE: Nothing.

BRANWELL: Love notes. I knew it.

(He dies on top of the desk/book. During the following monologue Charlotte lays him out on the desk, smoothing his clothing and hair.)

CHARLOTTE: *(She speaks to the audience.)* I wept for the wreck of talent, the ruin of promise, the untimely dreary extinction of what might have been a burning and a shining light. My brother was a year my junior. I had aspirations and ambitions for him once, long ago—they have perished. Nothing remains of him, but a memory of errors and sufferings. There is such a bitterness of pity for his life and death, such a yearning for the emptiness of his whole existence as I cannot describe. *(Charlotte crosses to the basin with the water and the rag. She wrings out the rag and wipes Branwell's forehead with it.)* My unhappy brother never knew what his sisters had done in literature—he was not aware that they had ever published a line. We could not tell him of our efforts for fear of causing him too deep a pang of remorse for his own time misspent, and talents misapplied. Now he will never know.[11] *(Charlotte throws the rag back into the basin.)* September 24, 1848, we buried Branwell under the house with Mother, and my two older sisters, Maria and Elizabeth.

MR. BRONTË: Bang!

CHARLOTTE: Are you alright Father?

MR. BRONTË: Charlotte, Emily is coughing all the time.

(Charlotte crosses back to the basin and lifts the wet rag up into the air, watches it drip, then drops it and runs to her cart/writing desk. During this scene Mr. Brontë, on his rolling chair, with a bloody rag in his hands, rolls back and forth between Charlotte and Emily, who is off left. Charlotte works at her cart/ writing desk.)

CHARLOTTE: I'm working on my next novel. It is titled *Shirley.*

MR. BRONTË: Emily refuses to sit down and rest, Charlotte. Will you talk to her?

CHARLOTTE: It is set in the time of the Luddite riots, Father you must remember, 1811 and 1812.

MR. BRONTË: Emily seems to be out of breath most of the time.

CHARLOTTE: I have sent for old copies of the Leeds *Mercury* to research the period.

MR. BRONTË: She's not eating enough.

CHARLOTTE: There is also of course the romantic element.

MR. BRONTË: Emily refuses to see the doctor.

CHARLOTTE: There are two stories really, the story of Shirley, the title character, and the story of Caroline Helstone.

MR. BRONTË: Emily's too tired to read, she wants you to read to her.

CHARLOTTE: *(Charlotte takes the bloody rag from her father.)* Shirley knows how to be a successful woman in a man's world, she owns a mill. Caroline has no idea where her worth lies.

MR. BRONTË: *(Mr. Brontë crosses the stage slowly toward the basin of water holding a bedpan brimming full of water straight out in front of him with his arms extended. Charlotte is fixed upon his movement.)* I told Emily to stay in bed today, but she insists on carrying on with her chores.

CHARLOTTE: There are, of course, two worthy men.

MR. BRONTË: Charlotte, Emily wants to go for a walk out on the moors.

CHARLOTTE: I'll be there in a moment.

MR. BRONTË: She keeps coughing up blood Charlotte.

CHARLOTTE: It is difficult for me to write fearlessly now as I did when I wrote *Jane Eyre.*

MR. BRONTË: Emily didn't make it to the privy, she needs to get cleaned up.

CHARLOTTE: I am also bringing into the novel the issue of women.

MR. BRONTË: She shakes constantly.

CHARLOTTE: Is there not a terrible hollowness, mockery, want, craving, in that existence which is given away to others, for want of something of your own?[12]

MR. BRONTË: That doctor you wrote to in London sent some medicine, but she refuses to take it.

CHARLOTTE: Does virtue lie in the denying of self?

MR. BRONTË: Emily is lying on the couch in the parlor Charlotte.

CHARLOTTE: I think not.

MR. BRONTË: Emily said we could send for the doctor now. *(Mr. Brontë lowers his straining arms and pours out the contents of the bedpan into the wash-basin.)*

CHARLOTTE: *(To the audience.)* December 19, 1848, we buried Emily under the house with Mother, Maria, Elizabeth, and Branwell.

(The following scene is a repetition of the previous one for Mr. Brontë. This scene builds from the last one until the dialogue takes on an extremely urgent tone, accompanied by music. On the final word Charlotte and Mr. Brontë hold out a long sustained wail.)

MR. BRONTË: Charlotte, Anne is coughing all the time.

(Mr. Brontë gets another full bedpan and begins another slow cross toward the washbasin.)

CHARLOTTE: I find it hard to concentrate.

MR. BRONTË: Anne refuses to sit down and rest.

CHARLOTTE: Keep writing and working.

MR. BRONTË: Anne seems to be out of breath.

CHARLOTTE: Keep writing and working.

MR. BRONTË: She's not eating enough.

CHARLOTTE: Don't keep George waiting.

MR. BRONTË: Anne says she'll see the doctor.

CHARLOTTE: What would Emily say.

MR. BRONTË: Anne wants you to read to her.

CHARLOTTE: Read books, write more books.

MR. BRONTË: I told Anne to stay in bed today.

CHARLOTTE: Keep writing and working.

MR. BRONTË: Anne wants to go for a walk out on the moors.

CHARLOTTE: What would Emily say.

MR. BRONTË: She's coughing up blood Charlotte.

CHARLOTTE: What would Emily say.

MR. BRONTË: Anne didn't make it to the privy, she needs to get cleaned up.

CHARLOTTE: Don't keep George waiting.

MR. BRONTË: She shakes constantly.

CHARLOTTE: Keep writing and working.

MR. BRONTË: Anne wants to go the sea.

CHARLOTTE: We'll go to the sea.

MR. BRONTË: To Scarborough.

CHARLOTTE: I said we'll go to the sea.

MR. BRONTË: You must take her to the sea.

CHARLOTTE: Keep writing and working.

MR. BRONTË: May 28, 1849. Dear Father…

CHARLOTTE: I buried Anne, I'm coming…

MR. BRONTË: *(Mr. Brontë pours out the second bedpan into the washbasin.)* When
   are you coming...
CHARLOTTE: hoooooooome.   Mr. Brontë: hoooooooome.
   *(Charlotte plunges her hands into the clear glass washbasin now full of water.
   There is a long silence while they are both alone in their isolated spaces.)*
MR. BRONTË: Charlotte, Charlotte!!
CHARLOTTE: Yes, what is it?
MR. BRONTË: I had a dream. I fell asleep.
   (Charlotte picks up her cart/writing desk and begins to exit.)
CHARLOTTE: I'm going to London Father to visit George Smith.
MR. BRONTË: Charlotte, don't go now.
CHARLOTTE: I have to leave here Father.
MR. BRONTË: Who?
CHARLOTTE: George Smith, Father, my publisher, George.
MR. BRONTË: Please Charlotte...don't go.
   (She pushes her cart offstage, leaving a bewildered Mr. Brontë alone.)

END OF ACT I

ACT II

London, 1849. Charlotte is thirty-three years old. Lights up on Charlotte and George as they are at the end of dancing a waltz together. They exit from the dance floor.

GEORGE: Well, that was quite wonderful.

CHARLOTTE: Yes it was George.

GEORGE: You didn't like the food.

CHARLOTTE: It was magnificent.

GEORGE: Like I said, you didn't like it.

CHARLOTTE: I'm not used to it, that's all. You've been a very gracious host.

GEORGE: You deserve a gracious host Miss Brontë. I admire what you've done, I don't believe I've ever told you that.

CHARLOTTE: Thank you Mr. Smith.

GEORGE: How are you Charlotte?

CHARLOTTE: I'm fine. I worry about my father. All alone now.

GEORGE: He has you.

CHARLOTTE: Yes.

GEORGE: I wish you'd stay in London.

CHARLOTTE: I'm not fit for London and you know it.

GEORGE: No I don't.

CHARLOTTE: We've managed not to talk about my book all evening.

GEORGE: Let's talk.

CHARLOTTE: Do you think it reveals me as a woman writer? More so than *Jane Eyre* did.

GEORGE: Yes.

CHARLOTTE: We shall see.

GEORGE: Shirley is quite a fascinating woman. Not like Jane Eyre at all.

CHARLOTTE: Jane wasn't fascinating?

GEORGE: Of course she was. I meant Shirley is different from Jane Eyre.

CHARLOTTE: Shirley is Emily.

GEORGE: Oh…

CHARLOTTE: Emily was a beautiful woman, too stupid and stubborn to realize it or do anything about it. When she got terribly excited about what she was writing and she wanted my opinion, she would get a particularly demanding look in her eyes. She would glare at me while she spoke. If my concentration slipped for a moment, even if while looking directly at her, she would lose her composure entirely. She would wait until she thought she once again had my complete attention, then she would berate me for having broken the spell, and insist on starting over again with whatever it was she was trying to tell me. She was definitely the kind of woman a man would want, but she never gave one the chance.

GEORGE: She's very modern.

CHARLOTTE: Emily?

GEORGE: Shirley.

CHARLOTTE: Because she has her own money?

GEORGE: Yes…and the things she says.

CHARLOTTE: She says she wants to be a man.

GEORGE: That's right.

CHARLOTTE: What's on your mind George?

GEORGE: It's not the book *Jane Eyre* was Charlotte.

CHARLOTTE: No, it's a different book, did you want me to write the same book?

GEORGE: It's not as good.

CHARLOTTE: I don't believe that.

GEORGE: Charlotte, I'm your publisher, I have your best interest in mind.

CHARLOTTE: George, you sell books for a living.

GEORGE: In the opening scene, you are mocking the church, people are not ready for that.

CHARLOTTE: My father is a man of God. I am telling the truth George, it is as simple as that.

GEORGE: I want you to take that opening scene out.

CHARLOTTE: No. Whatever now becomes of the book, the occupation of writing it took me out of the reality I was living in. I simply don't care what people have to say about it.

GEORGE: That's not true.

CHARLOTTE: A year ago—had a prophet warned me how I should stand in August 1849—how stripped and bereaved—had he foretold the autumn, the winter, the spring of sickness and suffering to be gone through—I should have thought—this can never be endured. It is over. Branwell—Emily—Anne are gone like dreams—gone as Maria and Elizabeth went twenty years ago. One by one I have watched them fall asleep on my arm—and closed their glazed eyes—I have seen them buried one by one and—thus far—God has upheld me.[13] All I have, had, was the book George. And thank God I had it. I know it's not perfect, but it's honest and people will recognize that. And if they don't, I can't make them and I don't want to.

GEORGE: I appreciate that Charlotte, I do, but there are certain passages that concern me. The scene where, after she's been bitten by a dog, Shirley cauterizes her arm with a red hot poker? Please reconsider that.

CHARLOTTE: George, Emily did that, I was there. I saw it with my own two eyes. She didn't flinch, she just did it!

GEORGE: That was Emily. This is publishing.

CHARLOTTE: I will not change this book George. Not for you or anybody else. It stays as it is.

(*Pause.*)

GEORGE: Are you working on anything else?

CHARLOTTE: Staying healthy. Keeping my father quiet and settled.

GEORGE: I meant another novel.

CHARLOTTE: I know what you meant George.

GEORGE: Charlotte, let me introduce you to the writing world here in London. There are so many people that want to know you.

CHARLOTTE: It's important to me to remain anonymous as long as possible.

GEORGE: Why?

CHARLOTTE: People that want to know me?

GEORGE: Yes.

CHARLOTTE: They'd be awfully disappointed, wouldn't they. I didn't write my books so people would know who I was.

GEORGE: I realize that. But it's a consequence of being a good writer.

CHARLOTTE: You speak as though I have a choice. As though I could leave my family...my father, and live the life I choose. Who would take care of him?

GEORGE: I want you to receive some of the attention that you deserve.

CHARLOTTE: I don't feel comfortable with attention.

GEORGE: Give yourself some time.

CHARLOTTE: I don't mean from you.

GEORGE: I know.

CHARLOTTE: Because I do feel very comfortable with you.

GEORGE: My mother and sisters love having you here.

CHARLOTTE: I know they wonder who I am.

GEORGE: I told them you're a good friend of mine, that's enough.

(*Pause.*)

CHARLOTTE: You've been kind.

GEORGE: I'm not kind. I like you. Must you go tomorrow?

CHARLOTTE: I must, my father will be...he gets very excited if I change my plans...he worries about me a great deal.

GEORGE: You'll be back soon I hope.

CHARLOTTE: Do you?

GEORGE: Well, of course. I love having you here, I told you that.

CHARLOTTE: George...

GEORGE: Charlotte?

CHARLOTTE: George…please…

GEORGE: What is it?

CHARLOTTE: Do you suppose that…Do you know what I'm asking?

GEORGE: No.

CHARLOTTE: I care for you.

GEORGE: As I do for you Charlotte.

CHARLOTTE: No…that's not what I mean.

GEORGE: Oh, well.

CHARLOTTE: What has all this been? All these years of corresponding and you sending me every book the firm has published, and inviting me to London over and over again, practically begging me to come, to stay at your home and live with your family. What has all of it meant George? All these wonderful evenings to the opera and the theatre and the parties we went to, what was all that?!

GEORGE: A publisher taking care of his most famous author.

CHARLOTTE: Oh George…that's not true, you're not like that.

GEORGE: Yes I am. I'm in love with your work Charlotte.

CHARLOTTE: I'm not wrong about this, we could make a wonderful partnership, you and I.

GEORGE: That may be true, but I don't want just a partnership with a woman.

CHARLOTTE: I'm not asking you to be in love with me. I know what I am George. I would never expect that…I…I don't know what I'm asking. I've made a terrible mistake.

GEORGE: Charlotte, don't go, don't leave now. I can't be that for you.

CHARLOTTE: Well then who can be George?

GEORGE: No one. No one can be Mr. Rochester to you.

CHARLOTTE: I didn't say anything about Mr. Rochester.

GEORGE: I'm not a fool. That is what you want, it's obvious. You created him, you are more him than any man could possibly be.

CHARLOTTE: That is not true. I'm not like him at all.

GEORGE: Charlotte you are so blind. So brilliant and so blind. Everything you want is right in front of you.

CHARLOTTE: Yes, it is.

GEORGE: No, I don't mean me. You don't need a man Charlotte, you have a brilliant career. You create fascinating men, there is not a man alive that would dare to court you. You are courageous and daring and honest and willful. You're not like most women Charlotte. You weren't made to be someone's wife.

CHARLOTTE: I don't understand what you are saying?

GEORGE: Men are afraid of you Charlotte. They don't want to marry you. You silenced William Makepeace Thackeray, one of the most outspoken, overbearing, hotheads God ever created, you, little Charlotte Brontë, you silenced him in a room full of his closest friends. You didn't even know what you had done.

CHARLOTTE: I just told him the truth.

GEORGE: Yes. You are not of this world Charlotte. You are a powerful, powerful woman. The last thing you should be doing is looking after a man. Besides, no man could satisfy that passionate heart you've got beating in there.

CHARLOTTE: I beg your pardon.

GEORGE: Charlotte, please, you are perhaps the purest lady I have ever known, I mean no disrespect, but you can't hide. You wrote these books Charlotte, they came from you and they are full of desire and romantic passionate love with the kind of men that do not inhabit the real world.

CHARLOTTE: They are full of love, real love. You cannot tell me it does not exist on this earth and that there are not intelligent, strong, brave, men in this world. I am looking at one right now.

GEORGE: Only in a little girl's mind...

CHARLOTTE: I am not a child.

GEORGE: Only in a little girl's mind do such men exist.

CHARLOTTE: I desire to share my life with someone, is that childish?

GEORGE: It's not your desire, it's what you expect out of a man Charlotte. I can't...

CHARLOTTE: I can't George. I can't do it another minute. Please, please don't leave me to do it myself. One more day up there in that house with my father and I will go stark raving mad.

MR. BRONTË: Charlotte.

CHARLOTTE: Yes Father.

MR. BRONTË: Bang! What are you doing?

CHARLOTTE: I'm writing Father.

MR. BRONTË: Are you going back to London again?

CHARLOTTE: No...George Smith is engaged to be married Father.

MR. BRONTË: Good. I'll be in my room. *(He begins to exit.)*

CHARLOTTE: Why is it good?

MR. BRONTË: What dear?

CHARLOTTE: Why is it good?

MR. BRONTË: What?

CHARLOTTE: Why did you say it was good that George is getting married?

MR. BRONTË: No reason. Good for him!

CHARLOTTE: He wrote me letters. He invited me to London. He treated me like a lady.

MR. BRONTË: Yes.

CHARLOTTE: We had an understanding and a heightened ability to converse.

MR. BRONTË: Yes.

CHARLOTTE: I liked him Father.

MR. BRONTË: Yes.

CHARLOTTE: I like him very much.

MR. BRONTË: Yes. *(Silence.)* You wanted to marry him?

CHARLOTTE: *(Pause.)* Yes.

MR. BRONTË: It's best you stay here.

CHARLOTTE: Why?

MR. BRONTË: Your family is here Charlotte. This is where you belong. *(He exits.)*

CHARLOTTE: *(Charlotte speaks to the audience.)* I shall be thirty-seven next birthday. What have I done these last thirty-six years? Precious little. I've been thinking a great deal lately about leaving Haworth and finding another situation in London. Perhaps now is the time. After all I am a published author, that is something.

(Charlotte is seated. The lights focus in on her so she is very isolated and small on the stage.)

CHARLOTTE: When I sit in the evening and write as has always been the custom in this house, I sometimes try very hard to imagine that Emily is still here. I don't mean imagine as it was in the past, I mean imagine she is here now in whatever form she would take. I listen for anything that might be the smallest signal that she is with me. Although it is ridiculous because Emily wouldn't come back if she could. She would stay out there and roam about. It's just very quiet here…and still…very quiet…and very still.

(Mr. James Taylor steps onto the small platform carrying a large sign which says "Proposal Number 2. Mr. James Taylor of Smith, Elder & Co." He speaks into the microphone.)

MR. TAYLOR: Charlotte.

(She gasps.)

MR. TAYLOR: Did I startle you?

CHARLOTTE: No. That's alright.

MR. TAYLOR: The housekeeper let me in.

CHARLOTTE: George sent me a note that you were coming. How was the journey from Scotland?

MR. TAYLOR: Wet.

CHARLOTTE: Oh, I'm sorry. *(Pause.)* Relatives you were visiting?

MR. TAYLOR: Aye.

   (Pause.)

CHARLOTTE: Well I'm sure you'll be glad to get back to London.

MR. TAYLOR: When George suggested I stop here on my way back to check on the progress of your manuscript, I was really delighted to make the trip.

CHARLOTTE: You can tell George when you go back it's not necessary for him to send someone after me. I'm quite capable of writing novels all by myself just like an adult.

MR. TAYLOR: Well, I'll…

CHARLOTTE: I'm sorry Mr. Taylor. I know it's not your fault. I'm afraid you'll have to tell him the progress is slow. Good day. *(She tries to escort him out.)*

MR. TAYLOR: Charlotte I want to speak to you.

CHARLOTTE: Of course.

MR. TAYLOR: *(Pause.)* Your new book…what's it about?

CHARLOTTE: Oh. It's about a woman who…

MR. TAYLOR: What's the title?

CHARLOTTE: *Villette.*

MR. TAYLOR: What's that?

CHARLOTTE: A town in Belgium.

MR. TAYLOR: I didn't know that.

CHARLOTTE: There is no real town Mr. Taylor, I made it up.

MR. TAYLOR: Oh. *(Pause.)* Charlotte…

CHARLOTTE: Yes.

MR. TAYLOR: You are an incredibly exciting, brilliant woman…and I'm going to India soon.

CHARLOTTE: India?

MR. TAYLOR: Yes and I thought you and I could…

CHARLOTTE: How truly wonderful for you Mr. Taylor, traveling all the way to India. And here I was worried about you coming to Haworth and yet you'll be making a trip like that.

MR. TAYLOR: Marry me.

CHARLOTTE: What?

MR. TAYLOR: I want you to marry me.

CHARLOTTE: Mr. Taylor it is hardly appropriate for a man to enter the home of a woman whom he barely knows and ask her to marry him. I have a father and I have responsibilities.

MR. TAYLOR: And I have such overwhelming feelings for you.

CHARLOTTE: I can't possibly respond to you in any way at this moment.

MR. TAYLOR: I'll be in London for another month. I shall hope to hear from you—your letters have been, and will be, a greater refreshment than you can think or I can tell. *(He drops his sign and steps off the platform.)*

(Charlotte and George take up a pair of tea cups that are attached together with a string. They use the tea cups as a communication device, holding the cup to their mouths when they speak and their ears when they listen.)

CHARLOTTE: Dear George, finally, enclosed is my next book *Villette.*

MR. SMITH: Dear Charlotte, I received the first two volumes of *Villette.* Where's the third?

CHARLOTTE: Dear George, well, what do you think? What do you think of the female character, Lucy Snowe?

MR. SMITH: Dear Charlotte, she is an odd fascinating little puss, but I am not in love with her.

CHARLOTTE: Dear George, oh.

MR. SMITH: Dear Charlotte, I received the last volume.

CHARLOTTE: Dear George, well?

MR. SMITH: Dear Charlotte, the transfer of interest in the third volume from one romantic hero to a new, from the dashing, handsome Graham Bretton to the serious, unlikely Monsieur Paul Emmanuel troubles me.

CHARLOTTE: *(During this monologue Charlotte sets down her tea cup and cuts the string with scissors. She then grabs George's tea cup and puts both cups on the prop table. She pulls off George's coat or whatever costume piece is used to signify George, and dresses the male actor in the Rochester riding cloak.)* Dear George, it is not pleasant, and will probably be found as unwelcome to the reader as it was, in a sense, compulsory upon the writer. The spirit of romance would have indicated another course, far more flowery and inviting; it would have fashioned a paramount hero, kept faithfully with him, and made him supremely worshipful; he should have an idol, and not a mute, unresponding idol either, but this would have been unlike real life—inconsistent with truth—at variance with probability.[14]

ROCHESTER: *(Rochester grabs Charlotte from behind and passionately strokes her body during his next speech.)* Are you anything akin to me, do you think, Jane?

CHARLOTTE: Mr. Rochester, you're here again.

ROCHESTER: Because, I sometimes have a queer feeling with regard to you Jane—especially when you are near me, as now: It is as if I had a string somewhere under my left ribs, tightly and inextricably knotted to a similar string situated in the corresponding quarter of your little frame. And if that boisterous channel, and two hundred miles or so of land come broad between us, I am afraid that cord of communion will be snapt; and then I've a nervous notion I should take to bleeding inwardly. As for you—you'd forget me.

CHARLOTTE: That I never should, sir: you know—

ROCHESTER: *(He crosses away from Charlotte.)* Jane, do you hear that nightingale singing in the wood? Listen!

CHARLOTTE: I wish I'd never come to Thornfield.

ROCHESTER: Because you are sorry to leave it?

CHARLOTTE: I grieve to leave Thornfield: I love Thornfield—I love it, because I have lived in it a full and delightful life—momentarily at least. I have not been trampled on. I have not been petrified. I have not been buried with inferior minds, and excluded from every glimpse of communion with what is bright and energetic, and high. I have talked, face to face, with what I reverence: with what I delight in—with an original, a vigorous, an expanded mind. I have known you, Mr. Rochester; and it strikes me with terror and anguish to feel I absolutely must be torn from you forever. I see the necessity of departure; and it is like looking on the necessity of death.

ROCHESTER: Where do you see the necessity?

CHARLOTTE: Where? You, sir, have placed it before me.

ROCHESTER: In what shape?

CHARLOTTE: In the shape of Miss Ingram; a noble and beautiful woman—your bride.

ROCHESTER: My bride! What bride? I have no bride!

CHARLOTTE: But you will have.

ROCHESTER: Yes—I will!—I will!

CHARLOTTE: Then I must go—you have said it yourself.

ROCHESTER: No: you must stay! I swear it—and the oath shall be kept.

CHARLOTTE: I tell you I must go! Do you think I can stay to become nothing to you? Do you think I am an automaton?—a machine without feelings? and can bear to have my morsel of bread snatched from my lips, and my drop of living water dashed from my cup? Do you think, because I am poor, obscure, plain, and little, I am soulless and heartless? You think wrong!—I have as much soul as you—and full as much heart! And if God had gifted me with some beauty and much wealth, I should have made it as hard for you to leave me, as it is now for me to leave you. I am not talking to you now through the medium of custom, conventionalities, nor even of mortal flesh—it is my spirit that addresses your spirit; just as if both had passed through the grave, and we stood at God's feet, equal—as we are!

ROCHESTER: As we are! So, so, Jane!

CHARLOTTE: Yes, so, sir, and yet not so; for you are a married man—or as good
as a married man, and wed to one inferior to you—to one with whom you
have no sympathy—whom I do not believe you truly love; for I have seen
and heard you sneer at her. I would scorn such a union: Therefore I am
better than you—let me go!

ROCHESTER: Where, Jane? To Ireland?

CHARLOTTE: Yes—to Ireland. I have spoken my mind, and can go anywhere
now.

ROCHESTER: Jane, be still; don't struggle so, like a wild, frantic bird.

CHARLOTTE: I am no bird; and no net ensnares me: I am a free human being
with an independent will, which I now exert to leave you.

ROCHESTER: And your will shall decide your destiny, I offer you my hand, my
heart, and a share of all my possessions.

CHARLOTTE: You play a farce, which I merely laugh at.

ROCHESTER: I ask you to pass through life at my side—to be my second self,
and best earthly companion.

CHARLOTTE: For that fate you have already made your choice, and must abide
by it.[15]

NICHOLLS: Charlotte…I have for some time…

CHARLOTTE: Mr. Nicholls!? *(Charlotte stunned, crosses away from Rochester who
has become Nicholls by dropping the cloak.)* Is there something you wanted?

NICHOLLS: I have read your books Miss Brontë. I have a great respect for you,
more than I can say and I can no longer endure this suffering. Please tell
me Miss Brontë if I should continue to hope that you might some day
return my feeling.

CHARLOTTE: Father…Father…Arthur Nicholls, your curate Mr. Nicholls, says
he loves me.

MR. BRONTË: What?

CHARLOTTE: He told me just now, well, he didn't say that exactly, but that was
the gist of it.

MR. BRONTË: What did he say to you?

CHARLOTTE: Papa, calm down. He was perfectly polite, he just wanted to know
how I felt about him.

MR. BRONTË: Bang! You will tell him immediately that you harbor no such feelings toward him whatsoever, and that when and if you do marry, it will be
to a man fit to marry a published, acclaimed, renowned authoress, who has
traveled and had numerous accomplishments. Bang!

CHARLOTTE: Father…

MR. BRONTË: Charlotte, you can't possibly…

CHARLOTTE: Father I was struck dumb. It was the last thing I expected, I had no idea how to reply. He was in a state of agitation and feeling.

MR. BRONTË: Unmanly driveller.

CHARLOTTE: I will speak to him tomorrow.

MR. BRONTË: *(Hands her a letter.)* Another letter from your publisher.

CHARLOTTE: The reviews of Villette… *(Charlotte reads to herself.)*

> *(Nicholls steps onto the small platform with the microphone carrying his traveling bag and a sign that reads "Proposal Number 3. Arthur Bell Nicholls, curate of Haworth".)*

NICHOLLS: Charlotte…

CHARLOTTE: Mr. Nicholls?

NICHOLLS: I'm not good with words, so I'll just say it. I want you for my wife. I've wanted it for some time. I can't promise you anything more than providing for you and giving you a home, and I will always treat you with respect Charlotte, in every way. A woman would be a great help to me with ministering to the parish, on Sundays after sermon you could visit the sick and the women with small children that need our help, my clothes always need mending, and I'm not much at feeding myself. And I'm sure with your writing skills you'd be a great help to me with my sermons. And I would always be there for you Charlotte.

CHARLOTTE: Alright.

> *(Nicholls excitedly drops his sign and leaps off the platform.)*

CHARLOTTE: Father, Mr. Arthur Nicholls is coming, he wants to see you.

MR. BRONTË: Charlotte, this is ridiculous. You can have any man you want, a man with wealth and position.

CHARLOTTE: Any man I want! Father, I never was pretty. I now am ugly. You are seventy-six years old. At your death I will have 300 pounds besides the little I have earned myself—do you think there are many men who would want me?

MR. BRONTË: So, you will marry a curate? Bang!

CHARLOTTE: Yes I must marry a curate if I ever marry at all; not merely a curate but your curate: not merely your curate but he must live in the house with you, for I cannot leave you.

MR. BRONTË: Never. I will never have another man in this house.

CHARLOTTE: I have spent my entire life taking care of you.

MR. BRONTË: Be very careful how you are speaking to me young lady.

CHARLOTTE: I am not a young lady Father. Look at me.

MR. BRONTË: You don't want him Charlotte, you are simply giving up.

CHARLOTTE: Maybe I am Father, that is my right. And I don't believe you are one to speak about giving up.

MR. BRONTË: I will not be spoken to in that tone by my child.

CHARLOTTE: You gave up on life a long time ago Father. I could have gone to London and had a productive, artistic, involved full life, with other writers and artists and people who understood me, but I stayed here.

MR. BRONTË: I had nothing to do with the choices you made or didn't make. You will not charge me with that responsibility!

CHARLOTTE: You have never understood me...

MR. BRONTË: Having a wife and six children to support is not giving up, it is reality.

CHARLOTTE: What is this life you have led, locked up in your room? What do you do in there?

MR. BRONTË: It is absolutely no business of yours what I do up there.

CHARLOTTE: Why is it no business of mine. Are you not my father? Are we not the only two people left living in this house together?

MR. BRONTË: My existence has been for you children.

CHARLOTTE: There are no children left.

MR. BRONTË: You must not marry this man. I forbid you to marry.

CHARLOTTE: You can't.

MR. BRONTË: I can and I do. You are forbidden.

CHARLOTTE: Papa, you can't control me anymore.

MR. BRONTË: I am your father until the day I take my last breath and you will not leave this house.

CHARLOTTE: I told you I won't leave you Papa, Mr. Nicholls and I will live here with you.

MR. BRONTË: Mr. Nicholls is not part of this discussion.

CHARLOTTE: Mr. Nicholls is going to be my husband.

MR. BRONTË: Charlotte, stop it!

CHARLOTTE: You cannot keep this from me.

(The following lines should overlap and move very quickly.)

MR. BRONTË: I created you Charlotte. You are mine. You are mine.

CHARLOTTE: You must listen to me.

MR. BRONTË: Do you understand me. I will not have you taken from me. You are mine. You understand me young lady. I will be damned...before I will watch you slip away. I will be damned. Bang!

CHARLOTTE: I have no other choice.

MR. BRONTË: I will be damned. I will be damned. I will be damned to hell before another one of my children get out of this house. Bang!

CHARLOTTE: Stop it Father!

MR. BRONTË: Damned! Do you hear me. You are not going to get another one.

CHARLOTTE: I hate you.

MR. BRONTË: You devil. I will kill you first. Bang! Bang! Bang! Bang! Bang! Bang! Bang! Bang!…

CHARLOTTE: Stop it Papa!

MR. BRONTË: He's trying to take you Charlotte. We've got to stop him. Bang! Bang! Bang! Bang!…

CHARLOTTE: Stop it! *(She grabs his pistol away from him.)* There is no devil Papa. It's me.

MR. BRONTË: There's a devil my little girl. There's no question there is a devil in this world.

CHARLOTTE: Papa what's happened to us?

MR. BRONTË: The devil has gotten into this house is what has happened to us… and his name is Arthur Nicholls.

CHARLOTTE: Oh Father.

MR. BRONTË: He's going to take you with him Charlotte if I don't stop him. Give me my pistol.

CHARLOTTE: Arthur Nicholls is not the devil. Your children died of a disease. It has nothing to do with the devil. Many people's children have died of consumption Father.

MR. BRONTË: My wife and all my children died…except for you.

CHARLOTTE: Yes Papa and I'm not going to die now.

(Mr. Brontë sits on the floor and cradles the clear washbasin full of water.)

MR. BRONTË: You stayed as a reminder. Every day I look…there's your mother in those black eyes…your sisters Maria, Elizabeth, and Anne are all there. Emily, my beauty, Emily lurks right behind your sharp tongue…and my boy Branwell, who should have written books…

CHARLOTTE: Every corner of this house, every stick of furniture, every picture on every wall reminds me of them. And the fact I'm still the one alive, and the fact I never did what I wanted and the fact I've wasted my life which they never had.

MR. BRONTË: You wrote books Charlotte, your life is not a waste.

CHARLOTTE: Yes, I wrote books.

MR. BRONTË: You wrote amazing, wonderful books. That's a great accomplishment.

CHARLOTTE: I wanted something more.

MR. BRONTË: There is nothing more.

CHARLOTTE: I don't believe that.

MR. BRONTË: You live your life, you do the best you can.

CHARLOTTE: How do you know you did the best you can?

MR. BRONTË: Charlotte, you're making my head ache.

CHARLOTTE: How do you know? I want to know Father. What is your best?

MR. BRONTË: You're talking like a dead woman now.

CHARLOTTE: I wanted a man to live for my voice. I wanted a man to tremble when I walked into the room. I wanted to change a man's life forever…to be the only thing that mattered… *(Charlotte puts on Rochester's riding cloak, stands on the small platform, and addresses an imaginary Jane speaking into the microphone.)* Jane, my dear Jane, I have for the first time found what I can truly love—I have found you. You are my sympathy—my better self—my good angel—I am bound to you with a strong attachment. I think you good, gifted, lovely: A fervent, a solemn passion is conceived in my heart; it leans to you, draws you to my centre and spring of life, wraps my existence about you—and, kindling in pure, powerful flame, fuses you and me in one.[16]

(Nicholls enters and lifts the Rochester cloak off of Charlotte.)

NICHOLLS: Charlotte, dear.

CHARLOTTE: Yes Arthur! I'm sorry.

NICHOLLS: I want to speak to you about the wedding trip.

CHARLOTTE: Yes, go ahead.

NICHOLLS: I thought we would go to Ireland so you can meet the family. We'll spend our wedding night at Conway in Wales. My Uncle has a house in Banagher in the south of Ireland. We'll spend some time in Dublin before we go there. And I thought we'd stay with my family about a month.

CHARLOTTE: Sounds fine.

NICHOLLS: Charlotte are you listening to me?

CHARLOTTE: Yes. I heard everything.

NICHOLLS: What are you working on?

CHARLOTTE: Another novel, I think.

NICHOLLS: After we're married Charlotte…there's going to be a great many things to do, I'll need your help. You don't have to write anymore. There's no need to publish books, you'll be my wife.

CHARLOTTE: I do enjoy it, it's given me a great deal over the years, my books, and I would hate to…

NICHOLLS: Charlotte, *I'm* going to give you that now.

CHARLOTTE: You are?

NICHOLLS: Yes, I love you. I mean to take care of you. You will have a full life. I'm not a smart man, but I know what's in your books Charlotte. I know how much you want a man that is truly a man for you in every way. I intend to be that. No more waiting and wondering and hoping for you my dear.

CHARLOTTE: Arthur, I want this to be a good marriage, but I'm afraid...

NICHOLLS: Of what?

CHARLOTTE: Of not being everything you want.

NICHOLLS: That's ridiculous. You are more than I ever thought I could have. Now stop your worrying, I'm going to send a letter off to my family and tell them to expect us...Mrs. Nicholls.

(He goes, Charlotte puts on a lace wedding veil.)

CHARLOTTE: Father, Father, are you almost ready?

MR. BRONTË: I'm not going Charlotte.

CHARLOTTE: What?

MR. BRONTË: You heard me.

CHARLOTTE: What's gotten into you Father, you have to go, it's my wedding day.

MR. BRONTË: I'm not feeling well, I think it's best I stay home.

CHARLOTTE: Father, the ceremony is in your own church, one hundred feet across the yard.

MR. BRONTË: Charlotte, I've stated my intention.

CHARLOTTE: Yes you have. And I've stated mine. I'm marrying Arthur Nicholls this morning with or without you.

MR. BRONTË: As you wish.

(Arthur takes Charlotte by the hand, they walk down the aisle toward the audience repeating the choreography done earlier in the Heger walk-in-the-garden scene, they wait listening, they exchange rings, they wait again, they face each other, Arthur slowly lifts the veil and kisses Charlotte.)

CHARLOTTE: Arthur, I am thirty-eight years old.

NICHOLLS: I know.

(He takes her hand and escorts her to the desk/book. They go through a series of very stylized movements depicting initial physical contact. Nicholls stands on the upstage side of the desk/book, and Charlotte lies on her back on the desk/book with her head downstage. Then he lifts her skirt and puts her legs against his chest. Charlotte, with her head bent back downstage, begins her monologue.)

CHARLOTTE: I grieve to leave Thornfield: I love Thornfield—I love it, because I have lived in it a full and delightful life—momentarily at least. I have not been trampled on. I have not been petrified.

NICHOLLS: Look at me Charlotte.

CHARLOTTE: I have not been buried with inferior minds, and excluded from every glimpse of communion with what is bright and energetic, and high.

NICHOLLS: Charlotte, look at me!

CHARLOTTE: I have talked, face to face, with what I reverence: with what I delight in—with an original…

NICHOLLS: Charlotte…

CHARLOTTE: …a vigorous,…

NICHOLLS: I am here!

CHARLOTTE: …an expanded mind.

NICHOLLS: I am here!

CHARLOTTE: I have known you, Mr. Rochester; and it strikes me with terror and anguish to feel I absolutely must be torn from you forever.

NICHOLLS: Look at me.

CHARLOTTE: I see the necessity of departure; and it is like looking on the necessity of death.[17]

(Nicholls kisses her and walks away. Charlotte slowly collects herself and begins speaking to the audience.)

CHARLOTTE: The first morning on our honeymoon we went out on to the cliffs and saw the Atlantic. I did not know whether I should get leave to take the matter in my own way, I did not want to talk, but I did want to look and be silent. Covered with a rug to keep off the spray I was allowed to sit where I chose, and he only interrupted me when he thought I crept too near the edge of the cliff. So far he is always good in this way—and this protection which does not interfere or pretend is I believe a thousand times better than any half sort of pseudo-sympathy.[18] Since we came home I have not had an unemployed moment; my life is changed indeed—to be wanted continually… *(She continues addressing the audience as she assists Arthur.)*

NICHOLLS: Charlotte, could you help me arrange these prayer books.

CHARLOTTE: …to be constantly called for and occupied seems so strange…

NICHOLLS: And where is my collar?

CHARLOTTE: …yet it is a marvelously good thing.

NICHOLLS: We must visit the Taylors' after the sermon today, their son is very ill. *(He sits at her desk/book to work on his sermon.)*

CHARLOTTE: As yet I don't understand how some wives grow so selfish. As far as my experience of matrimony goes, I think it tends to draw you out, and away from yourself. During the last six weeks, the colour of my thoughts is a good deal changed: I know more of the realities of life than I once did. I think many false ideas are propagated perhaps unintentionally. I think those married women who indiscriminately urge their acquaintance to marry much to blame. It is a solemn and strange and perilous thing for a woman to become a wife. Man's lot is far, far different. Mr. Nicholls gained twelve pounds during the four weeks we were in Ireland. To see this improvement in him has been a main source of happiness to me, and to speak truth a subject of wonder too.[19]

(There is a long silence as Charlotte studies him.)

NICHOLLS: You're not working on your novel.

CHARLOTTE: I'm scattered.

NICHOLLS: Why is that?

CHARLOTTE: I don't know.

NICHOLLS: Why are you smiling at me?

CHARLOTTE: I don't know.

NICHOLLS: I think you do. You're making fun of me because I attempt to understand your writing.

CHARLOTTE: Arthur, not at all. You completely misunderstand.

NICHOLLS: They why are you laughing at me.

CHARLOTTE: I wasn't laughing.

NICHOLLS: You were. You weren't making any noise but you were laughing.

CHARLOTTE: Arthur…your wife had a moment when she enjoyed looking at you, so she smiled. This is quite a ridiculous discussion.

NICHOLLS: Enjoyed looking at me?

CHARLOTTE: Yes.

NICHOLLS: What were you enjoying?

CHARLOTTE: Your cheeks. Rather the hollow in your cheeks.

NICHOLLS: Really?

CHARLOTTE: Yes. I find them quite attractive.

NICHOLLS: You do?

CHARLOTTE: Yes.

NICHOLLS: You find my cheeks quite attractive?

CHARLOTTE: Yes Arthur.

NICHOLLS: Charlotte…

CHARLOTTE: What is it?

NICHOLLS: I've waited so long for this. Charlotte…we've been living together as man and wife, but I've wanted you to look at me and see not just the man you married, but the man you wanted.

CHARLOTTE: I've been a bit slow, eh?

NICHOLLS: It doesn't matter.

CHARLOTTE: I was actually also looking at your hands, and this particular scar on your right hand…

NICHOLLS: I was working with some tools and it slipped…

CHARLOTTE: …and imagining the way these rough, masculine hands feel against my skin, and I was definitely looking at those green eyes… Arthur…

(They kiss.)

CHARLOTTE: I love you, I love you, I love you, I love you…

(She addresses the audience as Nicholls lies beside her.)

CHARLOTTE: Haworth is a very quiet place; it is also difficult of access and unless under the stimulus of necessity or that of strong curiosity—or finally that of true and tried friendship—few take the courage to penetrate to so remote a nook. Besides, now that I am married I do not expect to be an object of much general interest. Ladies who have won some prominence (call it either notoriety or celebrity) in their single life—often fall quite into the background when they change their names; but if true domestic happiness replace Fame—the exchange will indeed be for the better.[20]

NICHOLLS: I must run along to the church. Are you coming?

CHARLOTTE: In a moment. *(Charlotte lets out an audible moan, grabbing her abdomen.)*

NICHOLLS: Darling, what is it?

CHARLOTTE: Arthur, I was waiting to tell you until I was absolutely sure, I have no doubts now…

NICHOLLS: What?

CHARLOTTE: We're going to have a child.

NICHOLLS: Oh, thank God. You beautiful woman.

(Charlotte begins to furiously dry-heave, this turns into stylized movement as her body convulses in pain.)

NICHOLLS: Charlotte, you're coughing all the time. Please sit down and rest. You seem to be out of breath. Charlotte, you're not eating enough. Charlotte, the doctor is here to see you. Do you want me to read to you? I told you to stay in bed today. I'll take you for a walk out on the moors. You're coughing up blood Charlotte. You didn't make it to the privy, I will clean you up. You're shaking constantly. That doctor we wrote to in London sent some medicine. Please Charlotte! Lie down!

(Charlotte collapses, and Nicholls arrives near her just in time to catch her in his arms, he cradles her as they play the final scene.)

CHARLOTTE: Arthur don't leave me.

NICHOLLS: I'm not leaving, I'm right here.

CHARLOTTE: Where have you been all day?

NICHOLLS: Right here my dear.

CHARLOTTE: I don't remember seeing you.

NICHOLLS: You were sleeping.

CHARLOTTE: Oh.

NICHOLLS: How do you feel now.

CHARLOTTE: Tired.

NICHOLLS: You need your rest.

CHARLOTTE: The baby Arthur, I'm so worried about the baby.

NICHOLLS: You and our baby are going to be fine. I promise.

CHARLOTTE: You are so handsome you know that.

NICHOLLS: Charlotte.

CHARLOTTE: You are the most beautiful man in the world.

NICHOLLS: You might get some argument there.

CHARLOTTE: I didn't always think so you know. Remember that day you walked into the kitchen…was it the kitchen?

NICHOLLS: The parlor.

CHARLOTTE: Yes, I was writing. I had just finished *Villette*. And you told me you loved me. Remember that.

NICHOLLS: Of course.

CHARLOTTE: I thought you were silly.

NICHOLLS: I know.

CHARLOTTE: I told my father and he screamed.

NICHOLLS: I know.

CHARLOTTE: He said he wouldn't have it. And look at us now.

NICHOLLS: Married almost nine months.

CHARLOTTE: I love you so Arthur. I love you more than I ever realized I could.

NICHOLLS: Charlotte…

CHARLOTTE: I'm not going to die now…not when we've been so happy.

NICHOLLS: No. I won't let you. My beautiful girl. We are going to have a big healthy baby, and we're both going to be ninety years old when we die.

CHARLOTTE: Only ninety?

NICHOLLS: We have many, many more things yet to do.

CHARLOTTE: Arthur, I always thought my whole life would be in my books. But it wasn't. I love you Arthur Nicholls, don't you ever forget that.

NICHOLLS: Of course.

(Charlotte repeats convulsing choreography.)

CHARLOTTE: I'm very tired.

NICHOLLS: You need your rest.

(Nicholls lifts Charlotte to a standing position from behind her, in the same pose that Rochester holds her in when he confesses his feelings. She becomes limp in his arms and slowly collapses to the floor. He lifts her again and she collapses again. They repeat this many times, increasing in speed each time. On the final lift Nicholls holds the limp body of Charlotte in his arms. Slowly the lights fade out.)

END OF PLAY

FOOTNOTES

[1] Journal entry by Charlotte Brontë, August 11, 1836.

[2] Passages in both letters taken from actual letters written by Henry Nussey and Charlotte Brontë in the Spring of 1839.

[3] Spoken by the character of Jane Eyre in Charlotte Brontë's novel of the same name, published 1847.

[4] Letter written from Charlotte Brontë to Monsieur Heger, dated January 8, 1845.

[5] Letter written to Charlotte Brontë from Robert Southey, dated March, 1837.

[6] Excerpt from letter written by Charlotte Brontë, March, 1847.

[7] From a poem written by Charlotte Brontë.

[8] Conversation between Charlotte and Mr. Brontë from a letter written by Mrs. Gaskell to Catherine Winkworth, August 25, 1850, as told to Mrs. Gaskell by Charlotte Brontë.

[9] Scene between Rochester and Charlotte from Charlotte Brontë's novel *Jane Eyre,* published 1847.

[10] All the above reviews were actually written upon the publication of *Jane Eyre* by various reviewers in different publications.

[11] Charlotte's monologue from a letter written by Charlotte Brontë to Mr. Williams, 1848.

[12] This sentence is spoken by Caroline Helstone in Charlotte Brontë's novel *Shirley,* published 1849.

[13] Paragraph from a letter written by Charlotte Brontë, June, 1849.

[14] From "Dear Charlotte, she is an odd, fascinating…" through Charlotte's monologue was taken from letters written between George Smith and Charlotte Brontë in November and December, 1852.

[15] Beginning with Rochester's first line "Are you anything akin to me…", this is a scene from Charlotte Brontë's novel *Jane Eyre.*

[16] Rochester's monologue taken from Charlotte Brontë's novel *Jane Eyre.*

[17] "I grieve to leave Thornfield…" (Charlotte's lines only) taken from *Jane Eyre.*

[18] Described to Catherine Winkworth by Charlotte Brontë on July 27, 1854.

[19] Monologue taken from a letter written by Charlotte to Ellen Nussey on August 9, 1854.

[20] Monologue taken from a letter written by Charlotte to Miss Wooler, September, 1854.

Kicking Inside
by Jeannie Zusy

THE AUTHOR

Jeannie Zusy writes, acts, and directs. She has performed her one-woman pieces *Talkin' to my Girlfriends* and *Ladies Room* at the Ensemble Studio Theatre and various Off-Off-Broadway theaters. Her plays *Ladies Room Manhattan, Ladies Room Queens, Zen and the Art of Making It* and *Kicking Inside* were produced by the Flock Theater Company, NYC. She has written a screenplay adaptation of *Ladies Room Manhattan*. Recent plays include *Petrol Man* and *Girls Jefferson Junior High*. She is currently at work on a full-length play titled *Jimmy Moves Out*.

AUTHOR'S NOTE

Two years ago I wrote in my journal: "My uterus is dying. It needs life." And from this I gave birth to a play. I took what was right in front of me and put a time bomb underneath it. You could call this a story about a woman who wants a baby, which it is, but it is also a story about a person who wants something— needs something—to fill the empty place inside. Actually, all the characters are looking for something, searching for something to fill them up. Imperfect and afraid, they keep searching...I also wanted to explore how people can love each other but miss, how our inadequacies and egos can lead to our biggest losses, how paralyzing fear can be.

Exactly nine months after I finished this draft I gave birth to my first child, Olivia. I dedicate this play to her and to my husband John Cote who dared with me to create a new life.

I am grateful to Playwrights Horizons, Ensemble Studio Theatre and Flock Theater Company for the parts they played in various stages of this play's development.

ORIGINAL PRODUCTION

Kicking Inside was first produced by the Flock Theater Company at the Greenwich Street Theatre in New York City. It opened December 5, 1996. It was directed by Frits Zernike, assistant director/stage manager David Benson, with the following cast:

JESSICA	Jeannie Zusy
DAVID	Frits Zernike
ELAINE	Irene Glezos
MARIE	Grace Miglio
PATRICIA	Tanya Greve
THOMAS	Hugh Hunter

Kicking Inside

ACT I
SCENE I

Jessica and David's apartment, Manhattan's Upper West Side. Living room/kitchen. Christmas tree is lit. Presents under it. Jessica looks out the window. It's evening and it's snowing. David enters, returning from work. He's in a suit and carries a brief case. He shakes off the snow.

DAVID: Man!
   (She turns to him and smiles.)
DAVID: Man. *(He smells dinner cooking, goes to kitchen, opens pot.)* Mmmmmm-mmm. Planes will not be flying. No way will planes be flying. Have you called the airline? Jess? Okay. I'm gonna go call the airline.
   (He exits to bedroom. She waits, he returns.)
DAVID: We'll have to check before we leave in the morning. *(He opens lid to pot again.)* Do I need to do anything with this?
JESSICA: Stir it.
DAVID: Three feet.
JESSICA: Hmm?
DAVID: We're supposed to get three feet. Christmas Eve Eve. What a mess.
JESSICA: …I think we should move upstate.
DAVID: And do what?
JESSICA: Milk horses.
DAVID: We'll go visit Kevin and Marie in the Spring. So is this pretty much ready? Can we eat?
JESSICA: Bread. *(She goes to kitchen and puts bread in oven. Kisses him.)* Merry Christmas.
DAVID: We have to call in the morning. Our flight might be canceled.
JESSICA: Might not.
DAVID: Might.
JESSICA: You'd give anything to not have to visit your parents.
DAVID: There's the snow storm of the century out there.

JESSICA: It's exciting to fly in the snow. Big flakes dancing by your window. A nice warm airplane meal on your tray.

DAVID: Turbulence and nausea.

JESSICA: Soaring over snow-capped mountains.

DAVID: Try snow-capped factories, Jess. We're going to Detroit.

JESSICA: Factories look beautiful in the snow

DAVID: You're delusional...What's this?

JESSICA: A collection of short stories.

DAVID: Good?

JESSICA: Thomas Lauren wrote them. You met him, used to work in fiction? Went to Paris for a couple of years?

DAVID: Oh yeah, to work for that big publishing house.

JESSICA: Anyway, he's back. We might publish them.

DAVID: Early writer's angst, huh?

JESSICA: What makes you say that?

DAVID: You're in never-never land. *(Pause.)* Today was Tom Van Bloom's last day at work. I can't believe he's getting the hell out of there.

JESSICA: Good for him.

DAVID: I'm getting half his accounts.

JESSICA: Bad for you.

DAVID: It'll be good for us in the long run. *(Pause.)* So, you didn't go in today?

JESSICA: I worked at home. I made dinner. I wrapped presents. I spoke with Dr. Vulvar.

DAVID: Yeah?

JESSICA: Yeah.

DAVID: And?

JESSICA: And. He gave me a prescription for love.

DAVID: Oh really?

JESSICA: Really.

DAVID: What'd he do, give you some aphrodisiac?

JESSICA: Love making today makes the cramps go away.

DAVID: I like this Dr. Vulva.

JESSICA: Vulvar.

DAVID: Will it be okay?

JESSICA: Mm-hmm...We have to make a baby. Doctors orders.

DAVID: What are you saying?

JESSICA: I'm saying there is nothing wrong with me that can't get fixed by a baby. I need a baby in my body.

DAVID: This is what he said?

JESSICA: Sweetie, this is what they say. Pregnancy induces a hormonal change that will arrest the growth.

DAVID: Yeah, but that first doctor, she was gonna put you on those hormones?

JESSICA: David, Dr. Vulvar said we are very lucky. We've caught it early enough. He said I'm very lucky that I'm in a situation where I can try to get pregnant right away. He wants to meet with us both next week to discuss the best course of action.

DAVID: Course of action?

JESSICA: Plan of attack. Whatever. So that we can do everything that is in our power to get pregnant.

DAVID: Sweetie, what about the three year plan?

JESSICA: Sweetie, we said three years five years ago when we got married.

DAVID: Jess. Take a good long look at my parents this Christmas and you'll see why the last thing we need to do is to rush into having kids.

JESSICA: We need to do it now or it will be too late. If I don't get pregnant now my uterus will be devoured by this disease and I'll become infertile. The pregnancy will stop the growth, see. He thinks we've caught it early enough.

DAVID: You're not dying or anything? You're not dying?

JESSICA: My uterus is dying. It needs life. A baby is what my uterus needs.

DAVID: But it's your uterus, not you.

JESSICA: It's my uterus.

DAVID: Vulvar.

JESSICA: Yes?

DAVID: Vulvar, Vulvar. How can you trust a gyno named Vulvar anyway? I mean why did he become one in the first place—so he could make jokes at parties?

JESSICA: I'm gonna get you some wine.

DAVID: Come on, Jess, there must be other options. The other doctor said…

JESSICA: A hysterectomy is a last resort, not an option…if I don't get pregnant in the next two years I'll have to get one anyway.

DAVID: We should get another opinion.

JESSICA: And a fourth and a fifth…

DAVID: I'm sorry, Jessica, I'm just surprised…Just let me sit with the idea for a few days, okay?

JESSICA: Sure.

DAVID: My mother will be thrilled.

JESSICA: At least somebody will be.

DAVID: Little Miss Tragedy. That book's gotten to you.

JESSICA: Yeah.

DAVID: Have you packed yet?

JESSICA: No.

DAVID: Let's have dinner and then we can pack and open presents.

JESSICA: Okay.

DAVID: I know which one I'm gonna open first. Do you?

JESSICA: Yeah.

DAVID: Merry Christmas, Sweetie.

SCENE II

The publishing house where Jessica works. Her boss Elaine's office. Jessica waits while Elaine is on the phone.

ELAINE: Gracias Maria. I'll be casa a diez. Si, Maria. Gracias Maria. *(She hangs up.)* My nanny is driving me crazy. Jessica. Are you feeling better?

JESSICA: Yes, thanks.

ELAINE: Good. You did an excellent job editing Thomas Lauren's stories. Excellent.

JESSICA: Thanks.

ELAINE: I like that you took it upon yourself to take on his book. I want you to do that more often, take the initiative.

JESSICA: Okay.

ELAINE: I'm meeting with him today to discuss a publishing schedule. This is largely due to your high praise of his work. I want you to know that. I probably never would have gotten to it.

JESSICA: Well, he did work here for two years. I thought someone should cover it.

ELAINE: Oh, I probably would have flipped through it. He is a mench.

JESSICA: He's a very good writer.

ELAINE: Yes he is. He is a very good writer. And you are a very good editor. I didn't know you had such a knack for fiction.

JESSICA: Well, yes, that's what I got my Masters in. Fiction writing.

ELAINE: And you are one of the few people who can say that they actually make a living in their chosen field.

JESSICA: Well, editing non-fiction is hardly fiction writing.

ELAINE: But I'm moving you. I want you on the fiction staff. Would that interest you? There's no salary change of course. Just a department switch.

JESSICA: Yes that would interest me. I consider fiction my forte.

ELAINE: Oh?

JESSICA: Remember when I first interviewed with you? I had submitted the first thirty pages of my novel—you said I was a natural fiction writer.

ELAINE: I probably said you were a natural at fiction—

(Phone rings.)

ELAINE: What was it called? Excuse me, Jessica. *(She answers it.)* Elaine Strom. Barney. I still think the ending needs some work. Barney. Barney: calm down. I'm sorry, but I still think somebody has to change! Real life? Who wants to read about real life? If you let Taylor grow…then the wife, let the wife grow…I don't care who grows—it's slot for April you have a Christmas release. Christmas is about hope, Barney. Barney? Jesus. *(She hangs up.)* Sorry, Jessica.

JESSICA: *Mother Expecting.* My book.

ELAINE: Health? Self-Help?

JESSICA: A novel.

ELAINE: Honey, I read so much crap.

JESSICA: But we talked about it…

ELAINE: Do you think I have the time to read every unfinished novel written by the staff here? Let alone every young talented go-getter interviewing for a job? Sweetie, I must have had it covered. I hired you because you are an extremely bright young woman and an excellent editor, and that'll get you a lot further in this world, believe me.

(Her phone rings, she answers it.)

ELAINE: Elaine Strom. Thomas…Hello, my darling. That's okay. That's okay. I'm running late too. I don't know about you but I'm starving. Alfredos. Excellent. Fifteen. Caio. *(She hangs up.)* Mmmm, I'm having lunch with the mench. Let me give you some things to get you started. We'll talk this afternoon. *(She hands Jessica a huge stack of books.)* Cover these. This one I'd like special coverage and this is a possible go for the fall so let me know what you think. ASAP.

JESSICA: Okay.

ELAINE: *Mother Expecting,* huh? Have you done any more work on it?

JESSICA: So many books, so little time.

ELAINE: You're a doll. Welcome to fiction, Jessica.

JESSICA: Thanks, Elaine.

(Elaine runs out to her lunch meeting leaving Jessica standing with her huge stack of books.)

SCENE III

Jessica and Marie are lunching at Saks Fifth Avenue. Marie has lots of shopping bags with her.

JESSICA: He said I should try yoga.

MARIE: That sounds good.

JESSICA: Yoga? I don't need some guru telling me what to do. Besides, it's offensive.

MARIE: What? What's offensive?

JESSICA: The suggestion that a little stretching and breathing is all I need to get over this.

MARIE: I don't think that that was what he meant.

JESSICA: Well, what do you think he meant?...Then he had the nerve to suggest that I start keeping a journal again, get back to my writing...I want another drink, how 'bout you? *(She tries to flag down the waiter.)* You?

MARIE: One's my limit.

JESSICA: Oh, right.

MARIE: Jess—

JESSICA: Yeah?

MARIE: Jessica, there was a time in my life when I thought about leaving Kevin.

JESSICA: What?

MARIE: I'm not kidding.

JESSICA: What are you talking about? When?

MARIE: I don't want to say when.

JESSICA: Why not?

MARIE: It was about the time of your wedding.

JESSICA: Bullshit.

MARIE: No, it's not. When you two were island hopping in Greece, Kevin and I were figuring out who would get the silverware and who would get the cats.

JESSICA: I don't believe you.

MARIE: It's true. I was miserable. I thought I had made a mistake with Kevin. I thought I made the wrong choice. I thought we got married too young. I was having fantasies about every man I encountered. I was obsessing about the doorman.

JESSICA: Ricardo?

MARIE: No. Another one. He worked the night shift. I got crazy. I would think up excuses to go down to the lobby between midnight and eight AM. I would purposely leave the mail or the dry cleaning. I would go to the deli.

Once when Kevin was out of town on business I told him I was locked out.
I stood down there watching bad cable tv with him for two hours pre-
tending I was really pissed off. I told him I was waiting for a friend who
had a set of my keys to get home from her restaurant job.

JESSICA: This doesn't sound like Marie.

MARIE: Every client I had I wanted to fuck the shit out of. It wasn't just fucking
though. There was this one guy—my zillion dollar account? We were
gonna sail the world together. And he wanted me too I could tell. It was
that night though, that night with the doorman that really got me. I
walked around the block four times at three o'clock in the morning so he
would think I picked up my keys from my friend. When I got back to the
building, he was making out with one of my neighbor's daughters in the
storage room. I got home and I was too depressed to masturbate. I realized
something was wrong with my life.

JESSICA: God, I always thought you guys were so happy. I thought you had this
perfect sexual relationship.

MARIE: Not always.

JESSICA: So when I was coming to you with pre-wedding jitters and you were
telling me about the beauty of marriage, it was all a lie? It was all bullshit,
wasn't it?

MARIE: No, it wasn't like that. It was a very confusing time in my life.

JESSICA: Mine too.

MARIE: I'm trying to open up to you—

JESSICA: So what's the matter? Is he back in your life? Is the doorman back in
your life?

MARIE: God, no!

JESSICA: So what's up?

MARIE: So I started going to church.

JESSICA: What?

MARIE: I started going to church.

JESSICA: Yeah, right.

MARIE: I mean it. I started going to church every Sunday. Sometimes in the
middle of the week in midtown. I'd just pop into some church and pray. I
didn't go to Catholic school, I didn't know how to pray. I just knew I had
to go someplace quiet where I could think or not think. And then one day
Kevin came with me. And one day during our lunch hour we met at this
little church on 52nd Street and we decided it was time for us to leave the city.

JESSICA: Wow.

MARIE: You see, that night, that night when I found myself walking around my block at two o'clock in the morning I realized I was investing myself in something that wasn't real, that wasn't my life. That's what inspired the big change. That doorman has no idea the influence he had on my life.

JESSICA: You never told me you went to church.

MARIE: I thought you might think we went Bible belt. I don't know. I didn't even tell Kevin until I'd been doing it a few months. I guess I was embarrassed at first.

JESSICA: So are you still going? Do you go to a church in Rhinebeck?

MARIE: Yeah.

JESSICA: Wow.

MARIE: Maybe you should try it.

(Pause.)

JESSICA: You think something is wrong with me, don't you? That's why you brought up this whole thing.

MARIE: I'm not saying that at all.

JESSICA: You know, I'm not imagining these pains. I've been to Dr. Vulvar.

MARIE: I know that.

JESSICA: He's a good doctor. He's on Park Avenue.

MARIE: I know, Jessica.

JESSICA: There are books written about this.

MARIE: I know that.

JESSICA: But you think a little prayer will make the problem go away.

MARIE: Look, I turned to prayer when I didn't know where else to turn. It gave me guidance. Maybe for you yoga could help or I don't know…getting back to your writing or something…Miracles can happen, that's all I'm saying. Don't be mad.

JESSICA: Where is our waiter?

MARIE: You're mad.

JESSICA: No I'm not. I'm just tired and I wish he would check in with us once in a while.

MARIE: I know you have a real disease. I don't doubt that.

JESSICA: Whatever. Do you want another drink?

MARIE: I need to catch the 2:15.

JESSICA: Well, then we'll get the check. (She signals waiter for check.)

SCENE IV

Middle of the Night. David and Jessica's apartment. David comes out of the bedroom. He's wearing boxers, robe and socks. Goes to kitchen to get a glass of water. He's shaking. He drinks the whole glass looks down, realizes he's still shaking. He looks to bedroom door. He gets more water. Still shaking. He walks to bedroom door, peeks in. She's still sleeping. Hesitates closing it. Closes it. Shaking like mad. Almost drops glass. Catches it. Looks to door. Thinks about dropping it. Decides not to. Sits on couch. Holding glass. Shaking. Door. Puts on tv. Tv doesn't help. Door. Turns up volume. Still no Jessica. Shaking. Waits. Cranks up volume. Door. Knob starts to turn, he turns back to tv. Jessica emerges disheveled in pjs.

JESSICA: That's loud.

DAVID: Huh?

JESSICA: LOUD.

DAVID: Oh. Oh, Jess. I'm sorry. *(He turns volume down.)* I'm sorry.
(She turns back to bed.)

JESSICA: What time is it?

DAVID: 4:30.
(She stops and tries to get her focus.)

JESSICA: 4:30?

DAVID: Yeah.

JESSICA: In the morning? In the middle of the night?

DAVID: Yeah.

JESSICA: What are you watching?

DAVID: I dunno.

JESSICA: Why are you up?

DAVID: Couldn't sleep.

JESSICA: Oh.
(She sits down next to him on couch and they stare blankly at the volumeless middle of the night tv.)

JESSICA: Come back to bed.

DAVID: No.

JESSICA: Come on.

DAVID: I can't.
(They continue to stare blankly at tv.)

JESSICA: Water.

(He hands it to her. He's shaking.)

JESSICA: You're shaking.

DAVID: No I'm not.

JESSICA: Yeah, you are, look at your hand, you're shaking.

(He is shaking. He puts the glass quickly on the coffee table and spills in the process. He gets up to get a towel. Jessica turns off the tv. She starts to wipe up with the end of her robe.)

JESSICA: Stop it. Stay here. It's just water.

(He sits back down. He reaches for the water again.)

JESSICA: Look at you.

DAVID: I know.

JESSICA: Why are you shaking?

DAVID: I dunno.

JESSICA: Why are you shaking?

DAVID: Bad dream.

JESSICA: What was it?

DAVID: Jesus Christ. Leave me alone. *(He heads towards the kitchen again.)*

JESSICA: Where are you going? I wiped it up.

DAVID: To get a drink!

(He exits to kitchen. Jessica sits and waits. He returns with a brandy.)

DAVID: I'm sorry. It's stupid. I dunno. I just can't sleep. Probably something I ate. Why don't you go back to bed, I'll be there in a minute.

JESSICA: What was it?

DAVID: It's dumb. Stupid. Nothing.

JESSICA: You are really shaking. I'm getting you a blanket.

DAVID: I'm not cold.

(She stares at him.)

DAVID: It's cliché. A plane crash. I dreamed I was in a plane crash.

JESSICA: Yeah? *(She sits back down.)*

DAVID: I was on a plane. I was by myself. I think I was the only one on the plane. Except the stewardess. I was scared. It was raining. Thundering and lightning. And windy. I could see the wing from my window and pieces of metal were flying off. I said I want to get off and she said it's too late. We were already in the air. And then something happened. A big jolt. My laptop went flying. And I looked out the window and the wing had broken off and we were spinning and the plane started to dive.

JESSICA: And that's when you woke up?

DAVID: Yeah.

JESSICA: Wow.

DAVID: It was pretty vivid.

JESSICA: I can see that.

DAVID: This is good. *(The drink.)* Do you want one?

> *(She nods yes then shakes no.)*

JESSICA: The new painkillers.

DAVID: I'm sorry about earlier and I'm sorry I woke you.

JESSICA: Oh, David.

DAVID: I just can't.

> *(She pulls him to the couch and cuddles him.)*

JESSICA: Come here you big balooka.

DAVID: Stop.

JESSICA: You schnuggle-bum, honey-bun, sweet-potato-pie.

DAVID: Stop it.

> *(She messes his hair.)*

JESSICA: You're my sweetie-pie, do you know that?

DAVID: I mean it. *(He gets up.)*

JESSICA: David, we're not flying anywhere anytime soon.

DAVID: I know that.

JESSICA: David. Come to bed. I can put your mind at ease.

> *(He's pacing.)*

JESSICA: You know something interesting? Apparently when people have children they get over their phobias. I mean, it's a fact. I guess it puts everything in perspective and their little everyday fears get washed away. I read that once.

DAVID: Statistically?

JESSICA: Statistically what?

DAVID: Is that statistically proven?

JESSICA: I don't know I just read it in a magazine somewhere.

DAVID: In Dr. Vulva's office?

JESSICA: Would you stop pacing, you're making me dizzy.

> *(He sits down. Puts his head in his hands. Jessica goes up behind him and starts to rub his shoulders.)*

JESSICA: God, you are so tense.

> *(He pushes her away.)*

DAVID: Stop. Stop, would you stop?

JESSICA: What is the matter with you?

DAVID: What is the matter with you? Where are you going?

JESSICA: To bed.

DAVID: My life! My life! Something is the matter with my life!

(She stops. They are at a stand still.)

JESSICA: Oh?

DAVID: It's not you. It's. It's my life. It's not going the way I planned it. It's not going. Anywhere. Work. I work every weekend, I work late nights and I still don't make enough money.

JESSICA: You make a lot of money. Do you realize you make more money than most Americans ever dream of? You make more money than most of the people I know ever dream of. I'd be thrilled if I made even half of what you make.

DAVID: Yeah, so would I.

JESSICA: Well, I'm sorry if my chosen career doesn't come with a million dollar salary attached to it.

DAVID: I don't love my work. But I keep hoping I'll get promoted and maybe then I'll love it.

JESSICA: Then get a new job.

DAVID: How?

JESSICA: What do you mean, how?

DAVID: I mean "how"? Go back to school? Take a job building houses for twenty thousand a year? Will you support me in that?

(She doesn't answer.)

DAVID: Not with a fucking baby to feed! Not when nursery schools cost fifteen thousand dollars a year! Get real, Jessica. How could any of this be at all plausible?

JESSICA: You send them to public schools.

DAVID: And watch them get shot in the cross-fire on the evening news.

JESSICA: I don't know how, you move! People do it. Your parents did it.

DAVID: On food stamps.

JESSICA: And you turned out okay. You didn't starve to death. Poor people have been having kids since the beginning of time.

DAVID: And are they happy, these poor people? Working shit jobs, getting minimum wage?

JESSICA: I bet that most of them would say that having children was the best thing that ever happened to them.

DAVID: That's because they haven't got a life!

JESSICA: You just said your life isn't where you wanted it to be. So maybe this is a great opportunity to change. To change your life. Maybe the path you are on is taking some unexpected turns that will take you to a greater place than you ever imagined.

DAVID: Somehow having a baby doesn't seem like taking a turn. It seems like jumping off a cliff.

JESSICA: You'd be doing it with a friend.

DAVID: I don't even know if I like kids. I don't know. I just don't know. *(Pause.)* See, I'm still shaking…I do love you, you know.

JESSICA: I know. I love you, too.

SCENE V

Jessica is waiting on a bench outside a coffeehouse. Thomas approaches.

THOMAS: Hi.

JESSICA: Hi.

THOMAS: Good to see you.

JESSICA: Yeah. You too. You look good.

THOMAS: So do you. Let me get a coffee—do you want one—anything?

JESSICA: I'm okay, thanks.

(He goes. She waits. He returns.)

JESSICA: So, how are you?

THOMAS: I'm okay. You?

JESSICA: Okay.

THOMAS: It's good to see you. You look great.

JESSICA: Thanks.

THOMAS: How long has it been?

THOMAS: Two years?   JESSICA: Two years.

JESSICA: I just remember because wasn't it the Christmas party at work? Everyone was wishing you a Bon Voyage. Yeah, it was two years ago.

THOMAS: Your hair was shorter then.

JESSICA: Yeah, yeah, it was.

THOMAS: I blew on your neck by the eggnog.

JESSICA: That was you?

THOMAS: You wore a silver gold dress. You said it was your mother's.

JESSICA: Yeah. It was. So how was Paris?

THOMAS: Great. I'm going back.

JESSICA: Oh, great.

THOMAS: Not anytime too soon. Maybe in a year or so.

JESSICA: I'd love to live there.

THOMAS: Yeah ?

THOMAS: Parlez vous francais?   JESSICA: Do you speak French?

THOMAS: Oui.   JESSICA: Une petite per.

THOMAS: You'd learn over there.

JESSICA: Yeah.

THOMAS: Great day, huh? Winter in New York.

JESSICA: You can't beat it.

THOMAS: You can't beat it with a stick. Boy I'm glad you got me uptown today. Great day for a walk in the park. Would you like another coffee?

JESSICA: No thanks.

THOMAS: Tea?

JESSICA: No thanks. *(Pause.)* I really enjoyed editing your stories.

THOMAS: Yeah?

JESSICA: I thought they were beautiful.

THOMAS: Thanks.

JESSICA: I thought maybe we could collaborate on future projects.

THOMAS: Great.

JESSICA: I'm taking more initiative.

THOMAS: Great. *(Pause.)* You're shaking.

JESSICA: I am? I am. Oh. Oh God. This is crazy.

THOMAS: What?

JESSICA: This is the craziest thing I've ever done in my life.

THOMAS: What? What are you doing?

JESSICA: Are you seeing anybody?

THOMAS: I dunno. Kind of. Are you still married?

(Lights up on David, sitting at his desk at home, staring into his laptop. He looks worried. He goes to phone book. Searches through it, muttering.)

DAVID: Vulvar, Vulvar, Vulvar…Vulvar, Vulvar, Vulvar… *(No luck.)* Shit. *(He dials information.)* Yeah, I'm looking for a Doctor Vulvar on Madison Avenue…No, Park Avenue…Vulvar…V-U-L-V-A…Yeah, I know. That's funny. R. V-U-L-V-Yeah, he is believe it or not…Park—Oh, thanks, uh… *(He jots down number.)*

(Lights up again on Jessica and Thomas at coffeehouse.)

JESSICA: You're attracted to me. I mean you have been in the past attracted to me. It's not my imagination, right?

THOMAS: Since the first time I laid eyes on you.

JESSICA: Still?

THOMAS: Yeah. Still. But you're married.

JESSICA: Yeah. I know. Did you think about me in Paris? I mean of course you had affairs with beautiful French girls, but did you think about me?

THOMAS: Yeah.

JESSICA: I thought so.

THOMAS: You mean you've been obsessing about me?

JESSICA: I didn't say obsessing.

THOMAS: There were times when I was thinking about you and I know you were thinking about me. I could feel it.

JESSICA: This is crazy. This is nuts. God I'm insane. I should commit myself right now.

THOMAS: Why are you so nervous? Look. The answer is yes. Whatever it is you asked me here for, my answer is yes.

JESSICA: You don't know why I asked you.

THOMAS: You have a project you wanted to talk to me about? Is that really it? Look, I was hoping. I was hoping and praying that you were gonna tell me you divorced your husband or he died in a car crash and you just needed contact with another man. I worked up all kinds of scenarios.

JESSICA: We're very married and he is very healthy.

THOMAS: Well maybe you still need contact with another man.

JESSICA: You would have an affair? You would have an affair with a married woman?

THOMAS: If that's the best you can offer me, yes. I've been obsessed with you. I've lusted after you. I could fall in love with you in about two seconds. This girl I'm kind of seeing now—I met her in France—it's been six months and I haven't gotten close to saying I love you and I don't think I ever will. It's not there. Whatever it is that is supposed to be there, it's not there. So, yes. Yes. Yes, I would have an affair with you.

JESSICA: I don't believe in affairs.

THOMAS: Oh.

(Lights up on David dialing phone. Attempts a British accent.)

DAVID: Uh, yes, my wife and I have just moved here from the, uh, British Isle, yes, and well, she is very shy, but pregnant, and we wanted to know the credentials of a Mr. Dr. Vulvar…Mayo Clinic, Oxford, Mount Sinai…Yes, very well, very good. We'll be in touch. *(He hangs up.)* Shit.

(Lights up on Jessica and Thomas.)

JESSICA: I can't believe you would have an affair with me like that. I mean what kind of moral standards do you keep? Have you been with other married women? Is that a thing with you? You fear commitment, you don't want the real thing. Fight and conquer is that what you're after? I mean what kind of person are you? You just want to have some down and dirty sex and you can tell the boys about how you sexually awakened some repressed married woman? Chew and spit me out so you can move onto another. Is that what you want? I didn't ask you here to ask if you would have an affair.

THOMAS: Oh.

JESSICA: I mean I don't even know you really. I've worked with you on a couple of projects, seen you at meetings and parties. From what I can tell you drink too much. You're a pot-head. Why are you laughing?

THOMAS: I haven't touched a drug in two years.

JESSICA: Oh.

THOMAS: Look. I went to Paris to clear my head after Sarah and I broke up. It was a good job but mostly I went because I needed to get away. Mostly I worked. I wrote. I took really long walks and I had good French food. I drank wine—I still drink wine but I can go without it, too. I don't know why I should, but I could.

JESSICA: I like French wine.

THOMAS: Why did you ask me here?

(Lights up on David, on the phone.)

DAVID: Kevin. You're home! How are ya? I'm working. Working on a Saturday, what else is new. At home…Well, I'm sure Marie told you about Jessica's diagnosis…what was that? Oh, yeah, do you wanna call me…sure… Diaper duty, huh? Where's Marie? Oh sure, go ahead…

(Lights back up on Jessica and Thomas.)

JESSICA: Really, I just thought we should, you know, touch base. I could give you feedback on your work and you could give me feedback on my editing.

THOMAS: You just wanted to exchange feedback?

JESSICA: I don't know if you know that your book was my first fiction job.

THOMAS: Oh? No, I didn't.

JESSICA: Yeah, I guess I felt a real connection to your work, I—

THOMAS: You liked my work?

JESSICA: Do you like kids?

THOMAS: Excuse me?

JESSICA: You've been around the world, met a lot of women, do you have kids anywhere? Bambinos?

THOMAS: Bambinos?

JESSICA: I love kids. You strike me as the kind of guy that probably loves kids, right?

THOMAS: Yeah, I love kids.

JESSICA: I loved that story you wrote "My Son and Me." Was that based on reality?

THOMAS: No, I don't have a son. I have a vivid imagination.

JESSICA: So you imagine yourself with kids.

(Lights up on David again. He's still holding.)

DAVID: The little guy sure has some big lungs…Huh? I was just saying…Oh, that's cool. Yeah, she's fine…Oh, Yeah, we're trying. That's okay. Hey, birthday parties will not wait. Three? In one weekend? Wow. Just called to say hey. Give my best to Marie and the little tyke. *(He hangs up.)* Jesus.

(Lights up on Jessica and Thomas.)

JESSICA: I mean my biological clock isn't ticking, it's kicking! You know what I mean?

THOMAS: Yeah.

JESSICA: So here he has this great opportunity to make a baby with me and he's not sure he wants to do it. Isn't that nuts? Isn't that crazy?

THOMAS: Crazy.

JESSICA: I mean I just think babies are a part of life, you know?

THOMAS: Yeah.

JESSICA: I mean I just really liked your stories, you know? The ambiguities, the moral dilemmas. You ask real questions, you know. No answers, just questions.

THOMAS: Yeah, I ask questions.

JESSICA: So I just thought this was a situation you could appreciate, from a dramatic standpoint.

THOMAS: I appreciate it.

JESSICA: See, I knew you would…I think we're gonna work really well together.

THOMAS: Yeah.

JESSICA: So, I'll see you Wednesday, at the office. You, Elaine and I have a meeting, right?

THOMAS: Wednesday, right.

JESSICA: Good seeing you again, Thomas.

THOMAS: Yeah, Jessica.

(Jessica leaves Thomas alone on the bench. He watches her go.)

THOMAS: Oh, man.

(Lights back up on David.)

DAVID: Oh, man, oh, man, oh man.

SCENE VI

David visits his sister Patricia at the institution. She's playing solitaire. Through the entire scene she never stops playing solitaire.

DAVID: Hi Patricia.

PATRICIA: David Michael Miller.

DAVID: How are you?

PATRICIA: I'm winning.

DAVID: I brought you a present.

PATRICIA: Do you like my sweater? Joe gave it to me for Christmas. You know Joe? Big black Joe? He gave it to me. I like it. I like him. I have a crush on him. He likes me too but he's married. The wife and kids. Signed sealed delivered. I like the sweater though. Do you like it?

DAVID: Yeah. Yeah. I like it.

PATRICIA: Joe gave it to me. Big black Joe.

DAVID: That's nice.

PATRICIA: What? What? You don't believe me?

DAVID: I believe you. Joe who works the front desk?—

PATRICIA: Oh, he didn't break any rules, David. Not if that's what you're thinking. He's not a rule breaker. He's a rule maker! That's what I call Joe. He's a ruler! King! King of the Jungle! No he didn't break any rules David.

DAVID: I didn't think—

PATRICIA: He was my secret Santa. Picked me on purpose too. I know. I know. A woman's intuition. A woman knows. I'm a woman now. I'm not a girl. I'm a woman.

DAVID: I know that. Why don't you open the present I brought you, Patricia.

PATRICIA: Later. Busy.

(He watches her play solitaire.)

PATRICIA: So we didn't come here to talk about me, we came to talk about you! You! You! You with a capital "Ye."

DAVID: No, I just came to see you.

PATRICIA: How are you? How's the wife and kids?

DAVID: Jessica's fine. We don't have any kids.

PATRICIA: I know that. I know that. But she wants 'em doesn't she? Wants a whole house full of 'em.

DAVID: How are your paintings going? Have you done any paintings?

PATRICIA: I don't paint anymore. Don't wanna chop my ear off. Don't wanna self destruct. Gonna get out of here soon. Get a real life. No more paintings. Just reality.

DAVID: Oh?

PATRICIA: Don't believe me? That's okay. It's my reality, not yours. It's my reality. So why did you come here?

DAVID: I came to see you, to see how you're doing.

PATRICIA: No you didn't.

DAVID: Patricia.

PATRICIA: No you didn't David Michael Miller. No you didn't.

DAVID: Do you want to play a game?

PATRICIA: Huh?

DAVID: A game. Hearts? Spades? Go Fish?

PATRICIA: I hate Go Fish.

DAVID: How 'bout Hearts or Spades? Or do you know another game? Saw Mom and Dad for Christmas. They're real happy about your progress…I've been getting these flashbacks lately. Flashbacks of these memories. You, me, Matt, and Kelly waiting on the corner for the school bus to come. Remember how Dad made that rule how we had to wait an hour before we could go home to get Mom to give us a ride? We'd stand there for ten minutes knowing we missed the bus or it just wasn't coming that day but we'd have to stand there another fifty so we wouldn't piss off Dad. Some days we wouldn't get to school until lunch time. It seems like we spent most of our childhoods just waiting. Waiting to get punished, waiting for Mom to leave Dad, waiting for a bus that we knew would never come. Do you remember that? It's funny you said that, you know. About Jessica wanting a house full of kids. She wants a kid, you know. She's got this health condition where if she wants one she supposedly has to have it now. And I'm sure if she has one, she'll want another. She always said she envied kids from big families. So I guess I'm trying to figure this out. I mean. I don't think I want to do that. I don't think. I want. To. Do you think that's…Do you think. I mean, I don't think, not everyone wants kids, you know? I mean I'm not a bad guy, you know? We just want different things. She wants this house full of kids and I have my career to worry about. I have things I still want to do. It's funny, don't you think, she's got some romantic notion about this family. Like it's this recipe for a happy life. Happy brothers and sisters playing twister together.

PATRICIA: I like twister.

DAVID: It's just. It's just. I don't think I want that. And I'm afraid I'll lose her.

Afraid I'll lose her if I don't give in. I guess it's just. I don't know. I don't know if I'm doing the right thing here. And you could always see things clearly. You always saw the truth. I mean Mom and Dad, they were miserable, right? You always saw that they were miserable. Even when the rest of us didn't want to. They were miserable then and they're miserable now. They're just poorer. I mean, kids are cute for a while but they're a pain in the ass, too. I mean look at us. I visit them twice a year, send an occasional check, flowers on Mother's Day. Was it worth it? Was I worth it?

PATRICIA: Maybe you're not in love with her.

DAVID: I love her. I love her deeply. I've never loved anyone the way I love her.

PATRICIA: Maybe you're just plain splat not fucking in love with her.

(Silence.)

DAVID: I think you should try painting again, you know? I think you had a real talent there. I wish you'd open your present.

PATRICIA: I thank you for it. It's exactly what I wanted.

DAVID: Yeah. It's good to see you. You look good. I'll talk to Dr. Rosen on my way out. We'll see you soon, okay? *(He starts to leave.)*

PATRICIA: Do you like my sweater? Joe gave me this sweater, Big Black Joe. I'd have his baby but he's married. Signed sealed delivered. He was my secret Santa. Secret.

SCENE VII

Upper West Side. Outside Jessica and David's apartment building. Evening. It's cold out. Jessica is walking down the street with a grocery bag. Thomas runs up to her, breathless.

THOMAS: Happily.

JESSICA: Huh?! Thomas, what are you doing?

THOMAS: Happily.

JESSICA: Yeah?

THOMAS: You left out a word. Happily. Very happily married. That's the phrase. Very happily married.

JESSICA: What?

THOMAS: Very married. That's what you said. My husband and I are very married and he is very healthy. Very married. You left out happily. You didn't say very happily married.

JESSICA: Well, that's what I meant.

THOMAS: It's not what you said.

JESSICA: It's a word. Semantics. I left out a word.

THOMAS: Yeah. You left out a word.

JESSICA: What—have you been waiting for me out here? You're supposed to meet us Wednesday, remember? At the office?

THOMAS: Yeah, well, something came over me. I had a revelation and I couldn't wait. I couldn't wait til Wednesday. I couldn't wait another minute.

JESSICA: Wait a minute. This is my neighborhood. David could be coming home any minute and I'm in the middle of making dinner and I just came out to buy an onion.

THOMAS: An onion. An onion. I know. I saw.

JESSICA: So my husband might be coming down this street any minute and I don't need him to see you talking to me like this.

THOMAS: Like what?

JESSICA: Like you know me. Like we aren't just friendly acquaintances. Like we have a relationship.

THOMAS: We do have a relationship! You just confided in me this weekend that your husband doesn't want to make a baby with you!! Remember? That was you wasn't it? I'm pretty sure that was you?

JESSICA: Look. Lower your voice or I'm walking away. Just act casual like we're friends having a conversation and we've just run into each other, okay? Is that too much to ask? Just be cool.

THOMAS: Can we walk around the corner? Would you feel safer around the corner?

JESSICA: Yes, but stay cool or I'm outta here. Do you hear me?

THOMAS: I can be cool. I am cool. I am the personification of cool.

JESSICA: Oh God.

(They walk around the corner.)

THOMAS: Is this good? It's dark—we're off the beaten track. Good?

JESSICA: Yes. Now tell me. What is this revelation? This revelation that was so big it couldn't wait until Wednesday?

THOMAS: It was this. You tell me you love your husband.

JESSICA: I do.

THOMAS: You keep telling me you love your husband. You would never be unfaithful to him. He's the love of your life, right?

JESSICA: Right.

THOMAS: So why did you leave out happily? Okay, okay, you said it's just a word—semantics—whatever—but very happily married is the phrase. The phrase we grew up with. It wouldn't be the same without the word happily. My parents were very happily married. I hope someday to be very happily married. "Happily" is the key word here. It is what we strive for, what we dream of. "Very" is the icing on the cake. We hope to live happily ever after. Not very happily ever after. That would be asking for too much. I mean it would be great to be very happily ever after but we'll more likely get happily ever after—if we're lucky. So my point is. My point is. By leaving out the word happily and just saying very it's like saying you've got the bad stuff but not the good stuff. It's a significant word to be left out of a phrase—a phrase where it naturally belongs.

JESSICA: So, yeah?

THOMAS: So all this leads me to believe that maybe you're not happily married and maybe he's not the love of your life and maybe this disease you've got—health condition—whatever you call it—maybe it was a gift from God to you saying get out of this marriage while you can—you deserve to be happy.

JESSICA: What a presumptuous thing to say. Who do you think you are? You don't know the first thing about me.

THOMAS: I think I know a little about you.

JESSICA: So this is some concoction God came up with to reward me to forewarn me to wake me up?

THOMAS: Maybe.

JESSICA: This is a crisis situation, do you understand? I love this man I'm married to. Do you get it? I love him and I want to grow old with him. But I want children too and he's not sure if he wants that.

THOMAS: So you wonder if you could love someone else. You wonder if you could love someone else and grow old with someone else who wants babies too. You wonder if there is someone out there that you could love more, that could love you more. Maybe you could have a passionate sexual relationship with a man who wants children too? Isn't that what you wonder? It doesn't have to be me, it just happens to be me.

JESSICA: You're way off base. I liked your stories. I thought you could offer some insight.

THOMAS: If you just wanted to discuss your situation you could have called a friend, a therapist, a family member, a priest. I'm sure you have plenty of friends who would be thrilled to share with you their insight. I could hook you up with my girlfriend, the two of you could get together and have a girls talk. But you called me. Someone you haven't seen in two years. Someone you really barely know.

JESSICA: So she is your girlfriend? Not just someone you're kind of seeing?

THOMAS: Well, yeah—I guess.

JESSICA: She calls you her boyfriend? You call her your girlfriend?

THOMAS: I mostly call her Corrine.

JESSICA: I don't know what I was thinking. You're right. I shouldn't be here. I shouldn't be here talking to you. I shouldn't be confiding in you. I don't even know you. David would be—This is crazy. You must think I'm crazy. I'm sorry. Please don't tell anyone if you can help it. *(She starts to rush away.)*

THOMAS: Jessica.

(She turns back.)

JESSICA: Yes?

THOMAS: I don't think you're crazy. I think you have a lot to figure out.

JESSICA: You do?

THOMAS: Yeah. It's big stuff.

JESSICA: Yeah.

THOMAS: You asked for my insight, I offer my insight. I'm honored that you turned to me, I really am honored.

JESSICA: Yeah? *(Jessica starts to cry.)* I'm just so tired.

THOMAS: Get some rest, okay? Sleep on it.

JESSICA: Yeah.

THOMAS: I'll sleep on it, too.

JESSICA: Yeah. Yeah, I'll sleep on it.

(David has approached, laptop, briefcase in hand.)

DAVID: Sleep on what?

JESSICA: Honey.

DAVID: Hi Sweetie. *(He gives her a kiss.)*

JESSICA: Hi. You remember Thomas? He used to work in fiction? You met at a couple of parties.

DAVID: Ah, the aspiring writer. How ya doing Thomas? Didn't you go to Europe for some great job?

THOMAS: Yeah. Paris. I'm back. How are you?

DAVID: Okay. So what are you gonna sleep on?

JESSICA: The meaning of life.

THOMAS: Yeah.

DAVID: Sleep on it? I can't get away from it. It's on my mind every waking minute and I still can't figure it out. I thought that was the kind of thing you were supposed to figure out in Paris.

JESSICA: Thomas was just telling me about his French girlfriend Corrine.

THOMAS: Yeah, she has friends in the neighborhood. I'm going over there for dinner.

DAVID: Good night to be inside. Man, it's cold. Look at you, your eyes are tearing.

JESSICA: I know. I'm making dinner.

DAVID: That's nice.

JESSICA: I just came out to buy an onion.

THOMAS: Well, it was nice seeing you again, David. You too, Jessica.

(David and Jessica turn to leave.)

THOMAS: Let me know if you figure it out.

(Jessica turns back.)

JESSICA: Huh?

THOMAS: The meaning of life and all that.

JESSICA: Oh, yeah. Bye.

(They walk away.)

DAVID: Nice guy.

SCENE VIII

Jessica and David's apartment. They're eating dinner.

JESSICA: You're quiet tonight. Rough day at work?

DAVID: Yeah. Rough day. You?

JESSICA: Yeah. But I thought it'd be nice to have a home-cooked meal. I thought it would be nice.

DAVID: It is. It is nice.

JESSICA: I spoke to Marie today.

DAVID: Oh?

JESSICA: They're doing great. The business is doing great. She said they're the top non-commercial salad dressing distributors in upstate New York.

DAVID: That's exciting.

JESSICA: Yeah. Things are really taking off for them. Little Max is getting stronger every day. He ripped her earring out. She has to get it sown up.

DAVID: What?

JESSICA: Her ear.

DAVID: That's funny.

JESSICA: She says she's almost through the first trimester and she's feeling pretty good.

(*Pause.*)

DAVID: That was a good dinner.

JESSICA: Good.

DAVID: New recipe?

JESSICA: I've made it a hundred times.

DAVID: No, I thought there was something different this time.

JESSICA: No.

DAVID: Some special kind of onion?

JESSICA: No.

DAVID: Oh, I thought it was some special onion.

JESSICA: Just your basic onion.

DAVID: You could have gotten a basic onion at the deli downstairs but I ran into you over on West End.

JESSICA: Well, it felt cool and crisp and I figured I'd just take a walk over to Fairway and get one.

DAVID: An invigorating idea.

(*She gets up to clear the table.*)

JESSICA: I didn't have any cramps today. Those painkillers he gave me are really helping.

DAVID: That's good. You shouldn't be drinking wine.

JESSICA: I know, but just one glass.

DAVID: I thought that was such a big deal with that prescription.

JESSICA: Honey, you're not supposed to drink alcohol with aspirin. Sometimes a girls gotta do what a girls gotta do.

DAVID: Nice to run into old friends.

JESSICA: Huh?

DAVID: Thomas.

JESSICA: I wouldn't call us old friends.

DAVID: He seems like a nice guy.

JESSICA: Yeah.

DAVID: Isn't he the one that toured Africa for a while?

JESSICA: He's a writer.

DAVID: Nice life.

JESSICA: Sure, if you like rhinos. Aren't you drinking your wine?

DAVID: Gotta work.

JESSICA: What are you working on?

DAVID: Deals, deals, deals.

(*As she continues cleaning up, she starts to drink his untouched wine. She is getting drunk.*)

DAVID: We should go out with them sometime.

JESSICA: Who?

DAVID: Thomas and his French girlfriend.

JESSICA: Why?

DAVID: Why? You're always trying to get me to be more social.

JESSICA: We barely have time to see our best friends.

DAVID: It might be nice to get to know some people that are really living life.

(*Jessica's in the kitchen now with the dishes.*)

JESSICA: Our friends live life.

DAVID: No, I just mean, it'd be different.

JESSICA: If buying a house in the country, starting a family and a business isn't living life I don't know what is.

DAVID: Can we drop the baby thing for one night?

JESSICA: I'm not talking about the baby thing, I'm just saying that Thomas and that girl are probably not that much—Damn it!

DAVID: What?

JESSICA: Goddamn mother fucking piece of shit. I cut myself.

DAVID: You alright?

JESSICA: Yeah, yeah, yeah, yeah. I'm a klutz that's all.

(*She stops up her wound with a towel. Drinks some more wine. David gets up to help.*)

DAVID: Why don't we try a band aid?

JESSICA: Oh, yeah, that was smart. A blood-stained towel. Now I'm bleeding from both ends.

DAVID: Thanks for that imagery. (*He goes to get her a band aid and helps her put it on.*) Here.

JESSICA: Help me! Help me, doctor! I'm bleeding!

DAVID: Don't worry little Missy, we'll have you patched up momentarily.

JESSICA: Momentarily, momentarily. That is such a funny word.

DAVID: Now you've gotta hold still, Missy.

JESSICA: It's such a word from a memo. From a business call. I'll be with you momentarily. Please hold momentarily. The doctor will be with you momentarily. That's when you know you're gonna hear something bad.

(*He holds up empty wine glass.*)

DAVID: Ah! You disobeyed doctors orders! Drinking alcohol while taking prescription! For this you shall be punished!

(He stalks her around the couch. She runs. He grabs her and starts to tickle her. She's laughing. Finally.)

JESSICA: Stop! Stop! I can't breathe!

(He stops and holds her for a minute while they both catch their breath.)

JESSICA: David, are we happy?

(He lets go of her and walks away.)

DAVID: What a shitty thing to say.

JESSICA: No! I mean, I think we are. We're happy. I mean, you think we're happy, don't you?…

DAVID: What do you mean are we happy, of course we're happy!

JESSICA: I'm just so tired of fighting.

DAVID: Who's fighting?!!

JESSICA: Don't be mad, it's just. I feel we can't have a conversation without—

DAVID: Well, you keep bringing it up. Let it rest for a while.

JESSICA: You keep saying I'm bringing it up but I'm just talking. I tell you I talked to Marie you ask how she's doing and I say her pregnancy is going really well.

DAVID: I didn't ask how she was doing.

JESSICA: If you had it your way the word baby would just not be part of my vocabulary or anybody's that we know or anybody on the planet.

DAVID: Well, it's just not that interesting to me really.

JESSICA: I think they have a very exciting life. They're following their dreams, they're making things happen.

DAVID: I DON'T WANT TO BE MARIE AND KEVIN!! I don't want to be Fred-fucking-McMurray in the suburbs! The thought of pulling a baby carriage out of a car trunk at the mall is enough to make me sick. Having a baby would be throwing my life in the toilet. It's enough to make me sick!

JESSICA: Having a baby could make you sick? Well, you're making me sick right now. Do you know that you are making me sick right now? You know how important this is to me. Why can't you do this for me? With me? Why do I feel like we're enemies? I am not your enemy. I want the same things you do. A long happy passionate life. Together.

DAVID: And you don't think it's possible to have a long passionate life without kids?

JESSICA: We're talking about my health here. I feel like you're dumb to what we're up against here. Either that or you're incredibly selfish.

DAVID: It's not like your dying!...Having a baby would relieve you of these cramps.

JESSICA: Dr. Vulvar says if a woman wants to have children, it's the first thing they recommend.

DAVID: But he also says having a hysterectomy would have the same affect.

JESSICA: I don't consider that an option. I can't believe that you would consider that an option. It's like I'm a cat or a dog that you'd just assume get fixed.

DAVID: You say these pain killers are working. Why not keep taking the pain killers?

JESSICA: Because meanwhile, my uterus is getting eaten alive. In two or three years I'll be addicted to the drugs and pregnancy won't even be an option anymore.

DAVID: You keep saying that it's about your future. Your life. I'm the one that's selfish. What about my fate, my future? Why is wanting to live my own life and not the life of my parents selfish? Wanting to be happy? If that's selfish then I plead guilty. I'm selfish.

JESSICA: I just don't think you're aware of the ramifications of what you're saying. It was charming when we dated. Charming when you said for the first three years of our marriage you didn't want to discuss children. But it's not charming anymore.

DAVID: You seem to be saying that the only way we could reach a conclusion on this is if I go your way.

JESSICA: I don't know if that's even what I want anymore. That's what I'm saying. Because I don't want it to be my way. I want it to be our way. I want it to be full-hearted OUR way. I would want to go into it together. Together.

DAVID: I don't say mean things to hurt you. I say them because I'm scared and confused. I'm confused, I'm confused, I'm confused.

JESSICA: Well, you better think about your confusion. Because you just really better take a good look at it.

DAVID: I wish I was a little boy in footy pajamas and I could crawl into bed and pull up the covers tight around me.

JESSICA: But you're not a little boy. You're a man. You're a full grown man with facial hair and a job and a wife and a big decision to make. I must say in all this, I'm finding your cautiousness to be a real turn-off. You know, there's something you don't know: I have a nick-name for you and I think it in my head whenever you think you're being high and mighty. Cautious-Boy. Cautious Boy is so fucking paralyzed by his own fears that he never does anything. He's losing everything around him but he doesn't even know it. He thinks he's a big strong super-hero and he's gonna live a hero's life—when really he's just Cautious-Boy,

DAVID: You asshole.

JESSICA: I'm wondering if you really love me as much as you say you do.

DAVID: That's totally unfair. Just because I don't want to have children doesn't mean I don't love you.

JESSICA: Then I guess I'm wondering if I love you as much as I thought I did.

DAVID: Don't say that.

JESSICA: I just don't think I love you enough to sacrifice having children in my life.

DAVID: Well, I don't know if I love you enough to sacrifice my life.

JESSICA: Then I guess we have a problem here.

DAVID: Yeah, I guess we have a problem.

END OF ACT I

ACT II
SCENE I

Jessica is sprawled out under the messy sheets of a four post bed. She pulls on her underwear and does long delicious stretches.

JESSICA: I love this bed! *(She slips into a man's shirt and starts dancing around the bed, using it's four posts as ballet barres.)*
THOMAS: *(Offstage.)* Sugar?
   (He peeks his head in, she's dancing.)
JESSICA: Hmm? *(She stops dancing.)*
THOMAS: Oh, don't stop. I like it. Sugar?
JESSICA: Oh, yes.
   (He exits, she straightens sheets on bed and he returns with breakfast on a tray.)
JESSICA: I love this bed.
THOMAS: Do you?
JESSICA: I love it.
THOMAS: This bed has always brought me luck.
JESSICA: Oh, really?
THOMAS: Especially in the last twenty-four hours.
JESSICA: Let's hope it brought us both luck.
   (He kisses her.)
THOMAS: You're beautiful. I bought this bed from an old witch doctor I met in Thailand. He carved it from fruitwood and the whole time he was carving he chanted some song about love and good fortune. I sat with him the night he carved the final details. We smoked hashish and didn't exchange a word. He just carved and chanted. The next morning he sent two boys to carry it back for me to my little hut. He got on his knees and prayed to the skies and kissed my feet.
JESSICA: Wow.
THOMAS: Who knows what he said though. The boys couldn't stop giggling for about two miles.
JESSICA: What a great image.
THOMAS: Yeah, everything I own, everything in this apartment has a story.
JESSICA: You should write about that.
THOMAS: I have. I figure anyone who is willing to kiss my feet is worthy of a short story.
JESSICA: I'd love to read it.
THOMAS: I'd love for you to read it. But you know what I'd really like?

JESSICA: What?

THOMAS: I'd like you to continue your dance for me.

JESSICA: I'm not ready for an audience yet.

THOMAS: Come on, in India the women always dance for their men in the bedroom.

JESSICA: Well this is the lower east side of Manhattan…We'll see how I feel after breakfast.

THOMAS: Do you know what I think? David should be declared legally insane.
   (Jessica goes to get her pills. Takes some.)

JESSICA: I am amazed. I'm amazed at how good I feel.

THOMAS: Didn't you just take some of those?

JESSICA: That was four hours ago. I mean, you don't know, sex is usually painful for me. I guess I finally found the right prescription or something.

THOMAS: Or something.

JESSICA: Thomas?

THOMAS: Jessica?

JESSICA: I don't feel guilty. I thought I would, but I don't. I'm feeling no pain at all.

THOMAS: Well, why should you? Why should you feel guilty? The man, your husband, didn't want to make a child with you. Do you realize in the Catholic church that would be grounds for an annulment with no argument from the Pope? It's the natural order of things. Every religion—Catholicism, Judaism, the tribal klans of Africa—they all have their rituals. As I have observed there are eight basic steps in the life path that every religion believes in: Birth, Childhood, Initiation to Adulthood, Marriage, Childbirth, Raising Children, Old Age and Death. It's the natural progression to Nirvana. David is skipping two steps in the path of life. My little Thai friend would not approve.

JESSICA: Well, we've also skipped a step.

THOMAS: Which one?

JESSICA: Marriage.

THOMAS: Oh, I think in our society marriage is becoming more and more obsolete. It's much more important for the parents to be in love with each other than to be married, don't you think?

JESSICA: And you don't think we've skipped that step?

THOMAS: No, I don't think we've skipped it.
   (She works her way down to his feet and starts to kiss them.)

THOMAS: What are you doing down there?

JESSICA: Kissing your feet.

THOMAS: Now I'm going to have to write a short story about you. *(He slides onto the bed.)*

SCENE II

Coffee shop. David sits alone, his meal finished. Check paid. A menu sits across from him. Jessica enters.

JESSICA: Hi.

DAVID: You're late.

JESSICA: I'm really sorry.

DAVID: I already ate.

JESSICA: That's okay, I'll just get a—

DAVID: That's okay? That's okay that I ate?

JESSICA: I'm sorry. I said I was sorry.

DAVID: You're a half-hour late and it's okay that I ate.

JESSICA: I was held up at work. Do you want to do this another day?

DAVID: My time is precious. I have big deals happening at work. Really big deals.

JESSICA: Is that your water? May I have a sip of your water? Please. I'm sorry I'm late. I had to meet with one of our writers.

DAVID: Good?

JESSICA: Hm?

DAVID: Good writer?

JESSICA: Yes.

DAVID: And you're enjoying fiction? Editing and all? You find it fulfilling, satisfying, gratifying?

JESSICA: I find it helps pay the rent.

DAVID: That's good. Would you like to order some lunch?

JESSICA: I'm not feeling particularly hungry.

DAVID: Well, then, why don't we get this over with. *(He pulls out his laptop and gets to work.)* I've decided I don't care much about the furniture. I mean that old armoir of my grandfather's...it would make sense for me to take that, but you always appreciated that much more than I did. I suppose I could use a bureau, a chair, perhaps the desk, but that's negotiable. What I would like, if I may be so bold, are the paintings we got in the Southwest. And the encyclopedia set. I thought we could split the stocks down the middle. I think that's fair. Have you thought about what you want?

JESSICA: Excuse me?

DAVID: Do you know what you want? Have you thought about what you want?

JESSICA: Yes, Yes, I have.

DAVID: You want the Southwest paintings, don't you?

JESSICA: What I want you wouldn't give me.

DAVID: But you're getting it now, aren't you? Making up for lost time? Has Thomas impregnated you yet with his big French-loving cock?

(Jessica starts to leave.)

JESSICA: You know, I don't know who you are right now but you're not the man I married five years ago. You're not the sweet, loving man I fell in love with. How dare you? How dare you speak to me that way. What in your demented Wall Street mind do you think gives you permission to speak to me that way?

DAVID: I'm just calling it like it is, Jessica. You're shying away from responsibility. Putting it all on some disease you got, some diagnosis. Don't tell me when you went to Doctor Vulva there wasn't a part of you that rejoiced when he gave you the news. Emergency! Emergency! I must get pregnant right away!

JESSICA: I was relieved that I wasn't dying. That there was something real that we could do to make it all better.

DAVID: Oh, Jessica. You and your little dramas. Anything to make life more interesting.

JESSICA: You think I was looking for drama?

DAVID: You've always said you love a good drama.

JESSICA: Maybe I needed one to distract me from our miserable mediocre marriage.

DAVID: Excuse me?

JESSICA: You heard me.

DAVID: How about your miserable mediocre life? Maybe your life is miserable. Maybe that's why you have trouble getting out of bed. Maybe that's why you wake up crying. Walking around in your robe all day, your head buried in books, working at home. Maybe you need to get a life. What happened to your writing? To your book? *Mother Expecting?* You were so into your writing when we first met. You'd do those reading nights and enter your stuff in contests. What happened to your writing?

JESSICA: What happened was I grew up. I got a job and I realized my talents weren't that exceptional.

DAVID: You gave up. You gave up on your life, so now you want to start a new one.

JESSICA: Maybe I haven't gotten everything I set out for in my life, but I have hope. I have hope for a better future. Remember that word, "Hope"? It's a high-risk commodity. I know that's not your style. *(She starts to leave again and this time doubles over onto the floor.)*

DAVID: Shit. *(He runs to help her.)* Shit.

JESSICA: Goddamn mother fucking piece of shit.

DAVID: Shit. *(He helps her back to chair.)*

JESSICA: I'm okay. I'm okay.

DAVID: Shit. Are you okay?

JESSICA: Water.

(He goes to get her water.)

JESSICA: Pills.

(He goes to her bag for pills.)

DAVID: Shit.

(She takes the pills. He pulls out his pocket computer, his phone.)

DAVID: I'm calling Dr. Vulva. I'm taking you to Dr. Vulva. What's his number? Shit. Vulva, Vulva.

(She takes the phone from him.)

JESSICA: "R."

DAVID: Huh?

JESSICA: It ends with an "R." Vulvar.

(He's still looking for the number in his computer.)

DAVID: Vulvar. Right. Shit.

JESSICA: I don't want to go to the doctor.

DAVID: What?

JESSICA: I don't want to go to the doctor.

DAVID: Look at you.

JESSICA: I won't go, David.

DAVID: Don't be ridiculous. Look at you.

JESSICA: I know what he'll say. I won't go.

DAVID: This is ridiculous.

(She gets up. Grabs her bag. Leaves.)

DAVID: Jessica.

(She's gone.)

DAVID: Shit.

SCENE III

Bloomingdales restaurant, Le Train Bleu. Marie, as usual, has lots of shopping bags. They are sharing a bottle of white.

MARIE: So when are you bringing Thomas to Rhinebeck?

JESSICA: Soon, very soon. I've told him all about you guys, my inspiration.

MARIE: How's the baby making going?

JESSICA: It's going.

MARIE: Yeah?

JESSICA: It's going alright. Boy oh boy oh boy is it going!

MARIE: Really?

JESSICA: I just feel so good with Thomas, just sooooo good.

MARIE: Really?

JESSICA: Oh My God, we just fit so well together.

MARIE: Wow, Jessica, I've never seen you like this. I think you're blushing.

JESSICA: Am I? Oh God, I feel like I'm sixteen years old and the boy I've had a crush on all year has just asked me to go steady. I mean I still get nervous with him, sometimes I can barely catch my breath!

MARIE: Oh my!

JESSICA: Well, to be honest, we haven't been able to do it much in the past few days because I haven't been feeling that well, but—

MARIE: Do it *much?*

JESSICA: What can I say, he's an animal! And I guess I am too.

MARIE: My God!

JESSICA: Let me tell you, Marie, if he can't make me pregnant, nobody can. I want to make a toast. To a year from today. You and I will be sitting with our men in your new kitchen with newborns on our laps. I see it all so clearly.

MARIE: I'll drink to that.

JESSICA: Wait a minute…I thought one was your limit.

MARIE: It is. When I'm pregnant.

JESSICA: You're kidding.

MARIE: Miscarriage number three.

JESSICA: You're kidding.

MARIE: I didn't want to tell you over the phone.

JESSICA: I thought everything was fine.

MARIE: It happened Sunday.

JESSICA: Oh, Marie. That sucks.

MARIE: Who'd a thought something so natural would be so fucking difficult?

JESSICA: Wow.

MARIE: I'm okay. Really. Next time we're gonna be lucky. I can feel it.

JESSICA: How long do you have to wait?

MARIE: A couple months.

JESSICA: I'm sorry. *(Jessica pours them each more wine.)* Tell Kevin I'm so sorry. How's he doing?

MARIE: Okay.

JESSICA: You guys are gonna get it next time. I'm sure of it.

MARIE: Yeah.

JESSICA: So it looks like your ear is healing okay. How's little Max?

MARIE: He's a crazy kooky nut.

JESSICA: You're so lucky.

MARIE: I want him to have a brother or a sister. I don't believe in only children.

JESSICA: God.

MARIE: What?

JESSICA: Three months ago David and I were celebrating the New Year with you and Kevin and you announced you were pregnant.

MARIE: Yeah, I know.

JESSICA: So life is crazy.

MARIE: Yeah.

JESSICA: You know I'm really very happy with Thomas. I feel alive with him in a way I never felt with David. And I don't care about writing and career and all that shit anymore. I just don't care. I mean I could live with Thomas with fourteen children in a hut in Timbuktu. That's all I want. A very simple life.

MARIE: Uh huh.

JESSICA: I worry about David. I think he's going to grow old and bitter and alone. I worry that he'll be alone.

MARIE: Kevin called him again yesterday. He never returns our calls. It's like he's dropped off the face of the earth.

JESSICA: I'm worried about him. I haven't seen him since last month. He just sent me a packet full of paperwork.

MARIE: Paperwork?

JESSICA: You know, stuff for me to sign and whatever.

MARIE: Did you?

JESSICA: Not yet.

MARIE: Why don't you just sign them and get it over with? You don't want to string him along while you're making plans for Timbuktu.

JESSICA: I'm not stringing him along. You have a funny way of wording things.

MARIE: I just meant you know, so you guys can both move on with your lives.

JESSICA: I just don't know if he's ready yet.

MARIE: You don't know if David's ready?

JESSICA: I don't think he's ready yet.

MARIE: Jessica, I have something that I want to give you.

JESSICA: Oh?

MARIE: It's something I got for you this morning. I got one for myself too.
(Marie reaches into her various bags to find it.)

JESSICA: Oooh. Is it from Saks or Bendels?

MARIE: Maybe it will help us on our quests for pregnancy.

JESSICA: Victoria's Secret?

MARIE: Getting colder. Try Patricks. *(She hands a tiny wrapped present to Jessica.)*

JESSICA: Patricks?

MARIE: As in St. Patricks.

JESSICA: Huh? *(Jessica unwraps the gift.)*

MARIE: It's Mary.

JESSICA: Oh?

MARIE: The Virgin Mary.

JESSICA: Oh?

MARIE: You carry her with you. She watches over you.

JESSICA: Oh.

MARIE: She's my name sake. *(She sings.)* Ava Maria. Hey, she got pregnant, maybe she'll help us get pregnant! Would you stop looking so terrified? She's the Virgin Mary for Christ's sake!

JESSICA: I haven't been to church since my wedding.

MARIE: Just carry her in your wallet, okay? Every time you reach in to get a token or a quarter to call your French man you'll see her.

JESSICA: He's not French.

MARIE: Whatever. I have a strong intuition about this.

JESSICA: What if we can't get pregnant, Marie? What would we do if we couldn't get pregnant?

MARIE: Just keep her in your wallet, okay? And I'll keep her in mine.

SCENE IV

David's apartment. It's a bachelor's mess. He's working. Knocks on door. Then Marie singing "Winter Wonderland." He answers.

MARIE: Hi David.

DAVID: Marie. What a nice surprise.

MARIE: I was in town to catch some sales and I figured I'd drop in on you since you never call us anymore. *(She hands him something.)*

DAVID: What's this?

MARIE: Our soon to be world famous salad dressing. That's Kevin's favorite: Poughkeepsie Poppyseed.

DAVID: Gee, thanks.

MARIE: He's in Albany today getting it patented. And here, some lettuce. I know you don't have anything green in your house.

DAVID: Have you been spying on me?

MARIE: Actually, I think your skin is starting to turn a pale shade of green. You've looked better.

DAVID: I'll invite you in if you promise not to comment on my housekeeping.

MARIE: Deal. *(She comes in.)* Oh My God. *(She starts walking around the apartment, mindlessly checking dust.)* So, when are you gonna come see us in our new house? You know Rhinebeck is only a trainride away. Get some fresh air?

DAVID: It's hard, you know, with my hours.

MARIE: All work and no play.

DAVID: I know, but I'm looking for a new job, actually. Smaller firm.

MARIE: What about the Forbes 500? Deals, deals, deals?

DAVID: Marie, have you been drinking?

MARIE: Hey, I'm high on life. You should see the deals I got today. Check it out. One hundred ninety nine dollars—originally two fifty nine—I saved sixty dollars. And for Max. Is this cute or what? He hates hats but he looks so damn cute in them.

DAVID: Yeah, that's pretty cute.

MARIE: Check it out.

DAVID: Huh?

MARIE: Hold it, touch it, it won't bite.

DAVID: Yeah, Marie, it's really cute. You're tipped.

MARIE: Don't you think kids are cute, David? What? You think we're boring, suburban, van driving, church-going hicks. Is that it? Is that why you don't call us anymore?

DAVID: No, I don't think that.

MARIE: I had lunch with your soon-to-be-ex-wife today. A ladies lunch. Bloomingdales Le Train Bleu. We had a nice Californian Chardonnay. A middle class choice, I know, but we're on a budget and it was my treat. Then I caught a few more sales and stopped into a beautiful old pub for a hot toddy. The bartender thought I was pretty hot toddy so he served me doubles.

DAVID: Look, whatever she told you I said—it was in the heat of the moment, it wasn't what I really meant.

MARIE: She didn't tell me anything, David.

DAVID: Oh.

MARIE: But it's good to know all the same. You wanna have an affair with me, David? Kevin's always on the road, you're turning green, Jessica and her French man are doing it like rabbits. You wanna have an affair?

DAVID: Why did you come here, Marie?

MARIE: I'm a messenger from God, David. A messenger from God. Also, it's snowing and I'm in no condition to drive. *(She collapses on couch.)* I had a miscarriage Sunday. I'm not pregnant anymore.

DAVID: I'm sorry.

MARIE: I would never drink like this if I was pregnant. I'm a very responsible mother.

DAVID: I know that, Marie. You're a wonderful mother.

MARIE: You think so?

DAVID: And a wonderful wife. A wonderful, devoted wife.

MARIE: Yeah. A sensational business woman, too.

DAVID: Really sensational.

MARIE: Our business is going great. I'm doing a book of recipes. "Dressings for Dinner," "Salad Sensations" or "Dressing with Marie." What's your vote? Jessica's gonna help me get a publisher. *(She's slowly becoming part of the couch.)*

DAVID: That's great. How's Max?

MARIE: He's our little scrub-a-dub-dub. That's baby talk for sweety-peety.
(He puts a blanket over her.)

DAVID: Marie. Is Jessica pregnant?

MARIE: Oh no, David, Jessica's not pregnant either. Nobody's preggy, not today.

DAVID: Marie, I'm gonna call Kevin and let him know you'll be sleeping here tonight.

MARIE: Leave him a—

DAVID: I'll leave him a message.

MARIE: Tell him I'm hopelessly in love with him and to give sweety-peety an extra blankee.

DAVID: Okay, Marie.

MARIE: She's not happy, David. I mean she looked sexy and tousled and she's getting laid every night but somethings not right. She's not happy.
(She falls asleep as he dials the phone.)

SCENE V

Thomas's apartment. The bed.

JESSICA: Thomas, I'm sorry.

THOMAS: You're the one in pain. I'm sorry.

JESSICA: Maybe later?

THOMAS: Jessica, we don't have to do it every day.

JESSICA: But we're on a mission!

(He starts to massage her.)

THOMAS: Name a drink.

JESSICA: Absolute Martini. Extra olives. No. Stoli. Crystale. Straight up. Cold, very cold.

THOMAS: Ooooh. Good choice. I'm a Stoli Crystale martini—

JESSICA: Straight up.

THOMAS: I'm a Stoli Crystale. Straight up. Russia. Cold. Winter. A sleigh, weaving through snow banks. Icy. Rushing. Embankments of tall, white snow. Pre-Revolution. I'm with the woman I love under blankets. She's cold. Our noses touch, they're cold; our lips, hot. I am Doctor Zhivago and I am here to save the day!

JESSICA: That's pretty good. Now give me one.

THOMAS: Okay. Sweet sherry. Warm.

JESSICA: Hmmm. Zambizi desert. Along the Victoria River. White tents. Night. A party of ex-patriots. There's fire, dinners over, it's late. Music, a flute and drums. Some have gone to bed, some lie under trees, by the fire. But we, we dance under moonlight dressed in white, your pants are rolled up, barefeet. My long silk dress caresses my body. The sand is cool on our toes.

THOMAS: Where's the Victoria River?

JESSICA: I don't know, I made it up.

THOMAS: You lose points for cheating!

JESSICA: Poetic license.

THOMAS: And flute and drums. What a bizarre combination.

JESSICA: David and I heard a band at the Vanguard last year. Just flute and drums.

THOMAS: If you had your choice to go anywhere in the world for a year, where would you go?

JESSICA: Where the Victoria River meets the Zambizi desert.

THOMAS: No, really. A real choice.

JESSICA: Oh, we're talking reality here. Not fantasy.

THOMAS: Yes. Anywhere. A year.

JESSICA: I'd stay right here.

THOMAS: On this bed?

JESSICA: Well, we'd have to go out eventually, but yes, here, in New York City. With you.

THOMAS: Come on. What if you had your choice to go anywhere in the world? Say Africa, South America, the Far East or the Ex-Soviet Republic.

JESSICA: I'd need to make a living.

THOMAS: Say that's taken care of.

JESSICA: I thought we were being real.

THOMAS: Say it's taken care of.

JESSICA: It's strange. For the first time in my life I just want to stay right where I am. With you, near my doctor, and make a baby.

THOMAS: But what if you had an incredible opportunity to travel for a year. And I could write and you could come along as my personal editor?

JESSICA: But what about the baby?

THOMAS: Jessica, we can make babies anywhere. We'll have one in every country. They'll speak ten languages: Chinese, Swahili, Japanese, German, Spanish, Russian, English—

JESSICA: French.

THOMAS: The point is, we make our own reality, whatever we want it to be.

JESSICA: Thomas, do you think about Corrine anymore?

THOMAS: I left Corrine so I could be with you.

JESSICA: I know, but it's okay if you still think about her.

THOMAS: I put her on a plane back to France and wished her a Bon Voyage.

JESSICA: I know, but you still might think of her.

(He gets out of bed, singing.)

THOMAS: "Non, rien, rien…Non, je ne regrette rien…"

JESSICA: Where are you going?

THOMAS: To take a shower. Et toi?

JESSICA: Thomas, I'd go anywhere with you. *(She gets up and follows him to the shower.)*

SCENE VI

Institution. Flowers on table next to bed. Patricia, dressed in coat, stares out window. An old suitcase waits by the door. David stands there, watching her.

DAVID: Patricia Ann Miller. What are you looking at?

PATRICIA: The outside.

DAVID: The snow is finally starting to melt.

PATRICIA: I see that.

DAVID: It's a nice view.

PATRICIA: Yeah.

DAVID: You look like you're watching something.

PATRICIA: I am. I'm watching for something. I'm waiting for something to happen.

DAVID: Anything in particular?

PATRICIA: Yeah. Yeah, something in particular. As a matter of fact. I'll let you know when it happens.

DAVID: Okay. So you're packed and ready to go? *(Pause.)* Patricia.

PATRICIA: Yeah?

DAVID: Those are nice flowers.

PATRICIA: Mom and Dad sent them to me. Read the card.
     (He does.)

PATRICIA: What do you think?

DAVID: Sounds like them.

PATRICIA: Patricia, get well soon. Your Mom and Dad.

DAVID: I'm sure they didn't know what to say.

PATRICIA: You'd think I have a common cold.

DAVID: You know them, Patricia. It's the best they could do.

PATRICIA: Is it? Is it the best they could do?

DAVID: They're of a different generation. They don't know about these things.

PATRICIA: Is heartbreak a condition of modern times?
     (Pause.)

DAVID: Is that why you did it, Patricia? Because you have a broken heart?
     (She turns to him.)

PATRICIA: What did you say?

DAVID: I said did you do it because you have a broken heart?

PATRICIA: Yes. That's why I did it.

DAVID: I'm sorry.

PATRICIA: It's such a perfect image really, the image of a broken heart. Because that is exactly how it feels. Like it might break at any minute. Like it might just explode from the pain at any minute. I kept waiting for it to explode or to wake up one day and be dead from a heart attack but it didn't happen.

DAVID: So you decided to put it out of it's misery.

PATRICIA: Yeah, yeah, like remember when Murphy got old and started shitting all over the house and he could barely walk? We put him out of his misery.

DAVID: He was ninety-one years old in dog years.

PATRICIA: I started seeing my heart as a separate entity, like something I could put out of it's pain. I thought maybe I could stop the suffering. Have you ever felt that kind of pain? Be honest.

DAVID: Yeah. Only for me it's more a heaviness. It should be called a heavy heart. It's a heavy weight in my chest. The weight of it pulls me down, like gravity, into the floor, into the center of the earth. Sometimes I'm amazed I can get out of bed with the weight of it.

PATRICIA: You mean sometimes you've woken up with it?

DAVID: Yeah...Why are you smiling?

PATRICIA: It's good to see you, David.

DAVID: I'm glad you didn't die, Patricia. It would have killed me if you died.

PATRICIA: I want to give you something. *(She gets the sweater that she wore in the earlier scene and gives it to him.)* I want you to give this to Jessica.

DAVID: But isn't that the sweater Joe gave you?

PATRICIA: It's a nice sweater, look at the label. Don't you think she'd like it?

DAVID: Yeah, but...Big Black Joe?

PATRICIA: He's not in my reality anymore. Gone and left me. Got a new job, better salary, more money to support the wife and kids. I thought he'd stand by me in my time of need, but he didn't. He's gone and left me.

DAVID: I'm sorry.

PATRICIA: I thought he loved me but he's gone and left me. Couldn't take the hard times, couldn't meet the challenge.

DAVID: I'm sorry.

PATRICIA: Yeah, well...

DAVID: You know I worry about you.

PATRICIA: And I worry about you, David Michael Miller. I worry about you.

DAVID: Jessica and I have separated. She's with someone else now, she's trying to have a baby with someone else *(He collapses on the bed and starts to cry.)*

PATRICIA: Oh.

DAVID: Am I an asshole, Patricia? Did I let Mom and Dad get the best of me? Am I an asshole because I didn't want to have a baby? Why couldn't I do that for her? Why couldn't I do that?

PATRICIA: You're not an asshole.

DAVID: Why'd she have to have a baby so bad? Maybe it was just an easy excuse for her to get out. She's already on to somebody else. I don't think she loved me... *(Patricia takes some Kleenex from her pocket and puts it on the bed. He uses it.)*

PATRICIA: Big Brother.

(Silence. She goes to window and looks out. Her face lights up.)
PATRICIA: David. Look. *(She beckons him to window.)* Look. What I was waiting for.
DAVID: A crocus.

(They stand at the window, looking out.)
PATRICIA: You wanna know a fact? A statistically proven fun fact to know and
    tell that will intimidate the enemy and impress the friend?
DAVID: Yeah, tell me a fact.
PATRICIA: All of the best scientists of the world got together and after years of
    research and testing they have proven that of all the energy forces, of all the
    energy forces in the universe, they have proven that gravity is the weakest.

SCENE VII

*The ladies room at Jessica's work. Jessica is doubled over on the floor, dripping
with sweat. Elaine enters.*

ELAINE: Oh my God.
JESSICA: Elaine.
ELAINE: Oh my God. What are you doing on the floor?
JESSICA: Oh. Um. I'm okay.
ELAINE: You're dripping.
JESSICA: It's…
    (She is clearly in pain. Elaine gets wet towels and wets her face.)
ELAINE: Now tell me Jessica, what are you doing on the bathroom floor?
JESSICA: Nothing.
ELAINE: Meditating? Searching for the back of an earring?
JESSICA: I'm okay, I'm okay. It's passing.
ELAINE: What's passing?
    (Jessica struggles to seat herself on the couch.)
JESSICA: I'm okay.
ELAINE: You look like shit. I'm calling my doctor.
JESSICA: I'm just a little sick.
ELAINE: How often do you get just a little sick?
JESSICA: Once a month. It's a girl thing.
ELAINE: Uh huh. I'll have to remember to tell the office manager to lay down
    carpeting in the Ladies Room. *(She pulls some pills out of her purse.)* Here,
    take one of these. They're strong…So, this girl thing. Who have you seen?

JESSICA: Huh?

ELAINE: What doctors have you seen?

JESSICA: You know what it is.

ELAINE: Honey, been there. I had a hysterectomy right after we had Amanda.

JESSICA: I'm sorry.

ELAINE: Best thing I ever did. It's amazing how you get to the point when you take the pain for granted. I thought life was supposed to be painful.

JESSICA: Then why do you still carry pills?

ELAINE: I still get migraines.

(Elaine goes to sink for water. Gives it to Jessica, who takes the pill.)

ELAINE: Sex was a revelation. Jessica, is it always this bad?

JESSICA: Seems to be getting worse.

ELAINE: I want you to see my doctor. She's a specialist, one of the best.

JESSICA: I can't Elaine.

ELAINE: It's all the suffering of childbirth without the reward of a baby.

JESSICA: At this point I feel like I've given birth ten times, I can hold out a little longer. I only want one.

ELAINE: Are you and David trying?

JESSICA: It's complicated.

(Elaine joins her on the couch.)

ELAINE: Get the operation. You'll be in and out of that hospital smock in less than twenty-four hours and you'll be feeling no pain. Look at you. You feel miserable, your work is suffering, I'm sure your sex life is suffering. Do it and get on with your life.

JESSICA: You have Amanda.

ELAINE: Yes.

JESSICA: You make it sound so obvious, but you have Amanda.

ELAINE: I'm going to tell you a secret, Jessica. A secret between us girls. Having a baby isn't everything it's made out to be. You need to know that.

JESSICA: Yes, but it's easy to say when you have one.

ELAINE: Sometimes I hate her. And sometimes I hate my husband for making me have her.

JESSICA: I'm sure that's not true.

ELAINE: I thought having a baby would fill some void in my life, but all I got for it were raw nipples and sleepless nights…The night I found out I was pregnant Jonathan took me to Cafe des Artistes. He ordered champagne and kept toasting and I kept smiling and in the back of my mind I kept thinking I'll feel great about this when it sinks in, or maybe in a couple of weeks when I get over the queasiness. Finally I resigned myself to the fact that I didn't enjoy pregnancy and that when I held the little baby in my arms, my maternal instincts would kick in. But the delivery was so long and so painful that by the time she finally came out I think I hated her. I hated her for putting me in so much pain, I hated her for making me leave work when I was finally making headway. I hated her for making me feel plain and fat.

JESSICA: I think pregnant women are beautiful.

ELAINE: In my whole life I never felt so unattractive. And I'll tell you another thing: Men don't flirt with pregnant women. I was in Shakespeare and Company for a reading, trying to stay in touch with the literary world and this man—oh he must have been a model or an actor—he was gorgeous, he came around to the other side of the bookshelves, you know, opposite of me to check me out. We started flirting—dangerously, he said I had incredibly sensual eyes. And in between we talked about Kundera and Hemingway and menage a trois and finally he came around to get closer— we really were getting out of hand—and he saw that I was pregnant. His entire face changed. Suddenly I wasn't the woman he wanted to fuck. I was Mother Theresa! "Oh, when's the baby due? Boy or girl? My wife and I are planning on starting a family soon." He was so flustered. So trying to make up for his bad behaviour by showing the deepest concern for my health and well-being. I was sickened. I was so furious that I dumped my stack of books on his feet and said "Contrary to popular belief, pregnant women do fuck!" and I stormed out of the store. I hated her for that. For ruining a good flirtation.

JESSICA: A lot of women don't like the actual pregnancy, I know that.

ELAINE: But the worst part of it all—the part they don't tell you about—is having everybody come visit you in the hospital, all the phone calls, the first day I took her out in the stroller, all the doormen in my building, everyone, everyone is so excited, so goo-goo eyed over the whole thing and you have to play this role, this happy mother-oh-I've-never-been-so-thrilled-role. I tell you, I couldn't wait to get back to work. It was then that I realized I was starting to feel some sort of affection for her and that was promising. When I came home from a long days work and she would look up at me with a big smile—well, it does warm your heart. But still, even then, it was nothing more than coming home to a cute and needy puppy. She was sweet and I liked holding her and talking to her, but when she started crying or whining I just wanted to—

(A knock on the bathroom door, a voice says: "Elaine, Amanda on three.")

ELAINE: *(Calling.)* Hold it! Oh, I'm sorry Jessica, I'll be two secs— *(Elaine steps out.)* Where?

(The voice answers: "On three." We hear Elaine on the phone right outside the ladies room. Her persona metamorphosizes. Jessica listens and waits.)

ELAINE: Hi sweetie. Sweetie, Mommy's in a meeting. Sweetie. Leopard leggings? What color? Sweetie, Mommy is in a meeting. Mommy will call you later, okay? Kiss-kiss. Bye-bye. *(Elaine hangs up and returns.)* Now she's fun. Once they start walking and talking they become much more interesting. And she's fun to do girl things with. When Jonathan watches his football games we go into her room and play and read books and I like dressing her, she's acquiring a great sense of style. She dresses just like me. And it's fun teaching her things, having someone that looks up to me and respects everything I say and is on my side when Jonathan's a pain in the ass. But you see, Jessica, this is what they don't tell you in books and it's exactly what they should. The whole maternal instinct theory is one that was developed by men to keep women barefoot and pregnant in the kitchen. I just wish someone would have come out and told me when I was sick and trying so desperately to get pregnant. It's not all it's made out to be.

(Enter Thomas.)

THOMAS: Ladies. I was told I'd find you here.

ELAINE: Speaking of menches. Oh, Thomas, I'm running late for our lunch date. Jessica, do you feel up to joining us? We're going to talk about his next book. I spoke to your agent this morning.

THOMAS: Oh?

ELAINE: Very exciting. Let me go get my coat. *(She exits.)*

THOMAS: Powdering noses with the boss?

JESSICA: Not really.

THOMAS: Can you join us?

JESSICA: I'm not feeling very well.

(Elaine returns.)

ELAINE: So we've voted for Africa. You're hot, Africa's hot. Together you'll be hot, hot, hot. We think you should go next month.

THOMAS: That soon?

ELAINE: What are you gonna do, rest on your laurels? Jessica, we've got the Dostoyevsky of short stories here. A story in every port, a collection for every continent. Your discovery. Are you coming?

JESSICA: Is this reality?

ELAINE: Of course it's reality. Anything is possible.

THOMAS: But at this point we're just talking.

ELAINE: To be continued over fettucine alfredo. Coming?

JESSICA: No, Elaine, I'm thinking I should go home for the rest of the day.

ELAINE: Of course honey. Get some rest. *(Elaine hands Jessica a business card.)* Here's a phone number you might like. Think about it. *(Mouths.)* The Best.

THOMAS: Think about what?

JESSICA: The meaning of life.

ELAINE: Is it still snowing?

THOMAS: No, it stopped.

ELAINE: Jessica. R.E. *Mother Expecting:* I pulled it out over the weekend. I expected bullshit but what I read was beautiful.

JESSICA: Thanks.

THOMAS: *Mother Expecting?*

ELAINE: A little novel she's working on. *(Elaine's already down the hall.)*

THOMAS: Jess—

ELAINE: *(Calling.)* Come on, darling Thomas…

(He goes.)

SCENE VIII

Thomas's apartment. Jessica sits on the bed, writing. Thomas enters.

THOMAS: Working on your novel?

JESSICA: No, actually, I was working on a note to you.

THOMAS: Blank page.

JESSICA: I haven't written in a while. Long lunch meeting.

THOMAS: We had a lot to discuss.

JESSICA: Your itinerary?

THOMAS: Nothing's set in stone.

JESSICA: I know. *(Pause.)* You told me. You told me it was reality. We were discussing reality. I should have heard you. I guess I just thought that that word coming out of Mr. Romantic's mouth was a contradiction in terms.

THOMAS: I want you to come.

JESSICA: As your personal editor? What am I gonna do, follow you around with your typewriter—like the boys that carried your bed in Thailand? Giggling?

THOMAS: You'd be the woman I love, mother of my child.

JESSICA: Do you love me?

THOMAS: I just said.

JESSICA: But you didn't.

THOMAS: I just said you'd be the woman I love.

JESSICA: But can you say the words: I love you? *(Pause.)* You can't. I bet you've never said it. It's just that I've noticed that anytime you refer to the "L" word or any feelings you might have for me, you do it in the third person. "The woman he loves is under blankets." "It's more important for the parents to be in love." You're this highly passionate guy that can only go so far. You can't say "I love you"...You see, I don't want to have just anyone's baby. And I don't just want a baby. I want a father for my baby. One that's here. I want the father to love me and the baby. And of course I'd want to love them too. I mean this is ridiculous. It's crazy.

THOMAS: Why don't you just come to Africa with me and we'll find where the Victoria River meets the Zambizi Desert?

JESSICA: Because it's more important for you to write right now than it is for you to be with me. Isn't it?

THOMAS: Why can't I have both?

JESSICA: You want to have your cake and eat it too.

THOMAS: I never understood that expression. Why have cake if you can't eat it?

JESSICA: Anyway, I'm sure once you get to Kenya you'll meet some beautiful Kenyan woman. And in Zimbabwe, another. I mean what happened to Sarah and Corrine and a few years ago you were living with some Spanish woman. What happened to them? You never mention any of them. Thomas, I wonder why it is that you only write short stories.

THOMAS: I get bored.

JESSICA: You don't think it's possible to have one love, do you? One person that you fall in love with and can stay fulfilled with and committed to forever.

THOMAS: Do you?

JESSICA: I have to believe that that exists. I have to.

THOMAS: There's a world full of people. I think that in every building in New York City lives someone that I could fall in love with. And someone that you could fall in love with too.

JESSICA: That's not very romantic.

THOMAS: I think it is.

JESSICA: Well, my baby needs more than that.

THOMAS: But you don't have a baby.

JESSICA: Well then, I need more than that. I have this pain in me that I thought

could get eased by a baby, but maybe I was wrong. Maybe it's not a baby I
    need at all.

THOMAS: Then why don't you come to Africa with me?

JESSICA: Because I know that traipsing around the globe following my lover isn't
    what I need either.

THOMAS: What do you need?

JESSICA: I need to make a life here, for myself.

THOMAS: How are you going to do that?

JESSICA: I don't know, I don't know. *(Pause.)* I'm going to start by making an
    appointment…

THOMAS: Jessica, you don't want to rush into this.

JESSICA: Do I look like I've been rushing?…I'm probably infertile anyway.

THOMAS: Jessica.

JESSICA: You're relieved.

THOMAS: No, I…

JESSICA: It's okay. You should be…Hey, you gotta strike while the iron is hot and
    right now you're hot, hot, hot! I think you should go to Africa.

SCENE IX

The Church of the Immaculate Conception, Rhinebeck. Marie and Patricia
standing on the steps outside. Marie holds an infant. It's cold.

PATRICIA: He's real cute, Marie. He's cute.

MARIE: He likes you, Patricia, he's holding your finger.

PATRICIA: Teeny-Tiny.

MARIE: I'm so glad you could come.

PATRICIA: David's a Godfather.

MARIE: *(Calling.)* David! Rockabye baby, on a tree-top…
    (David enters, greets her. He's carrying a baby present.)

DAVID: Hi Marie.

MARIE: David, Alex. Alex, David, your Godfather.

DAVID: Hi little guy.

MARIE: So we finally got him to Rhinebeck!

DAVID: It's not a bad train ride.

MARIE: That's great about your new job, David.

DAVID: Yeah, smaller firm.

MARIE: *(Calling.)* And your Godmother!

(Jessica enters, very pregnant. She also carries a present.)

MARIE: World famous writer!

JESSICA: Hi.

MARIE: Remember your Godmother? Jessica?

JESSICA: Hi Sweetie. Good to see you Patricia.

PATRICIA: Wow. Look at you.

JESSICA: Yeah. Where's Kevin?

MARIE: He parked in the back. He and Max are getting the baby carriage out of the car trunk. We got in a fight this morning. He cut up one of my credit cards so I took the air out of one of his tires...

DAVID: Hi.

JESSICA: Hi.

MARIE: We're gonna go inside to wait. It's too cold for my sweety-peety. Patricia, do you want to hold him?

PATRICIA: I don't know.

MARIE: Come on, he won't bite.

(They go inside the church, leaving Jessica and David alone on the stairs.)

JESSICA: Congratulations on your new job. Words out that you really like it.

DAVID: Yeah, it's good. Smaller firm. *(Pause.)* You look really great.

JESSICA: Thanks.

DAVID: I mean you look good. You look healthy. You look—

JESSICA: Pregnant.

DAVID: It's strange for me to see you pregnant. I mean I thought about it, imagined it, but now to really see you, it's strange.

JESSICA: It's strange for me to see you, pregnant.

DAVID: So, how are you feeling?

JESSICA: Better than ever. I feel better pregnant than I ever did not pregnant.

DAVID: That's amazing.

JESSICA: Not so amazing. I mean it's what they said.

DAVID: *Mother Expecting.*

JESSICA: I'm getting published.

DAVID: I always thought you should get back to writing.

JESSICA: Yeah, well, with no men in my life I have the time.

DAVID: When does Thomas get back from Africa?

JESSICA: He's been back from Africa. Now he's in the Russia. He's working on a screenplay now—a follow-up to *Zhivago*.

DAVID: You're kidding.

JESSICA: He writes a good letter, though.

(Patricia peeks out from inside the church.)

PATRICIA: David Michael Miller. Jessica and child.

DAVID: Are they ready?

PATRICIA: Almost, but the most amazing thing just happened.

DAVID: Yeah?

PATRICIA: I'll tell you David if you promise not to think I'm crazy. Jessica will understand, she's a woman, like me.

DAVID: I don't think you're crazy.

JESSICA: What happened?

(Patricia steps out onto the steps with them.)

PATRICIA: I went into the church, I was by myself and I was looking up at the Virgin Mary—they have this beautiful statue of the Virgin Mary—and I thanked her for bringing me here, for giving me this life and I kissed her feet. And when I looked up at her she smiled. I swear to God on the steps of His house, she smiled.

JESSICA: That's amazing.

DAVID: We'll come see.

PATRICIA: Oh she's not doing it now, David. It was just an instant, a flash, just a moment in time. Probably happens once every hundred years or something. You'll just have to take my word for it.

DAVID: I do.

(Patricia goes inside.)

JESSICA: I guess we should go in.

DAVID: Yeah.

JESSICA: Oh! *(She doubles over in pain.)*

DAVID: Jesus, are you alright?

JESSICA: Gosh darn—

(She's still in pain, he goes to help.)

DAVID: Do you have a pill? Do you need to take a pill?

JESSICA: No, no, no, no, no. I'm okay, I'm okay.

DAVID: Water? Do you need water?

JESSICA: No, no, no…It's the baby, that's all.

DAVID: Oh.

JESSICA: Feel it.

(He places his hand on her belly.)

JESSICA: It's kicking.

END OF PLAY

Nine Armenians
by Leslie Ayvazian

TO SAM AND IVAN ANDERSON; FRED AND GLORIA AYVAZIAN;
GINA AND ANDREA AYVAZIAN; THE REV. A.A.
AND MARIE BEDIKIAN; SHNORHIG AND HAIG AYVAZIAN;
GRACE AND GEORGE BABAKIAN,
WITH LOVE AND GRATITUDE.

Nine Armenians by Leslie Ayvazian. ©1996 by Leslie Ayvazian. Reprinted by permission of the author. All inquires should be addressed to 164 Leonia Ave., Leonia, NJ 07605. Please refer to copyright page for caution notice.

THE AUTHOR
Leslie Ayvazian's most recent play, *Singer's Boy,* debuted at San Francisco's American Conservatory Theatre in May. Ms. Ayvazian's play, *Nine Armenians,* was presented at the Intiman Theatre in Seattle and at the Manhattan Theatre Club in 1996, subsequently opened at the Mark Taper Forum in Los angeles this summer, and at Denver Center Theatre in the Fall. Ms. Ayvazian is the recipient of the Roger L. Stevens and the Susan Smith Blackburn award for *Nine Armenians.* She would like to thank the New Harmony Writers Project for their help in developing *Nine Armenians.* Ms. Ayvazian is the recent recipient of a fellowship from the New Jersey Council of the Arts. Given the climate for national funding for the arts, this gift is even more precious. In addition, Ms. Ayvazian has spent the past twenty years working as an actress, writer and teacher. As an actress, she has appeared in Nicky Silver's popular play *Raised in Captivity* at the Vineyard Theatre in New York City. Ms. Ayvazian has also worked at the Manhattan Theatre Club in Richard Greenberg's one woman show, *Jenny Keeps Talking,* and Terrence McNally's *Lips Together, Teeth Apart.* On Broadway, Ms. Ayvazian stood by in the role of Bella in Neil Simon's *Lost in Yonkers.* In film, she has worked with Mike Nichols in *Working Girl* and *Regarding Henry,* with Woody Allen in *Alice* and with Doris Dorrie in *He and Me.* On television, she has worked on *Sunset Gang* with Uta Hagen, *Flour Babies* with Linda Lavin and various ethnic roles on *Law and Order.* As a writer, she has worked on *Footlights,* a one woman show produced at the Westside Arts Theatre and the Vineyard Theatre; *Practice,* a one-act play produced in the Marathon at the Ensemble Studio Theatre; *Emma in Concert,* a film for HBO, written in collaboration with four actresses, produced at the Cleveland Playhouse and published by Samuel French. *Voices of Earth* was created in company with Olympia Dukakis, Joan MacIntosh and Remi Bosseau, a group that investigates ancient myths of matriarchal societies and dramatizes them.

AUTHOR'S NOTE
The initial spark for this play was ignited in Aunt Kohar's driveway, where I stood with my family saying good-bye for forty-five minutes. We walked in and out of the house, we carried pans of food into the car, we sat in lawn chairs in the driveway to continue conversations, and so forth. And I thought, someday I want to write a play that starts in a driveway and begins with the word "Good-bye!" That thought went onto an index card, which went into a box that sat on my desk and gathered other ideas for six years.

What conspired in those six years were, roughly: 1) I gave birth to my son, ivan, and decided to relax my acting career and stay home more. 2) My sister

Andrea, travelled to Soviet Armenia and experienced the village in the mountains. 3) The nation of Armenia endured great hardship with the war of Nagoro-Karabagh. 4) The Armenians again felt they were not recognized in the global community and were suffering to an extreme degree: mass unemployment, starvation, unbearable living conditions. 5) I inherited and moved into my grandparents' house. The house contained all their belongings, including tapes of their stories from life in the Old Country, journals, diaries, sermons, and so on.

And so, the time came. I went into the room that had been my grandfather's study and sat down next to his Armenian typewriter and wrote this play.

I have been informed by many friends as this play moved from first draft to first reading to first workshop to first production, and then onto other beautifully realized productions in wonderful theatres with wonderful people.

I am grateful to everyone who have put their hands on this play and helped carry it into the world. To name a few: Olympia Dukakis, Charolette Colavin, Linda Levin and the New Harmony Project; Warner Shook and the Intiman Theatre; Lynne Meadow and the Manhattan Theatre Club; Gordon Davidson and the Mark Taper Forum, and all my ancestors who perched on my shoulder and whispered secrets. Thank you.

ORIGINAL PRODUCTION

Nine Armenians was first presented by the Intiman Theatre Company. It was directed by Christopher Ashley with the following cast:

Marie/Non	Barbara Andres
Armine/Mom	Charlotte Colavin
Ani	Julie Dretzin
Ari	Benjamin Fels
John/Dad	Sherman Howard
Antry/Pop	Bernard Kates
Aunt Louise	Lauren Klein
Virginia/Ginya	Mallery MacKay-Brook
Uncle Garo	Martin Shakar
Musician	George Mgrdichian

CHARACTERS
NON (MARIE): The Grandmother
POP (VARTAN): The Grandfather
ARMINE: Their daughter, the Mother
JOHN: Her husband, the Father
ANI: Their oldest daughter, 21 years old
VIRGINIA (GINYA): Middle child, 15 years old
RAFFI: Youngest child, 11 years old
AUNT LOUISE: John's sister
UNCLE GARO: Her husband
ARMENIAN MAN: Played by actor who plays Pop

All nine characters wear coats in every scene: fall coats, winter coats, spring coats and finally summer sweaters.

THE TIME
The time is 1992.

THE PLACE
The place is an American Suburb (probably in New Jersey) and Yerevan, Armenia.

THE SET
A simple set. Needs to include an offstage tree with branches visible on stage, a bush, a doorway, and a car. Armenian music is played on Armenian instruments.

Nine Armenians

SCENE I

A driveway. A car is parked in the driveway. There is a suggestion of a house: steps or a door, and so forth. A Rhododendron bush is downstage. A Tree is off-stage. We see a branch. Armenian music plays. Lights come up as members of the immediate family (all except Ani) are coming together to say good-bye. They are wearing their coats and carrying pans of food wrapped in aluminum foil.

JOHN: GOOD-BYE!

ARMINE: BYE, BYE, POP!

POP: MANOCK PAROV! (Good-bye!)

ARMINE: BYE, BYE, MA!

NON: YOU HAVE THE FOOD?

JOHN, GINYA, ARMINE: IT'S HERE!

NON: ALRIGHT.

RAFFI: IT'S SPILLING!

NON: YOU NEED A RUBBER BAND!

ARMINE: NO, NO.

GINYA: GOOD-BYE, NON!

RAFFI: GOOD-BYE, PAPA!

NON & POP: GOOD-BYE, DEAR!

JOHN: GOOD-BYE, GOOD-BYE EVERYONE!

(They all lean and kiss each other.)

JOHN: COME ON, ARMINE. LET'S GO!

(The clump breaks apart.)

ARMINE: See you Tuesday, Ma!

NON: Bye, bye.

ARMINE: Come on, Raffi.

NON: *(She squeezes Raffi's cheeks.)* BACHIGS! (Kisses!)

JOHN, ARMINE, RAFFI, GINYA: BACHIGS! BACHIGS! BACHIGS!

NON & POP: BACHIGS! BACHIGS! BACHIGS!

POP: I must go inside.

ARMINE: Bye, Pop.

POP: Marie!

NON: What?

POP: I'm going inside.

NON: Yes, Vartan, go. Armine!

ARMINE: What, Ma?

POP: Come in, Marie. That's enough.

NON: Yes, yes. I'm coming. I.O. (Yes.)

ARMINE: What, Ma?

NON: *(To Armine.)* Call when you get home.

ARMINE: Of course.

POP: Good-bye, Annushigus. (dear one)

ARMINE: Bye, Pop.

> *(Pop exits.)*

JOHN: Come on, dear!

ARMINE: Ma, good-bye. Go inside!

JOHN: Give regards to Sarkis…

ARMINE & JOHN: and VaVa.

NON: Ya. OK.

ARMINE: Ma, go!

NON: Ya. Ya. *(Non exits.)*

ARMINE: Where's Raffi? Raffi! Come on! Time to go!

RAFFI: OK, Mom. *(Raffi doesn't move.)*

GINYA: Look at this bird!

RAFFI: Mom, can I take my coat off?

ARMINE: No, no, dear.

JOHN: EVERYBODY IN THE CAR! LET'S GO!

ARMINE: Let me get a rubber band!

> *(Non enters carrying a rubber band.)*

NON: Here's a rubber band! Why not take the Tass Kebob? (lamb stew)

> *(John goes in house.)*

ARMINE: Ma, there's no room.

GINYA: Nonnie, look at this bird!

NON: Yavroom (darling), you can hold the Tass Kebob. Put it on the floor under your feet.

GINYA: BETWEEN my feet, Non. It's BETWEEN my feet.

NON: What is, darling?

ARMINE: Raffi! OK! Come on! Let's go!

GINYA: No! Look at the bird.

ARMINE: Where's Pop?

NON: Inside. What bird?

GINYA: Right there!

ARMINE & NON: Where?

GINYA: By the branch there. At the end. See?

(John enters carrying a big pot of food.)

JOHN: OK! EVERYBODY IN THE CAR!

ARMINE: What's that?

JOHN: I took the Tass Kebob.

NON: AFAREHIM! (Excellent!)

ARMINE: RAFFI!

RAFFI: OK, Mom. *(Raffi doesn't move.)*

ARMINE: Where's Pop?

NON: In the bathroom.

ARMINE: I want to say good-bye.

JOHN: ARMINE! YOU SAID GOOD-BYE!

GINYA: Dad, don't turn the car on.

JOHN: Why not?

GINYA: Come look at this bird.

NON: A cutie-pie!

JOHN: It's time to go!

GINYA: *(Pointing to bird.)* Look, Dad!

(Armine enters, still carrying tray of baklava.)

ARMINE: I think Pop is locked in the bathroom.

JOHN: Oh, Jesus.

NON: Vy Vy Vy! (My, my my!) Ah see inch chay? (What is it?) VARTAN! *(Non goes in house.)*

JOHN: Oh, Jesus!

ARMINE: You talk to him, dear.

JOHN: Tell your mother...Tell your mother to take the Goddamn locks off the doors!

(John goes into house. Armine follows, still carrying tray of food. Raffi stays by bush and takes out small pad and pen and draws. Ginya watches bird. From the house, we hear.)

JOHN: VARTAN! VARTAN! IT'S JOHN!

POP: JOHN!

JOHN: I'M HERE. YOU'RE LOCKED IN THE BATHROOM!

POP: JOHN! I'M LOCKED IN THE BATHROOM!

JOHN: IT'S OK, POP.

POP: WHAT DO I DO?

JOHN: PUT YOUR HAND ON THE LOCK.

POP: HELP ME!

(Ginya goes into house. Raffi takes off his coat and ties it around his waist.)

ARMINE: PUT YOUR HAND ON THE LOCK, POP.

POP: HELP ME!

JOHN: IT'S OK, POP.

GINYA: HI, POP! IT'S VIRGINIA!

POP: GINYA! I'M LOCKED IN HERE.

GINYA: IT'S OK, POP.

POP: WHAT DO I DO?

ARMINE: JUST RELAX, POP.

JOHN: TURN THE KNOB TOWARD THE WINDOW. TOWARD THE WINDOW!

POP: WHICH?

ARMINE: THE WINDOW!

GINYA: THE WINDOW, POP.

JOHN: NOT THE TUB!

NON: NOT THE TUB, VARTAN!

POP: MARE! ARE YOU THERE?

NON: I'M HERE, VARTAN.

JOHN: TURN IN THE OTHER DIRECTION FROM THE TUB!

POP: WHICH ONE?

ALL (INCLUDING RAFFI): NOT THE TUB!

JOHN: POP! LISTEN TO WHERE I'M KNOCKING ON THE DOOR. LISTEN, POP!

POP: OK!

(Knocking sound.)

JOHN: TURN TOWARD THE SOUND, VARTAN!

(Knocking continues.)

POP: OK.

JOHN: THAT'S IT, POP!

ALL: YAAAAAAAAAAAAAAAAAAAAAY!

NON: AFAREHIM! (Excellent!)

ARMINE: Alright now.

(Ginya enters. She goes to tree.)

GINYA: Bird's still there.

RAFFI: Where?

GINYA: See that white thing?

(Armine enters still with tray of food.)

ARMINE: MANOCK PAROV, MA. (Good-bye.) BE CAREFUL, PAPA. Come
on, kids. Raffi, put your coat on.

RAFFI: Why?

ARMINE: It's better.

(Non enters with another tray of food.)

NON: Don't forget the kata. (rolls)

(John following Non.)

JOHN: Marie, we have no room for any more food.

NON: On the trunk!

GINYA: IN the trunk, Non. It's IN the trunk.

NON: What is, darling?

JOHN: COME ON, KIDS!

ARMINE: Come on, kids. What are you doing?

RAFFI: Look at this bird.

NON: Aman. Shad Annushig! (So sweet!)

ARMINE: That white bird?

RAFFI: In the leaves.

JOHN: What bird?

GINYA: That's not a white bird. It's a little brown bird holding a Kleenex.

JOHN: A brown bird?

ARMINE: A Kleenex?

GINYA: It might be a paper towel.

ARMINE: Maybe he's taking it to his kitchen! *(Laughs.)*

(Pop enters. All are looking at the bird.)

POP: What is it? What are you looking at?

ARMINE: It's a bird, Pop!

JOHN: What's in his beak?

NON, ARMINE, GINYA: Toilet paper. Kleenex. Paper towel.

POP: What?

RAFFI: He's stepping on it!

JOHN: I think it's a napkin.

POP: What, Marie? What is it? Ah see inch chay? (What is it?)

NON: Ice Turchuna KLEENEX oonee! (The little bird has a Kleenex.)

POP: Turchuna Kleenex? BOH! *(Laughs.)*

RAFFI: He keeps stepping on it.

ARMINE: I bet he's taking it to that nest under the eaves.

RAFFI: I feel sorry for the bird.

NON: Yavroom, it's good! He's doing his work!

GINYA: He's bringing home a big white Kleenex for his family!

POP: Good for him!

(They all watch the bird fly over their heads.)

ALL: OHHHHHHHHHHHHHHHHHHH!

ARMINE: He's under the eaves!

GINYA: OH NO! IT RIPPED!

RAFFI: IT RIPPED?

ARMINE: No, no, it's alright! Now he has a more manageable piece in his mouth.

RAFFI: Why is he just standing there?

JOHN: He's waiting for us to leave!

POP: OK! Let's go!

JOHN: That's right! Let's go!

(They come together again, in a clump, and kiss good-bye. The clump breaks apart when Pop says.)

POP: Good-bye!

RAFFI & ARMINE: Bye, Pop!

(Raffi goes to bush and sits.)

ARMINE: Bye, Ma. Don't forget, on Tuesday, we go to the Podiatrist.

NON: Ya.

JOHN: Oh! Marie, did you sew my buttons?

NON: Aman, of course. I'll get.

JOHN: I'll get.

NON: I'll get.

(Non and John go in the house.)

POP: They went inside!…Ginya?

GINYA: Yes, Pop?

POP: When do you have your commencement?

GINYA: In three years, Pop.

POP: Ah. Are you successful, Ginya? Do you succeed?

GINYA: In life?

POP: BOH! *(Laughs.)* Life!

(Ginya laughs too.)

POP: Ahhh. *(Smiling.)* What's so funny?

GINYA: Life?

POP: BOH! *(Laughs again.)* Ya.

ARMINE: Pop, are you OK?

POP: Ya.

ARMINE: Do you want to go in the house?

POP: No dear. I'm enjoying my visit.

ARMINE: OK.

POP: Yavroom, what is your favorite pastime?

GINYA: I'm a pretty good athlete, Pop.

POP: Sports?

GINYA: Yea.

POP: *(Remembering.)* You run!

GINYA: Yea!

POP: And you write!

GINYA: Ani writes. I run. Raffi is the boy.

POP: Ya, of course. You run? Annushig! Who taught you?

GINYA: My gym teacher.

POP: Bravo!

GINYA: Yea

POP: Do they teach the history, Ginya, also, in the school?

GINYA: No, Pop.

POP: Shall I come to your school? Shall I speak?

GINYA: I don't know, Pop.

ARMINE: John! Where are you?

RAFFI: He's in the house!

POP: Raffi! There you are!

RAFFI: Hi, Pop.

POP: Hi. Are you content, Raffi, with your bush?

RAFFI: Sure, Pop.

POP: AFAREHIM! (Excellent!)

ARMINE: Raffi? What's going on?

RAFFI: Nothing, Ma.

POP: Ginya! We were speaking.

GINYA: Yes, Pop?

POP: Do you know? It is happening again.

GINYA: What is, Pop?

POP: The Armenians are starving. Do they tell you this, Ginya? Do you know? What is your age?

GINYA: Fifteen.

ARMINE: Ginya, where's your father?

GINYA: In the house. I'm fifteen, Pop.

POP: Armenia, Ginya, has one railroad. It goes through the country to the North. Do you know which country?

ARMINE: JOHN! COME ON!

GINYA: Turkey?

POP: Turkey? No. Georgia, Ginya, has the railroad that brings the supplies from the sea towns to Armenia.

ARMINE: Where's Raffi?

POP: It is stopped. It is dismantled. The country is starving.

GINYA: He's by the bush, Ma.

POP: Aman…We are dying.

GINYA: Yes, Pop.

ARMINE: Ginya! Get your father!

POP: Where's Ani?

GINYA: She'll be home soon. *(Ginya goes into house.)*

POP: What do you draw, Raffi, in your pictures?

RAFFI: Um. Aliens.

POP: Aliens?

RAFFI: Yea. *(Gives Pop picture.)*

POP: So this is what they look like!

RAFFI: Yea!

POP: I see. Raffi, do you ever draw a landscape?

RAFFI: You mean a picture of some land?

POP: Ya, some land. Perhaps also with a mountain?

RAFFI: Well, not usually.

POP: Perhaps, Mt. Ararat, Raffi. The mountain in Armenia where…

RAFFI AND POP: Noah's Ark landed.

POP: BOH! *(Laughs.)* Ya. Aman.

RAFFI: I'll draw it, Pop.

POP: Bravo!

ARMINE: JOHN!

(John enters. Non follows carrying pressed pants on a hanger. Ginya follows Non. They cross to the car.)

JOHN: I'm here!

POP: Marie! Where is Ani?

NON: Ginya, tell Pop.

GINYA: She's in Nevada. The desert.

POP: Why didn't she come today? Marie, shouldn't she come today?

RAFFI: She can't, Pop. She's in jail.

POP: She was arrested?

ARMINE: She's alright. She's in jail with two nuns.

POP: Why?

ARMINE: They prayed on the Test Site.

POP: Marie, what is it?

NON: Aneen Nevada AH Nuclear Bombs see head-day, (Ani is in Nevada with nuclear bombs.)

POP: Aman, Marie!

NON: She's alright, Vartan.

ARMINE: Ma! Did you sew John's pants?

NON: I did. I gave.

JOHN: I have. They're here.

ARMINE: OK.

JOHN: Let's go!

POP: Marie, should we write a letter? Should we write a letter to the jail?

NON: Armine, talk to Pop.

ARMINE: Pop, she'll be home soon.

POP: I'll write.

ARMINE: OK, Pop.

POP: Marie, I'll write.

NON: Alright, dear.

JOHN: OK! I'M COUNTING!

NON: Counting what, dear?

JOHN: MINUTES!

NON: Aman! The grape leaves!

ARMINE: We don't have time, Ma.

NON: Ginya, you go pick some grape leaves in the back for your mother. Vartan, you help her.

POP: Did you give Ani the book, Marie?

NON: What book, dear?

POP: My book.

NON: She has them, Vartan. She has them.

POP: My last book, Marie!

GINYA: Papa, let's go.

NON: Alright, dear, I'll give it.

POP: Marie, she should be here.

NON: I know, dear.

GINYA: Pop, let's pick the grape leaves.

POP: We are landlocked. We have no port.

NON: Vartan, what are you saying?

POP: The conditions, Marie. The Conditions!

NON: Yes, dear. It's true. Are you tired?

POP: I am not.

NON: OK...Go on, Vartan.

POP: Marie, one minute! Just one minute!

NON: Yes, dear. What is it?

POP: Where is my photograph? Have I asked you this, Marie? The photo, with my father. At the Church. In the frame. Where is it?

NON: The wire has broken, Vartan. It is being repaired.

POP: OK!...Marie...

NON: Yes, dear?

POP: We must make a gift to Ani, when she returns. She should have that photograph. The photo and the book.

NON: Alright, Vartan. We'll give them to her.

POP: Make sure.

NON: Yes, dear, of course.

POP: Alright.

GINYA: Come on, Pop.

POP: You don't go outside after dark, do you Ginya?

GINYA: No, Pop.

(*Pop and Ginya exit. Armine heads for house.*)

JOHN: ARMINE! WHERE ARE YOU GOING?

ARMINE: Bathroom!

JOHN: Let's go, Raffi!

NON: John, Louise is having heart pains.

JOHN: I know, Marie.

NON: Yavroom, she's your sister.

JOHN: Don't ask me, Marie.

NON: She wants you to listen to her chest.

JOHN: I have listened to her chest, Marie. LET'S GO, ARMINE!

NON: She's not sleeping well, dear.

JOHN: That's not new, Marie.

(*Armine enters.*)

ARMINE: Is your sister coming?

NON: She wants him to listen to her chest.

(*Raffi has walked up and joined them.*)

ARMINE: What do you need, dear?

RAFFI: Nothing.

ARMINE: OK. We'll go in a minute. Get in the car.

(*Raffi gets in car. Ginya enters with aluminum foiled package.*)

JOHN: Armine!

GINYA: Papa gave me the rest of the baklava.

NON: Where are the grape leaves?

ARMINE: John, please, Louise is having pain.

JOHN: I don't have my stethoscope! Do you think I have my stethoscope?

NON: Armine, never mind, dear. You're right, John. You go. RAFFI!

(Raffi sticks his head out car window.)

RAFFI: What?

NON: *(Surprised.)* Ah! You're hiding, Annushig! Good-bye, darling!

GINYA: Non, Pop didn't want me to pick the grape leaves.

NON: Ya. OK.

ARMINE: The sink! Oh, John, the sink!

JOHN: Jesus, Armine, Jesus.

(He storms into the house. Armine and Non follow.)

ARMINE: He never tells me why he's upset.

(Beat. Ginya and Raffi get out of car.)

RAFFI: What sink?

GINYA: Who knows.

(Ginya crosses to bush, takes a piece of toilet paper out of her pocket. She tears paper into little pieces, making a little pile.)

RAFFI: When we get home, I want to show you what I found.

GINYA: OK.

RAFFI: But don't talk about it, OK?

GINYA: OK.

RAFFI: Don't tell me things about it. Don't TELL me things.

GINYA: OK. Shut up.

(Non enters carrying her lightweight porch chair. She sits.)

NON: What do you study, darling, in your school?

GINYA: The regular stuff.

NON: Anything about the Armenians, darling?

GINYA: Not yet, Non. I'll tell you when.

NON: OK. That's perfect.

GINYA: Non, Papa didn't let me go through the gate to pick the grape leaves.

NON: Ya.

RAFFI: He thinks you'll get your thumb shot off, right, Non? Like his sister?

GINYA: Was it his sister, Non?

NON: It was his sister. First they shot her hand when she put it on the fence gate. Then they shot her in the back.

RAFFI: Oh.

GINYA: Non, will you move this to the windowsill, if it rains?

NON: Your little pile? Ya.

(John bursts out of house. Armine following.)

JOHN: I can't fix sinks! Call someone who fixes sinks! Call Ernie Breed! He fixes sinks!

ARMINE: Ma, I'll call Ernie Breed.

JOHN: I can't fix sinks.

LOUISE: *(Offstage.)* JOHN!

(Aunt Louise runs on. Her husband, Garo, follows. Both in coats.)

LOUISE: JOHN! PLEURISY! IRREGULAR PULSE, JOHN!

JOHN: That's not pleurisy, Louise.

LOUISE: I have the symptoms, John,

GARO: *(To Ginya.)* Hello, dear.

GINYA: Hello, Uncle Garo.

JOHN: Pleurisy is an inflammation of the lining of the lung, Louise. You don't have that.

LOUISE: I think I do, John.

JOHN: No, you don't, Louise. Go home.

LOUISE: Just listen to my lungs.

JOHN: You couldn't have run here, Louise, in fifteen minutes. You couldn't have run at all.

LOUISE: I need a shunt.

GARO: She thinks she needs a shunt.

JOHN: She doesn't need a shunt. Her brain is fine. Her heart is fine. Her lungs are fine.

LOUISE: My hands are swelling. My rings are tight.

JOHN: I'm going in the house.

LOUISE: JOHN!

(He exits.)

GARO: *(To Armine.)* How are you dear?

ARMINE: Busy.

LOUISE: He never listens to my heart.

GARO: *(To Ginya.)* How's my favorite dancing partner?

LOUISE: Garo, don't cha-cha!

GARO: Have you been practicing?

GINYA: Not really.

RAFFI: HI!

LOUISE/GARO: HELLO, YAVROOM! (darling)

GARO: Raffi, come watch. We're going to practice.

(Garo sings cha-cha music. They dance.)

ARMINE: *(To Louise.)* Hello, dear.

LOUISE: Where's Ani?

NON: Nebraska. Arrested on the grave site.

ARMINE: The TEST site!

NON: TEST site! Aman.

LOUISE: I thought she was coming today. Didn't she say she would be here? Didn't she say she would come for Sunday meal?

ARMINE: She was delayed.

LOUISE: Vy Vy Vy. (My, my, my.)

RAFFI: Mom, can I leave my coat in the car?

ARMINE: No, no dear. You need it.

LOUISE: Vartan has been waiting for Ani, you know, Armine.

ARMINE: Louise, for Pete's sake, I know, what should I do?

LOUISE: Tell her, there is disappointment! Tell her, Armine!

ARMINE: No no no…

(*John yells from house.*)

JOHN: WHERE'S THE ANNOUSHABOURG? (pudding)

ARMINE: She'll be home soon.

NON: Garo, how are you?

ARMINE: IT'S IN THE FRIDGE, JOHN!

GARO: Fine, Marie.

JOHN: I LOOKED IN THE FRIDGE! DON'T TELL ME THE FRIDGE!

LOUISE: Oh, my heart.

NON: (*To Armine.*) Maybe it's in the car.

ARMINE: No, Ma. JOHN! LOOK ON THE COUNTER.

GARO: Hey! Look at that bird!

LOUISE: What bird?

NON: On the LITTLE counter, Armine.

GARO: It's got a white thing!

LOUISE: Where is it?

ARMINE: LOOK ON THE LITTLE COUNTER!

GARO: What is that?

LOUISE: That bird?

(*John enters.*)

JOHN: Pop is dead.

GARO: What?

NON: That's a nap, dear. He's napping.

JOHN: No, Marie.

(*Armenian music plays. Lights shift and come up on.*)

SCENE II

A Church. The family sits, in their coats. John is at the pulpit.

JOHN: …and many of us were baptized by him, married by him, as he stood at
this pulpit, in this Church. I think of this and I think of the Church he
built in one night in Casaria. The Church he built with his father, in one
night, from sundown to sunrise, because the Turkish laws forbid the con-
struction of a Christian House of Worship. So, they built through the
night: an Altar, twelve benches, three and one half walls. Then the sun rose.
And they stopped building. But the people came. Even through the win-
ters, people came. And he preached to them. Remarkable. *(Beat.)* I have a
picture. *(Beat.)* I'll show you. *(Bows his head.)* Asht-vatz-hogeen Los Ah
Vor reh. (May God illuminate his soul.) *(Beat.)* Ani.
(John steps down. Ani goes to the pulpit carrying a piece of paper.)

ANI: My Grandfather. Papa. My Papa. The Minister from Armenia. Told stories.
When I was young enough to sit on my Papa's knee, I would lean my head
against his vest, and he would say: "Which, Ani, my Annushig, which
story?" And together, we would choose: The Noah's-Ark-Landing-on-Mt.-
Ararat-Story!

Or: The Margaret-Mead-And-Her-Armenian-Son-In-Law-Story.

Or: The Mesrop-The-Great-Who-Invented-The-Armenian-
Alphabet-in-400 AD—which-I-could-never-figure-out-when-that-was-
Story.

Or: The-Good-Turk-In-Istanbul-Story.

The Good Turk who sat on the porch with his chair and his gun. And
when the Turkish soldiers came with their orders to: "Kill All The
Armenians!" The Good Turk said: "These people are my neighbors. I love
them." And the soldiers moved on.

Papa told stories. Papa wrote sermons. Papa wrote letters. Non told
me that during World War II, Papa wrote to every Armenian soldier. Every
one. More than once.

Our Papa.

Who babysat on Sunday evenings and polished the copper bottoms of
the pots and pans while we watched the television. And before bed, he
would sit with us on the front steps, stirring honey into his coffee,
clinking, clinking. Papa. The Minister from Armenia.

Our Papa, who wrote fifteen books on Armenian History, on his

Armenian typewriter, which I now have in my room. Papa tried to tell us about the history. The massacres. But we resisted. So he waited.

He waited to tell his American grandchildren in American schools, playing on teams in American sports. I knew he was waiting and I didn't want to hear. My friends didn't know about the Armenians. Pam Hansen didn't know that my grandfather's family was forced to walk across a desert without food or water, until they dropped dead. My American friends who became more important to me than school. Or grades. Or Papa.

And now, again the Armenians are starving. And no one knows. I want to go to Armenia. I have to go. I want to witness. For Papa. I am going to Armenia.

RAFFI: Wow!

LOUISE & GARO: Shhhhhhhhhh!

JOHN: She can't do that.

ARMINE: John!

NON: Shhhhhhhhh!

(*Lights shift. Armenian music, Yerevan, plays.*)

SCENE III

Non's bedroom. Music plays throughout.

As Yerevan is being played, Non walks into her "bedroom." Ani picks up her backpack and follows. As the song continues, Non gives Ani several items. Each item is given with the intention of preparing Ani for her journey. First, she gives Ani a babushka, which she puts on Ani's head. Then Non gives Ani Papa's book. Non opens it to the first page. Together, they silently read the inscription. Then Ani puts the book in her backpack. Then Non gives Ani a beautiful Persian urn. Ani carefully puts the urn in her backpack. The last thing Non gives Ani is the shawl she is wearing. Ani folds it and places it on top of the urn in her backpack. Next Non takes Ani's head in her hands, kisses the top of her head, looks at her and then turns away from her. Ani stands a moment in silence. Then Ani exits, carrying her backpack.

Lights shift. We hear the sound of planes.

SCENE IV

An Airport waiting room. Entire family is gathered with exception of Non. They sit in their coats. Ani is wearing her backpack. She has removed her babushka. They are waiting.

LOUISE: Ani, do you know about your Great Great Uncle Mugerditch?

ANI: Uh-huh.

RAFFI: Great Uncle who?

LOUISE: Mugerditch!

RAFFI: Mugerditch?

LOUISE: Yes! He was Knighted by the Sultan in 1790!

RAFFI: What's a Sultan?

LOUISE: A Sultan is a Pasha, a Monarch.

GARO: A King.

RAFFI: Oh.

LOUISE: Ya. A fat king.

JOHN: They weren't all fat.

LOUISE: Usually, ya, they were all fat.

GINYA: A fat king knighted out great great Uncle Muger—who?

LOUISE & GARO: Mugerditch!

LOUISE: I can tell you this story! Somehow, in his village, your Great Great Uncle Mugerditch invented a precious thing! Something he knew the Sultan would want for his armies, and perhaps for himself also, this precious thing would be desirable!

RAFFI: What was it?

LOUISE: I will tell you. This is the suspense! Sit down.

RAFFI: OK.

GARO: Go on, dear.

LOUISE: Ya. So, he traveled with a caravan, all the way from his village in the mountains to Constantinople. He traveled by horseback, with his precious invention here, in his breast pocket.

GINYA: What was it?

JOHN: Tell them what it was, Louise.

LOUISE: I'm telling! So. The Caravan was attacked! More than once. Their horses were stolen! Their goods were stolen!

GARO: Everything was stolen!

LOUISE: Everything was stolen! But your Great Great Uncle Mugerditch was wily! And he arrived safely in Constantinople!

RAFFI: Then what?

GARO: He finds an acquaintance who can introduce him to the Sultan!

GINYA: How did he do that?

LOUISE: Through a friend.

GINYA: A friend of the Sultan's was a friend of an acquaintance that our Great Great Uncle Mugerditch knew?

LOUISE: Yes, he was.

GARO: Distant! A distant friend. You should say, Louise. It was distant. Go on, dear.

JOHN: Go on, Louise!

LOUISE: I'M GOING! So. He, your Great, Great Uncle Mugerditch, has an audience with the Sultan! And he walks in, wearing his Zavalla (pathetic) suit. Nothing in his hands. He bows.

GARO: A deep bow.

LOUISE: A deep bow. Then carefully, he removes from his pocket, his precious invention, which had weathered the journey in perfect condition. And with two fingers, he holds it up to the Sultan, so that he could see. What do you think?

GINYA & RAFFI: What?

LOUISE: BASTERMA!

GINYA & RAFFI: What?

LOUISE: Basterma!

JOHN: Beef jerky.

LOUISE: Ya.

GINYA: He was knighted for discovering Beef jerky?

LOUISE: Yes, he was!

ARMINE: The plane's so late. My goodness.

RAFFI: What is beef jerky?

LOUISE, JOHN, GARO: Dried meat!

RAFFI: Puke.

ANI: I thought he carried it in his cummerbund.

JOHN: That's correct.

LOUISE: It was the breast pocket.

ARMINE: Nevermind.

GARO: It was the cummerbund, because it had the taste of sweat.

LOUISE: That doesn't disqualify the breast pocket, Garo. You know that doesn't disqualify the breast pocket!

JOHN: You distort your facts! You consistently distort and misconstrue your facts! You misconstrue! You never listen!

LOUISE: You always say I misconstrue, John! When you took me to the pool and left me there and I almost drowned, you said I misconstrued!

JOHN: I can't fight with you.

GARO: Don't fight with her.

JOHN: No one can fight with her.

GARO: Don't fight.

JOHN: She's blameless. She's without blame!

LOUISE: Why should I be to blame? Never mind! Aman! Your daughter's leaving for Yerevan! Why? No one knows!

JOHN: IT WAS THE CUMMERBUND! HE CARRIED THE BASTERMA IN HIS *MAROON* CUMMERBUND! NOT IN HIS BREAST POCKET! NOR IN HIS MORE FAVORED *MAGENTA* COLORED CUMMERBUND, BECAUSE THE *MAGENTA* WOULD ATTRACT ATTENTION FROM LOOTERS! SO, THE BASTERMA WAS TUCKED IN THE *MAROON* CUMMERBUND. AND THE *MAGENTA,* WHICH HE BROUGHT IN PREPARATION FOR HIS AUDIENCE WITH THE SULTAN, WAS CAREFULLY FOLDED AND CARRIED IN HIS *BREAST POCKET!* THAT'S THE STORY! THE BASTERMA WAS CARRIED IN THE *CUMMERBUND!*

LOUISE: Never mind.

JOHN: Ani! Why are you going to Yerevan? For Pete's Sake! It is blockaded! There is no fuel! You are alone!

ANI: I'm not, Dad. I'm with a group bringing supplies.

JOHN: Where? Where is the group bringing supplies?

ANI: Dad! I meet their plane in Chicago!

ARMINE: We've been through this, John. She meets their plane in Chicago.

JOHN: How many? How many in this group?

ARMINE, ANI, GINYA: Twenty-two.

GARO: Twenty-two?

LOUISE: Ya.

JOHN: Why did I agree to this? I forget why I agreed to this.

ARMINE: You agreed.

GINYA: Cher went.

GARO: Cher who?

LOUISE: Cher Cher!

GARO: Cher Cher?

JOHN: Cher No Last Name Cher!

ARMINE: It was Sarkisian, dear.

JOHN: OK! CHER! CHER SARKISIAN! CHER SARKISIAN WENT TO ARMENIA! IT'S PATHETIC!

ANI: Dad, I told you.

JOHN: Witness! Witness, you said! I want to witness for Papa! This witness notion! KAR KHAN EH GEEN! (Turkish swear word) Cher wants to witness! Her publicist wants Cher to witness!

ANI: DAD!

JOHN: Our parents escaped! And you want to witness! *(Swears in Turkish.)* ES SHAG!

ARMINE: John!

JOHN: My Father! MY FATHER, THE ONLY DOCTOR OF HIS VILLAGE...

ARMINE: JOHN!

JOHN: WAS FORCED TO SERVE IN THE TURKISH ARMY...

JOHN & ANI: WITH NO SHOES!!!

JOHN: THAT'S RIGHT!

ANI: I know!

RAFFI: Why didn't he wear shoes?

JOHN: HE WAS FORCED, EVERY DAY...EVERY DAY, HE WAS FORCED TO ADMINISTER CARE TO THE TURKISH SOLDIERS, WHO WOULD RETURN TO CAMP, AFTER A DAY...

ARMINE: JOHN!!!

JOHN: OF KILLING ARMENIANS! *(To Raffi.)* So he couldn't run away.

RAFFI: Oh.

GINYA: Oh.

RAFFI: Did he have a horse?

JOHN: Armenia is dangerous, Ani. It's uncomfortable.

GARO: *(To Raffi.)* He didn't have a horse.

ARMINE: She's used to that, John. She's been to jail, John.

JOHN: JAIL! AMAN! FOR WHAT? THREE DAYS? SHE SANG SONGS WITH NUNS! SHE SLEPT IN A HEATED ROOM! SHE ATE COOKED FOOD! ARMENIA IS COLD! THE PEOPLE THERE WANT TO COME HERE!

ARMINE: Shut up, dear.

LOUISE: Good for you, Armine!

GARO: Shut up, dear.

JOHN: BRAVO, GARO! Does she do it? When you ask her to shut up, Garo? Does she?

GARO: Never mind.

LOUISE: Aman.

RAFFI: I liked your story, Aunt Louise.

LOUISE: Thank you, Annushig! (dear)

ANI: You agreed, Dad. You can change your mind and take back the money that I am borrowing, if you want. But I'll go eventually, Dad.

JOHN: Ani, you don't even speak Armenian! You think you understand it, Ani, but you don't. You think you speak Armenian, Ani, but you don't. You don't speak Armenian! You don't understand Armenian!

ANI: I know I don't! I know I don't know how to speak Armenian! How was I suppose to learn it? I could never hear it! The only time you spoke Armenian in the house was when you and Mom told secrets. YOU WHISPER IN ARMENIAN! YOU YELL IN ENGLISH! AND YOU CURSE IN TURKISH!

ARMINE: You're yelling in the Airport, dear.

ANI: YES, MOM, I'M YELLING IN THE AIRPORT! WE'RE ALL YELLING IN THE AIRPORT! WE ALL YELL EVERYWHERE! WE ARE YELLERS! WE YELL! AND WHAT ARE WE YELLING ABOUT? CUMMERBUNDS AND BASTERMA!!

ARMINE: Sit down, dear.

ANI: *(Sits down, then stands up.)* DAD!

JOHN: WE DON'T ALL YELL! Your Mother doesn't yell.

ARMINE: Sometimes I do, John.

JOHN: When, Armine?

ARMINE: In the evening, John.

JOHN: No dear. You don't yell, dear. In fact, you get quieter.

GINYA: There's no room for her to yell.

JOHN: What?

ARMINE: Never mind! Aman.

LOUISE: Ginya's right!

ARMINE: Shhhhhh, Louise!

JOHN: What were we talking about?

ANI: ME! We were talking about ME!

ARMINE: Yes, we were. You speak, Ani.

ANI: Dad! My friends, Dad, my friends don't even know where Armenia is. They think…

JOHN: Ani…

ARMINE: Please let her speak, John.

ANI: You have taught me, Dad. Papa taught me. 1915!

JOHN: Yes.

ANI: Over one million Armenians were killed.

JOHN: That's right.

ANI: And to this day, the history books make no mention—not one word of the genocide!

JOHN: And to this day, Ani, Armenia has no Allies! It is unprotected.

ANI: Because *no one has witnessed!*

JOHN: Aman.

ANI: I have to go to Armenia, Dad. I have to go so I can see things and write things. And then send the things I write to newspapers. I want to yell things in newspapers! I want to yell things in newspaper!

LOUISE: What is she saying, Garo?

GARO: She wants to yell things, dear.

GINYA: She did it in Nevada!

JOHN: What?

ARMINE: Yes, John!

GINYA: Remember? Remember that story?

ARMINE: In the newspaper!

GINYA: YEA!

ARMINE: They got attention! In Nevada!

RAFFI: YEA!

ARMINE: It was important, John.

RAFFI & GINYA: YEA!

JOHN: Aman.

GARO: BRAVO, ANI!

LOUISE: What, Garo?

GARO: I am moved.

JOHN: Garo! You are moved! I am worried!

GARO: I understand, of course.

JOHN: For Pete's Sake!

GARO: Of course. Of course.

ANI: Dad…Please.

JOHN: Ani. Do you understand…we…I…am frightened.

GARO: Now, it's said.

ANI: I know, Dad. Your family escaped. And you'll never go back. But I can go, Dad. I am ready!…Mom?…Mom?

ARMINE: She can go, dear. We cannot. But she…believes she can.

ANI: I know I can! Look at me!

JOHN: What will you do there?

ARMINE: She will help.

JOHN: How, Armine?

ARMINE: In her way, John.

JOHN: Aman…

ANI: Dad.

JOHN: *(Takes candles from his coat pocket.)* You'll need candles, Ani. You must take some candles. Here.

ANI: Thank you.

JOHN: Keep them for yourself.

LOUISE: Armine, did you give her food to eat on the plane?

ARMINE: Of course.

GINYA: Basterma?

ARMINE: No, no. Too much garlic.

GARO: *(Handing Ani a small box.)* Here, Ani. I made this. A gift. It's nothing. A small thing.

   (She opens box, it's a ring. She puts it on.)

ANI: Thank you, Uncle Garo.

GARO: Good-bye, dear.

LOUISE: I brought you some cheese beregg, darling.

RAFFI: I got you some Blow Pops, Ani.

GARO: When you come back, Ani, we'll YELL our heads off! *(He starts to dance.)* BRAVO! BRAVO!

LOUISE: Garo! Aman!

   (Flight announcement.)

GINYA: It's time to go, Ani. Here, I bought you a pen.

ANI: It's pretty. Thanks, Gin.

GINYA: Bye, Ani. Bye, bye.

ARMINE: Kazee guh serum, Ani… (I love you)

ANI: Mom…

ARMINE: I know, darling.

LOUISE: Bachigs, Yavroom. (Kisses, dear.)

   (Louise crosses to Ani and Armine. Hugs. Then Garo, Raffi and Ginya join hug.)

GARO: Good-bye, Ani.

   (Hug breaks up. Ani looks at her Father. She goes to him. They hug. Then Ani begins to leave.)

LOUISE: TAKE THE BERREGG!

   (Ani stops. Louise hands her the little shopping bag containing Beregg.)

ANI: Raffi!

RAFFI: Yea?

ANI: Thanks! *(Holds up the Blow Pops.)*

RAFFI: Cool.

ANI: Bye bye.

> *(They all raise their hands to wave a still wave. Lights shift.)*

SCENE V

> *The cemetery. Non, Ginya and Raffi. Raffi is poking the dirt with a stick. He has his coat tied around his waist.*

RAFFI: What do they do when they've run out of room?

NON: For what, dear?

RAFFI: To bury people.

NON: Oh. Well…let's see…

GINYA: Don't ask questions like that.

RAFFI: Why not?

NON: It's alright, dear. Raffi, I'll think about your question.

RAFFI: It's OK, Non.

GINYA: Do you have another stick?

RAFFI: Yup. *(Tosses her one.)* Don't forget to give it back.

GINYA: OK. Thanks. Put your coat on.

RAFFI: No. Why?

NON: It's better.

RAFFI: It is?

NON: Ya. *(Puts his coat on.)*

RAFFI: Non, did you tell Papa, Ani's in Yerevan?

NON: Not yet.

RAFFI: OH! *(Covers his mouth.)* Sorry.

NON: It's alright, dear. He knows.

GINYA: Duh.

NON: Shh shh.

RAFFI: Yea, Ginya, be quiet!

NON: You know what?

GINYA & RAFFI: What?

NON: I think soon there will be babies in the nest in our tree!

GINYA: The all white nest?

NON: Ya.

RAFFI: Awesome!

NON: It's browner now. Beege.

RAFFI: What?

NON: Beege.

GINYA: Beige, Non. It's Beige.

NON: What is, dear?

GINYA: The nest.

NON: Ya. OK.

RAFFI: Oh, brother.

GINYA: Raffi!!

NON: Shhhhhh.

GINYA: Do you talk to Papa, Non?

NON: Yes, but not out loud.

RAFFI: In what language?

NON: Armenian. Some Turkish.

GINYA: I don't like to think about Papa here, Non. I mean, here. *(Points to grave.)*

NON: Our Papa, darling, what shall I say…his Spirit is everywhere.

GINYA: Yea. But his body is in the ground.

(Raffi stops poking the dirt.)

RAFFI: Can we go now, Non?

NON: Soon, Raffi. Do you want some pistachios?

RAFFI: No, thanks. Isn't it time to go?

NON: In a minute. I think first, I must tell you my secret.

GINYA: A secret?

RAFFI: In English?

NON: Of course!

GINYA: Wow!

NON: Wow, ya! Your first big secret! An event!

RAFFI & GINYA: Yea.

NON: Are you ready?

RAFFI & GINYA: Yea.

NON: Do you want some figs?

RAFFI & GINYA: No thanks.

NON: OK. My darlings…I had Papa put in ashes.

GINYA: CREMATED?

RAFFI: WHAT? WHAT IS IT?

NON: Cremated! Ya. He is not in this grave. His body is ashes.

RAFFI: Ashes?

NON: Ya. And the ashes are with Ani.

GINYA: With Ani?

NON: In her packback!

GINYA: BACKpack!

NON: Ya.

RAFFI: AWESOME!

GINYA: Why?

NON: She is taking them back to his Church in Casaria, to be buried with his father.

RAFFI: And his mother.

GINYA: No, his mother was lost, right, Non?

NON: Ya. She was lost. His father built, with Papa he built, the three-walled Church in Casaria. So, Papa, I think, by now, he is there.

GINYA: Is the coffin in the ground here empty?

NON: No, no.

RAFFI: What's in it?

NON: Birch logs.

RAFFI: Birch logs?

NON: Ya. To make it heavy.

RAFFI: From birch trees?

NON: Ya. Papa liked birch trees.

GINYA: So, there are logs in the coffin, and Papa's in Armenia?

RAFFI: Yea. But he's dead.

NON: Ya. Too bad.

RAFFI & GINYA: Ya.

NON: Better dead than never! Right? Is that it?

GINYA: Not really.

NON: Never mind.

GINYA: You did all this, Non?

NON: Ya.

RAFFI: WOW!

NON: I deserve Ph.D.! It was difficult! Until a miracle! What do you think? The father-in-law of the funeral director. He was Armenian! DICHRAN PAPAZIAN! Aman! They call him Digger!

GINYA: Digger?

RAFFI: Gross.

NON: Digger, darling! He helped me!

RAFFI: I'm hungry. Can I have some Kata? (rolls)

NON: Of course, Annushig, it is for you! Here, darling. And for the birds, I brought Baklava.

GINYA: Baklava?

(She takes out aluminum foil package and sprinkles pieces of baklava on the grave.)

NON: Ya. I think Papa's grave is a good place for the birds to have a party! Here, now they can live, how you say, high hog?

GINYA: Ya. High hog.

RAFFI: This is our secret, Non?

NON: Papa? Ya!

GINYA: No one knows?

RAFFI: Digger knows.

NON: Just a little. Mostly, you, you, me. And Ani.

GINYA: Cool.

NON: AUKSOME.

RAFFI: Yea!

(Armine enters.)

ARMINE: Come on. Let's go. It's time to go. *(To Papa's grave.)* I love you, my Father. Kazee guh serrem. (I love you.) *(To them.)* Come on. Louise is in the hospital having tests. Dad's coming home early. Garo is missing. And we got a letter from Ani. Let's go. Say good-bye to Papa *(Armine exits.)*

(Non, Ginya, Raffi face out and yell.)

NON/GINYA/RAFFI: GOOD-BYE PAPA!

(Lights dim. We hear the distant sound of thunder.)

SCENE VI

A storm. Non sits at a table in her kitchen. She wears a shawl. Armine enters carrying candles. The lights in the room flicker and go out.

NON: Vy Vy Vy.

(They light more candles. Armine takes a letter from her pocket.)

ARMINE: From Ani.

NON: I.O.

(Ani enters on opposite side of stage. She is wearing a babushka and shawl, carrying a candle. During this scene, Ani is recalling the letter. She is in her hotel room. She has her journal, a pen, a hand mirror, and Non's shawl. Through the course of the scene, she walks around the small room, she looks out the window. She tries to dance. She remembers the song and sings.)

NON: OK.

ARMINE & ANI: Parev.

ARMINE: *(Reading.)* I'm here!

ANI: I'm fine.

ARMINE: Don't worry! I hope this letter makes its way to you.

ANI: There's so much to say.

ARMINE: Everyone here sounds like you, Nonnie. And the whole city smells like your house!

(Ani is looking out window.)

ARMINE: I have seen Mt. Ararat!

ANI: Mt. Ararat is beautiful. It's so easy to imagine the Ark on top! Also, from my window in the hotel, I can see the fountain in Central Square. It is enormous. But it has no water!

ARMINE: It has no water. There is no water, Mom.

NON: Go on, dear.

ARMINE: There is so little fuel.

ANI: We only have three hours of power a day.

ARMINE: Sometimes, at two o'clock in the morning, all the lights will go on and everyone will get up and cook, bathe, clean and read, until the system is exhausted. And then everyone goes back to bed.

ANI: There is so little fuel. All the trees have been cut down and burned for firewood. The ancient poplars that lined the roads are gone.

NON: Aman.

ARMINE: There are no trees, and no trees stumps.

ANI: There are no wooden doors or window sills left in the city.

ARMINE: And no wooden desks in the schools But the children continue to attend school. They go for half the day, for half the year. When it's not too cold… Tune garta asee, Myrig. (You read this, Mother.)

NON: I.O., of course. *(Reads.)* I must tell you what happened to us! Guess what! The owner of this hotel is the Mayor of a small village in the mountains.

ANI: He's been very kind to me.

ARMINE: Who is he?

NON: Don't worry. *(Reads.)* He invited me and all the members of our group to visit his village. So we traveled in a rusty van, three hours up the mountain roads, to his little town.

ANI: The first thing he showed us was the village farm.

NON & ANI: Sandy little rows of eggplants and onions, tomatoes and okra.

NON: The Mayor (His name is Zaven.) was so proud! He told us: "We made everything here! The hinges. The faucets. Even the peeps!"

ANI: He meant pipes!

NON: Peeps! Aman.

ARMINE: Go on, Mother.

NON: As we toured the Farm, it became obvious to all of us that we hadn't seen a single other person. The town was empty. But we didn't ask and the Mayor made no mention.

ARMINE: Read faster, Myrig.

ANI: Then we all went to the Village Church.

NON: The ancient Village Church. As soon a we arrived, the Church doors burst open and the entire town came out, dancing, singing and playing tambourines!

(Armenian music plays. Ani begins to dance as though she is learning. She continues to dance through the following section.)

NON: The last to come, was a Priest, dressed entirely in white robes. His hands were crossed in front of his chest and in each hand he was holding a white dove. He walked directly to me, bowed in greeting and then released the doves to the sky. They flew together like synchronized swimmers and perched on the Church steeple. Then again, the tambourines played, the women danced and they led us into the Church.

(Ani's hands move like the flight of birds. Non raises her arm, still seated, she dances.)

ARMINE: Mother. Continue.

NON: Ah.

(Ani and Non lower their arms at the same time.)

NON: Once we were inside the Church, we sat on the stone floors and were served a feast of the tiniest portions. All vegetables from the sandy, little garden. Then the children, two small children, stood in costume, and sang to us. As they sang, another child translated; from the Armenian to English.

(Ani begins to sing the first verse of Yerevan. She sings as Non reads the translation.)

NON: Yerevan.

The great dream of our little land.

Cherished for centuries. Centuries old

But youthful still.

The Beauty of Stone.

(Non hums the last few lines; or sings the second section of song. In either case, Non sings the last word "Yerevan".)

ARMINE: Mother, please.

NON: As we drove home, winding down the Mountain roads, it grew dark and we were silent. They knew Papa.

ANI: They knew Papa.

NON & ANI: So they did this for me.

NON: Aman.

ANI: So often, I think I see Papa's face. I hear his voice.

ARMINE: Mother.

NON: Most of the group is leaving tomorrow.

ANI: I've decided to stay.

NON: I'm going to stay.

ARMINE: What?

NON: I want to write something.

ANI: I want to go to people's homes.

NON: And to the libraries, the churches, the orphanages and record the conditions. The Conditions.

ANI: Don't worry.

NON: Don't worry. I have my candles, my blow pops, and my pen!

ANI: Love you.

NON: Love you. Bachigs, Ani.

(Ani begins to untie her babushka.)

NON: P.S.

NON & ANI: I found a thin pair of scissors in my room.

(Ani picks up a hand mirror. Armine takes letter from Non.)

ARMINE: Ancient sewing scissors.

(Ani looks at herself in mirror, she removes her babushka, her hair is gone.)

ARMINE: I'm thinking of cutting my hair...Good night.

ANI: Good night.

(Sound of thunder. Louise enters wearing a raincoat, carrying a pan of food.)

LOUISE: Oh my God, this storm! The Bazaar was canceled! The Church basement looked wonderful before the lights went out! All that food, sitting on tables, in absolute darkness! I brought you some Sarma, it needs lemon. VaVa is thinner, Sarkis is fatter, they send love. Rosine has a boyfriend!

NON: Armenian?

LOUISE: No. Odar! (a non-Armenian)

NON: Aman.

(Sound of thunder.)

LOUISE: Ah! This storm! It gives me palpitations.

NON: You want some coffee?

LOUISE: Garo is lost again.

ARMINE: My daughter…My daughter cut off all her hair.
LOUISE: Ah!
NON: Perhaps!
ARMINE: I know it.
(*Music. Lights shift.*)

SCENE VII

Lights come up to reveal Garo sitting on the curb in his coat. We hear Louise call: "Garo" Then Louise crosses out of kitchen, wearing a coat. She is carrying kata, wrapped in a napkin.

LOUISE: Garo! (*She walks to him.*) Do you want some Kata?
GARO: I.O.
(*He takes the kata and eats. She stands behind him.*)
LOUISE: What are you looking at?
GARO: Nothing.
LOUISE: How are you?
GARO: Fine.
LOUISE: Shall we go inside?
GARO: I.O. (*He stays.*)
LOUISE: Garo?
GARO: I'll stay here.
LOUISE: No, dear.
GARO: This is pleasant.
LOUISE: This is the curb, dear.…Are you a dog? Garo, are you a dog?
GARO: I am not.
LOUISE: That's correct. Come inside.
GARO: Do you know…the gift I gave to Ani. Louise, do you know?
LOUISE: For good luck.
GARO: Ya. Good luck. For safe journey.
LOUISE: It was very good.
GARO: It was a small thing. Nothing.
LOUISE: She will be alright, Garo. She is wily.
GARO: Wily. Your Uncle…
LOUISE: was wily. Ya.
GARO: I am not.
LOUISE: You are Garo. Garo on the curb.

GARO: That is me.

LOUISE: Are you alright? Are you cold?

GARO: I'm alright.

LOUISE: Alright. Come inside.

GARO: Alright.

    (She starts to exit.)

LOUISE: Garo, we will listen to the music. Come inside!

GARO: OK.

    (She exits. He stays. She turns up the music. Cha-cha music. Garo stands. He considers the house. Then he chooses to go for a walk. Raffi enters on rollerblades. They acknowledge each other. Garo exits.)

SCENE VIII

    Raffi enters on rollerblades, listening to a walkman. We hear contemporary music. He is rollerblade dancing. He's a pro. Ginya enters. Also on rollerblades. It's her first day. She stumble-skates across the stage to Raffi and plows into him.

GINYA: RAFFI!

RAFFI: HEY!

    (Ginya holds onto Raffi and skates around behind him. They skate, then Raffi turns off his walkman and the music stops.)

GINYA: Sorry. I'm sorry.

RAFFI: What are you doing?

GINYA: Raffi, come on. Just show me how to stop.

RAFFI: USE THE BRAKE!

GINYA: WHAT BRAKE?

RAFFI: Let go of me and I'll show you the brake!

GINYA: Promise?

RAFFI: Yea!

GINYA: OK. *(She lets go. She keeps skating. She can't stop.)*

RAFFI: Hey! Those are Ani's skates, Ginya.

GINYA: She said I could use them.

RAFFI: She did not.

GINYA: Just show me where the brake is.

RAFFI: Duh.

GINYA: RAFFI!

RAFFI: THIS IS THE BRAKE!

GINYA: WHAT DO YOU DO WITH IT?

RAFFI: You have to drag it. It slows you down.

GINYA: How do you STOP?

RAFFI: You jump up and pivot turn! *(He does it.)*

GINYA: That was good!

RAFFI: *(Lets go.)* Alright, See ya. *(He skates away.)*

GINYA: WAIT RAFFI WAIT!

RAFFI: WHAT DO YOU WANT, MY WHOLE LIFE?

GINYA: I want you to teach me to stop.

   (He takes her hands and guides her.)

RAFFI: Press down on the right foot. The RIGHT foot. Slide it.

   (She slides it.)

RAFFI: That's good. OK! *(Raffi turns Ginya around and pushes her downstage. On push.)* You're outta here!

GINYA: AHHHHHHHHHHHH!

RAFFI: BRAKE! BRAKE!

   (She brakes.)

RAFFI: OK!

GINYA: Was that good?

RAFFI: Well…You stopped.

GINYA: Yea. Thanks.

RAFFI: Sure.

   (They practice.)

GINYA: Did you pick something to send to Ani?

RAFFI: No and don't tell me anything.

GINYA: I bought her a new journal. You can send it.

RAFFI: Ginya, when's Ani coming home?

GINYA: Who knows.

RAFFI: Does Dad know?

GINYA: I don't know if he knows. Nobody speaks in English anymore.

RAFFI: I'll say. We live on PLANET ARMENIA!

GINYA: Don't yell!

   (Raffi skates in a circle and yells.)

RAFFI: PLANET ARMENIA!!

   (Beat.)

GINYA: PLANET ARMENIA!!!

   (Beat. They both chuckle.)

GINYA: OK, I'm gonna go home. I'm going home.

RAFFI: See ya. *(Raffi skate dances again.)*

GINYA: *(Skates and brakes.)* You coming?

RAFFI: Nope.

GINYA: *(Skating offstage.)* RAFFI, COME HOME BEFORE DARK!

> *(Raffi turns on Walkman and skate dances. Beat. He skates off in Ginya's direction. Lights shift.)*

SCENE IX

> *Evening. A hospital room. Garo is in the bed. Louise (in her coat) and John (lab coat) are on either side of Garo.*

LOUISE: Do you think it's the diet? Too much fat?

JOHN: No.

LOUISE: He eats so much fat, John. And he stopped moving. Except for those walks to Pal Park. Oh my God, those walks! His knees were swollen. John, his knees were swollen.

JOHN: It's his circulation, Louise.

LOUISE: His circulation and his nutrition, John.

JOHN: Louise, I'm not his Doctor. This isn't my Ward. I'm due at a conference. I stopped in to say hello. I didn't know you were here.

LOUISE: Where else would I be?

JOHN: I thought you'd left.

LOUISE: No. I'm here. Stop hating me.

JOHN: Garo, can you hear me? Squeeze my hand.

LOUISE: He can't hear you.

JOHN: Louise, please, I'm speaking to Garo.

LOUISE: He can't hear you, John. Why don't you speak to me?

JOHN: Garo, I've spoken to your doctors.

LOUISE: John! Me! Here I am! Talk to me!

JOHN: *(To Louise.)* They're going to run some tests. Noninvasive. He'll be comfortable. Don't worry.

LOUISE: Thank you.

JOHN: You're welcome. I'll stop in tomorrow, Garo.

LOUISE: John, listen to me.

JOHN: I have to go, Louise.

LOUISE: I need you to listen to my heart.

JOHN: Louise, if you're having pain, go see a Doctor.

LOUISE: I'm seeing a Doctor! I'm seeing a Doctor right in front of me, with his stethoscope in his pocket, John! I'm seeing a Doctor who is my brother, standing right in front of me.

JOHN: I'm not your Doctor, Louise.

LOUISE: Just sixty seconds, John.

JOHN: I'm late for the conference.

LOUISE: Half a minute!

JOHN: You're in a hospital, Louise! Ask a nurse!

LOUISE: JOHN!

JOHN: Ask some unsuspecting nurse, Louise. Ask a nurse!

LOUISE: John, you never listen to my heart.

JOHN: That's not so, Louise. I have listened to your heart. I have listened to your lungs. I have read your X-rays. You are fine! You're a horse, Louise. A Horse!

LOUISE: I'm not a horse, John.

JOHN: I'm sorry, Louise. I'm late.

LOUISE: You're miserable, John. You're miserable. You're a miserable man.

JOHN: That's true, Louise.

(John exits. Beat. Louise takes Garo's hand. She starts to sing a cha-cha. She makes his hand dance a cha-cha. Then she takes his arm and dances the cha-cha. She stops. She feels the weight of his slack arm. She puts his hand on her cheek.)

LOUISE: Garo. Let's go home, darling. *(She sits on the bed, facing him, wraps his arm around her, as she puts her head on his chest. She holds his arm around her.)* Let's go home.

(Lights shift.)

SCENE X

The cemetery. Garo's grave is next to Papa's.

LOUISE: Who would have thought?

ARMINE: I know.

LOUISE: Do you think I killed him?

ARMINE: SHHHHHHHHHH, Louise, ridiculous, don't say that.

LOUISE: With my craziness? With my craziness, did I kill him? Did he hate me?

ARMINE: Louise, Garo loved you. He showed you he loved you. Look at your hands! Look at all those rings on your hands. Think of all those anniversary presents! His pride and joy! You were his pride and joy!

(Louise looks at her hands.)

LOUISE: He was a jeweler!

ARMINE: And he made all those rings just for you! They are unique.

LOUISE: Armine! Tell me the truth! Did I ignore him? Was I a terrible companion? What was it? What happened?

ARMINE: Shhhhhhhhhhhhhhhhhhhhhh.

LOUISE: My heart. My heart is breaking.

ARMINE: He needed you.

LOUISE: No.

ARMINE: You know what, Louise? He had fun with you.

LOUISE: Fun?

ARMINE: Ya.

LOUISE: Huh…Garo. Was he fun?

ARMINE: He was a good dancer.

LOUISE: Ya.

ARMINE: And a good listener.

LOUISE: Ya. Why is there so much bird shit on Papa's grave?

ARMINE: Mother feeds the birds.

LOUISE: Oh. That's nice. I think he was running away. I think he died running away. What do you think, tell me.

ARMINE: I think he was going for a walk. He liked the blue sky.

LOUISE: Armine, Aman. Don't say that!

ARMINE: I'm sorry.

LOUISE: The sky? The sky? For Pete's Sake! Through the windows, Armine, he can see the sky! He doesn't have to walk to another town!

ARMINE: Perhaps he was…I don't know.

LOUISE: Tentative. Did you feel he was tentative?

ARMINE: Ya.

LOUISE: When we married, I thought, no matter, I'll back him up.

ARMINE: And you did.

LOUISE: I never did! I kept him tentative, Armine. I kept him that way, I'm sure of it.

ARMINE: Why do you say that?

LOUISE: I know it.

ARMINE: Do you want to say you're sorry?

LOUISE: We find ways, Armine, at all costs, we find ways to…what is the word…Like a pet!…What is it?…HOUSEBROKEN!…That's it!…We find ways to housebreak our husbands, Armine!

ARMINE: Why?

LOUISE: WHY?…So that…WHY?…So that…They will keep their eye on us!

ARMINE: Vy Vy Vy. (My, my, my.)

LOUISE: They will watch! They will stay! They will stand guard, Armine!

ARMINE: I.O. (Yes.) We have our reasons.

LOUISE: Oh, God…What do you say, Armine? What do you have to say, Armine?

ARMINE: About you?

LOUISE: Ya.

ARMINE: You'll be alright, dear.

(Armine puts her arm around Louise and rocks her. She rocks her more aggressively as the scene goes on.)

LOUISE: What else?

ARMINE: That's all.

LOUISE: And Ani? How is she?

ARMINE: She's there.

LOUISE: I know she's there! Why do you say that? It's so upsetting!

ARMINE: SHHHHHH, Louise, SHHHHHHHHHHH

LOUISE: And my brother? How is my brother?

ARMINE: The same.

LOUISE: The same! The same! He's going to have a HEART ATTACK!

ARMINE: SHHHHH, Louise, Shhhhh. Be Quiet!

LOUISE: What?

ARMINE: Don't talk.

LOUISE: Oh, my heart!

ARMINE: Ya, ya…

LOUISE: Who would have thought, Armine. Tell me! Who would have thought?

ARMINE: No one. Don't think. SHHHHHHHHHHHHHHHH…

LOUISE: STOP IT, ARMINE! STOP IT!

(Louise punches Armine in the arm. Armine punches Louise back. Then Armine stands up, they look at each other. Then Armine gently pats the spot where she hit Louise and exits. Louise sits alone. Cries. Then John enters.)

JOHN: It's time. Come on. Let's go. It's time.

LOUISE: John…

JOHN: Ya. Come. Shhhhhh.

(John helps Louise up. They exit with his arm around her, her head on his shoulder. Lights shift.)

SCENE XI

Ani is in her Hotel Room in Armenia. She is wearing her babushka. The other half of the stage is Non's front lawn. Ani is holding the book from Non. She opens it and reads.

ANI: "To my granddaughter, Ani, our sweet, Crusader: Whenever you open this book, my dear, take a moment to read or pray. Think of those of us who love you and take heart...Your devoted, Papa." *(Ani puts down book and picks up letter.)*
  (Lights up on other half of stage. Raffi skates on. He practices backward circles. Armine is planting pachysandra. She wears a little cap.)
ANI: *(Reading letter.)* Ani...
  (Raffi stops skating.)
ARMINE: Ani. I have realized.
  (Raffi skates again.)
ANI: I can no longer...
ARMINE: I can no longer imagine you there.
RAFFI: Do you still have candles?
ANI: Do you have food?
ARMINE: Are you warm enough?
ANI: Do you write?
RAFFI: What do you do there?
ARMINE & ANI: Life here is the same.
RAFFI: Ginya is wearing your skates.
ARMINE: Raffi—he is fine—
ANI: Always with his secrets.
ARMINE: Dad and I are planting pachysandra. Spring is coming.
ANI: It is warm.
ARMINE: We miss you.
ANI: Love, Mom.
ARMINE: Love.
ANI: Mom.
RAFFI: Mom?
ARMINE: What?
RAFFI: Nothing. *(Raffi skates off.)*
ANI: P.S. Write to us, Ani. Write.
  (John enters.)
JOHN: Do you have Ani's postcard?

ARMINE: Next year, John, I'd like to plant more grass on Mom's lawn.

JOHN: She likes pachysandra. Do you have Ani's postcard?

ARMINE: It's in my pocket. Grass is nice, John.

JOHN: You don't have to mow pachysandra. Can we read it now, Armine?

ARMINE: I don't mind mowing, John.

JOHN: Armine…

ARMINE: I mowed the lawn of the postman's house that summer in Hudson, New York. Remember that house we rented, John? When I was pregnant with Ani? Remember?

JOHN: Ya.

ARMINE: I mowed.

JOHN: I remember the backyard of the postman's house.

ARMINE: Ya.

JOHN: The postman!

ARMINE: Ya.

JOHN: Who was insane. Buried everyone's mail in his backyard.

ARMINE: Not everyone's mail, John.

JOHN: MOST of the mail.

ARMINE: The junk. The junk mail!

JOHN: NO MAIL SHOULD BE BURIED IN A BACKYARD!

ARMINE: Never mind.

JOHN: Let me read Ani's postcard, Armine.

ARMINE: In all this time, John, one letter. Two cards.

JOHN: Yes, dear.

ARMINE: This postcard, John, is very short. Not many words.

JOHN: Let me read it, Armine. Then you can put it back in your pocket.

ARMINE: John. Remember the bird in the chimney?

JOHN: Aman!

ARMINE: When I was pregnant with Ani. The bird. The thunderstorm. Remember, John? It escaped…John?

JOHN: Yes. The bird in the chimney. The bat in the bedroom!

ARMINE: The bat! You shooed the bat!

JOHN: I shooed the bat with your tambourine!

ARMINE: Ya. My tambourine. *(She waves her hand like a tambourine.)* John!

JOHN: Armine. *(He extends his hand for postcard.)*
      (Non yells from house.)

NON: ARMINE! DID YOU GET THE SPONGES?

ARMINE: UNDER THE SINK, MA!

NON: UNDER THE SINK?

ARMINE: IT'S EASIER THAN IN THE CUPBOARD.

> *(Beat.)*

NON: OK.

> *(Armine takes out comb. She combs the top of her head.)*

JOHN: She'll put them back in the cupboard.

ARMINE: I know.

JOHN: And continue to stand on the stool to get them.

ARMINE: Ya.

JOHN: Armine, my dear…

ARMINE: Ya.

JOHN: You are combing your hat.

ARMINE: Aman, John, inch khentz pannay. (how silly)

JOHN: It's alright. If you give me the postcard, I will look. I will give it back.

ARMINE: No.

NON: *(Offstage.)* TIME FOR LUNCH!

ARMINE: Ah! Lunchtime!

JOHN: Yes, I heard.

> *(Non enters carrying a plate of sandwiches.)*

NON: Here. Time to eat! I made my specialty.

JOHN: *(Taking one.)* Thank you, Marie.

ARMINE: What is this, Ma?

NON: *(Returning to house.)* TUNA!

> *(Non exits. Armine holds her sandwich.)*

JOHN: BOH! *(Laughs.)*

ARMINE: Don't laugh, John.

JOHN: Aman. *(He eats.)*

ARMINE: John, your chewing.

JOHN: What?

ARMINE: It is very loud.

JOHN: It is how I chew.

ARMINE: No. You can chew more softly, John. Chew more softly.

JOHN: Armine, this is not your concern. My chewing is not your concern.

ARMINE: I think it is John.

JOHN: Eat! You. Eat! Armine. That is the concern of the moment.

ARMINE: Ya. I am happy to eat.

> *(She doesn't eat. Non enters with her porch chair. She sits behind Armine.)*

NON: I made placemats. Do we know anyone who needs a present?

ARMINE: Lucy and Hagop.

NON: What is it?

ARMINE: Anniversary.

NON: OK...Any babies?

ARMINE: What?

NON: Do you have friends, Armine, with any babies?

ARMINE: No, Ma.

NON: Too bad. I made some mittens.

ARMINE: What color?

NON: Green.

ARMINE: Green?

NON: Ya.

ARMINE: Dark green?

NON: No, no.

ARMINE: Spring green?

NON: No.

ARMINE: What then?

NON: Like leaves, Armine.

ARMINE: Like that leaf there, that green?

NON: Which?

ARMINE: There?

NON: No.

ARMINE: There?

NON: No.

ARMINE: There? There?

NON: Where?

ARMINE: There.

NON: There?

> (*Armine looks at Non. Non looks at Armine. They end up staring in each other's faces.*)

NON: I don't see it.

ARMINE: Ah.

JOHN: Aman.

NON: Have you read Ani's postcard? Have you read Ani's postcard?

ARMINE: In a minute! Let me eat, Ma, for Pete's Sake. Just wait!

NON: Of course. We will wait, Armine. We will all wait.

> (*All three eat. Armine takes one bite.*)

ARMINE: Alright. (*She takes postcard out of her pocket.*) John.

> (*John takes postcard. Together she and John say.*)

JOHN & ANI: PAREV!

JOHN: It is unbearably cold.

ANI: There is no fuel.

JOHN: Some families are living in Cargo containers. Metal Boxes. No windows. No air. So hot in summer.

ANI: So cold now.

JOHN: Those who can, are leaving. So many Armenians are leaving!

ANI: What will happen?

JOHN: What will happen? Love, Ani.

(Beat.)

ARMINE: Ma. (Armine puts her head in Non's lap. She cries.)

NON: John, it's time. It's time now.

JOHN: I know, Marie.

NON: For Ani. It's enough now.

JOHN: Yes. I'll get.

NON: You can do this, John?

JOHN: I think so. I.O. (Yes.)

NON: Let me help you.

JOHN: I can manage, Marie.

NON: Let me help you, John.

JOHN: I can manage!

ARMINE: LET HER HELP! FOR PETE'S SAKE. LET MOTHER HELP! LET HER HELP, JOHN!

NON: Shhhhhhh.

JOHN: Of course.

NON: Shhhhhh.

JOHN: I apologize, Marie.

NON: It's alright, dear.

JOHN: Aman.

NON: It's alright.

(Lights shift.)

SCENE XII

Moonlight. Ani is still in her hotel room. She has one candle burning. She is holding a letter. She reads aloud.

ANI: "…These are your instructions, Ani. Enclosed, find your ticket." (She looks and finds ticket. Then picks up letter again.) "And two additional things I must tell you, dear…"

(An Elderly Man stands outside her door. The Actor who plays Pop also plays this man. He is cold. He knocks.)

ANI: Hello? Parev?

MAN: Hello? American? *(He knocks again.)*

ANI: Yes? I.O.? Yes?

MAN: Help. Please. *(He knocks.)*

ANI: What do you need?

MAN: Shad on oh te em!

ANI: What? AH SEE INCH CHAY? (What is it?)

MAN: SHAD KAGH TSAHTZ EM. (I am hungry.)

ANI: Um. INCH GOOZESS? (What?)

MAN: PLEASE. SHAD SHAD KAGH TS AHTZ EM! (I am very hungry.)

ANI: Shad Shad KAGH TS…? OH! HUNGRY?…Oh, I have nothing!

MAN: *(He knocks.)* BAHDAI MA HAHTS. (Piece of bread.)

ANI: What? What?

MAN: GURNASS INZEE OCKNELL! (Can you help me?)

ANI: GURNASS…GURNASS…INCHGOOZESS? (What?)

MAN: *(Knocking loudly.)* GERNASS INZEE OCKNELL! (Can you help me?)

ANI: PLEASE. SPEAK. MORE. SLOWLY.

MAN: MURSOOM MEM! (I'm cold.) *(Knocking.)*

ANI: I'M SORRY. I CAN'T…Oh.

MAN: HELLO PLEASE.

ANI: YES. I'M SORRY. I'M SORRY. I'M SORRY. I'm sorry.

MAN: SHAD MURSOOM MEM! (Very cold!)

ANI: I DON'T UNDERSTAND YOU.

(Silence. The Man turns to walk away. Then returns. And again, loud knocking.)

MAN: OCKNEH EENZ! OCKNEH EENZ! (Help! Help!) GERNASS INZEE OCKNELL!!

ANI: Oh God. Oh God.

(Ani looks in her room. She has nothing. Then she goes to door. Opens it. The Man steps into room. She gestures: "I have nothing." She looks at him. He is cold. She takes off her coat. She offers it to him. He accepts it. He bows his head. They stand opposite each other. Each one holding the coat.)

MAN: Shad Shad Shanor hag alem. (thank you so much)

(She releases the coat. He raises his head. She sees his face.)

ANI: Oh!

MAN: Munock Parov. *(He's backing away.)*

ANI: Sir…

MAN: Munock Parov. *(He leaves.)*

ANI: Bye, bye. Bye, bye. *(Ani stands alone in doorway. Cold. Then she puts on Non's shawl. She crosses to table. She picks up a letter. She turns to second page. She reads.)* ...two additional things I must tell you, dear.

(Lights up on John pacing in airport.)

JOHN: Your Uncle Garo has died.

ANI: Uncle Garo has died.

(Ani holds letter as John continues.)

JOHN: He suffered a heart attack. Your Mother spoke at his service. She said he was a gentleman. Proud of his family. Especially you, dear.

ANI: *(Continues to read.)* And last, Raffi asked me to enclose his picture of Mt. Ararat. Please correct it, he says, if it's wrong.

JOHN: Don't miss the plane, Ani.

ANI: Don't miss the plane.

(Ani blows out candle. We hear the sound of planes.)

SCENE XIII

The Airport waiting room.

John is waiting. Music. (Yerevan.) Ani enters. She is carrying her backpack. She is wearing the babushka. She sees her father. John opens his arms to her. She walks to him. She rests her head against his chest. He holds her. She cries. They are joined by the rest of the family. (With the exception of Non.)

Beat.

Louise enters last, carrying a pan of food. She finds Ani in the group hug and taps her on the back. Ani turns and hugs Louise. Then they all exit the Airport. Armine and Louise holding Ani between them. Ginya, Raffi and John follow. Lights dim and come up on:

SCENE XIV

Non's bedroom. Non sits, sewing Armenian lace. Ani stands in the doorway watching Non. Ani is still wearing her babushka.

NON: What do you need, darling?

(Ani enters room.)

ANI: I don't know.

(Armine enters. Stands outside room and listens.)

NON: Are you tired?

ANI: No.

NON: You're not hungry.

(Ani shakes her head no.)

NON: Did you watch the women sew?

ANI: Yes.

NON: In the darkness? They sewed in the darkness?

(Ani shakes her head yes.)

NON: Embroidering their lace around scraps of cloth.

ANI: They have no hot water. They can't cook. They can't bathe their children. They are all…tired.

NON: And still they sew.

ANI: The daughters. The daughters sewed.

NON: Do you want to learn, Ani?

ANI: And the children. The children in the orphanages. With no one.

NON: Yes. Did you speak with them?

ANI: I couldn't.

NON: Ah.

ANI: I looked at them. I tried to draw pictures with them.

NON: Yes?

ANI: The children draw black suns, Nonnie. Always black suns in the sky.

NON: They are frightened.

ANI: Oh, God. *(Shakes her hands in despair.)*

NON: Do you want to learn to sew the lace, Ani?

ANI: I can't.

NON: Come, Ani.

ANI: All the little knots, Non. I can't stand it.

NON: We will start with the big knots.

ANI: There are no big knots.

NON: I'll show you.

ANI: It doesn't suit my hands, Non.

NON: We'll teach them.

ANI: No, Non!

NON: Come, darling.

ANI: I can't sew the Lace, Non!

NON: Alright.

ANI: I can't speak the language! I can't sew the lace!

NON: I know. You never learned.

ANI: You never taught me.

NON: I wanted you to ask.

ANI: I needed you to teach.

NON: Ah! OK. What, Ani?

ANI: Non. In Yerevan. The library.

NON: Ya.

ANI: It has a room just for Papa's books.

NON: Yes. It is dedicated to him.

ANI: They have his sermons.

NON: Yes.

ANI: The people weep when they speak of him.

NON: He was a very important man. Even as a young man, he was important.

ANI: Did you love him, Non, like they do there?

NON: Ani…

ANI: Did you love him absolutely? Was he your first love?

NON: No, Ani.

ANI: Because I never felt you loved him absolutely.

NON: No, darling…He was not my first love. No one was. Until my children.

ANI: You married him, Non.

NON: Your Papa told me he would kill himself if I didn't marry him. I believed him.

ANI: Was he lonely?

NON: Yes. I'm sorry.

ANI: Were you lonely?

NON: Do you want to know?

(*Ani shakes her head yes.*)

NON: Darling…When I was a young girl, I found a Church…Ani, do you want to hear?

(*Ani shakes her head yes.*)

NON: It was deserted, the Church. And it was built into the side of a Mountain! Imagine! A Church built in the Thirteenth Century, into the side of a Mountain! I went there every day. And I stood on the stone floors and I sang. I sang! And my voice went into the Mountain!…I sang with the Ancient voices in the Ancient Choirs, in an Ancient Stone Church, in our Ancient Country. And I had joy. The greatest joy.

ANI: I can't write anything, Non.

NON: Let me tell you your heritage, Ani.

ANI: I know my heritage.

NON: Let me tell you!

ANI: Suffering! Suffering is my heritage!

NON: Yes.

ANI: Endless suffering!

NON: No!

ANI: Suffering! Hiding! Waiting!

NON: Ani! Listen!

ANI: Yearning! Silence!

NON: Ani!

ANI: Silence is my heritage!

NON: Stop it, Ani!

ANI: SILENCE!

NON: Ani, listen to me! I'm going to tell you about your papa's mother.

ANI: I know about Papa's mother!

NON: YOU DON'T KNOW! You've been told only that she was lost. There is more. Your papa's mother, your great grandmother, was taken by the Turks in a wagon and driven along the roads to be given to an officer in the Turkish Army. This officer—this man—had ordered her to be his mistress.

   She sat in the wagon and watched the women walk. They were walking, Ani, down the roads in the desert. They were walking to their death. Holding their children, vacant-eyed. Collapsing, bleeding, walking down the roads into the desert, where they died. And their children died. The Turks made the women walk. And the Turks stopped them to rape them. Cut them. Dismember them. And leave them to die in the roads on the way to the desert. Your papa's mother watched the women walk. Then she ordered her carriage to stop. She got out. And she joined them.

   (Ani is crying.)

NON: She died. Your papa lived. I married him. We came to America. We bore your mother. Our only child. She bore you. Her first child. Cry, Ani. Cry and cry and cry and then stop crying.

ANI: And what? Teach my hands?

NON: Teach your hands, I.0.

ANI: *(Crying.)* My hands…

   (Non begins rubbing her own hands.)

NON: Ani. Look.

ANI: What are you doing?

NON: Wringing. I'm wringing.

ANI: Wringing your hands?

NON: Ya. Wringing my hands. Like this, darling. Rub…Squeeze. Rub Squeeze. *(She does is more deliberately.)* RUB…SQUEEZE.

ANI: Rub? Squeeze?

NON: Ya. Rub…squeeze!

ANI: Rub…squeeze.

NON: Bravo!

ANI: Rub…squeeze!

NON: I.O. Now, darling. Step Two!

ANI: Step two?

NON: RUB! SQUEEZE! GROAN! MMMMMMMMMMMMMMMMM!

ANI: Rub. Squeeze. Groan. Mmmmmmmmmm.

NON: Perfect! Together!

NON & ANI: RUB! SQUEEZE! GROAN! MMMMMMMMMMMM

NON: AGAIN!

NON & ANI: RUB!…SQUEEZE…GROAN…

NON: INTO THE MOUNTAIN, ANI!!! PUT YOUR VOICE INTO THE MOUNTAIN!!!

ANI: AHHHHHHHHHHHHHHHHHHHHHHHHHH!

NON & ANI: RUB!…SQUEEZE!…GROAN! AHHHHHHHHHH! RUB!… SQUEEZE!…GROAN! AHHHHHHHHHHHH! RUB!…SQUEEZE!… GROAN! AAAAHHHHHHHHHHHHHH!

(They do this until it builds to release. Beat.)

NON: Let me see you, Ani. *(Looking at her babushka.)*

ANI: You mean… *(She touches her babushka.)*

NON: Ya. Let me see your head.

ANI: *(Unties and removes her babushka.)* Here it is.

NON: Ya. There it is! *(Non kisses Ani on the top of her head.)*

ANI: MOM?

ARMINE: *(From the hallway.)* Ya?

ANI: Were you listening?

(Armine enters and stands in doorway.)

ARMINE: Ya.

ANI: Do you like my hair, Ma?

ARMINE: You are beautiful, Ani. Come eat.

(Ani crosses to Armine.)

ARMINE: You go, dear, to the kitchen.

(Ani crosses out of Non's room. Now Ani listens in the hall.)

NON: What is it?

ARMINE: Mother. You never taught me to wring my hands.

NON: I couldn't teach you, Armine.

ARMINE: Because I didn't ask.

NON: Because I didn't know myself.

ARMINE: When did you learn?

NON: This evening.

ARMINE: So.

NON: What do you need, dear?

ARMINE: Nothing.

NON: OK.

   (Lights shift.)

SCENE XV

   The cemetery. Louise sits by Garo's grave. Armine and Ani enter.

ARMINE: Ani, do you think you could manage the house?

LOUISE: I can help her.

ANI: Can I manage the house?

ARMINE: Ya.

LOUISE: I can cook, Ani. You drive and clean.

ANI: For how long?

ARMINE: One month. Next month.

ANI: You mean…What do you mean?

ARMINE: Will you do my job for one month?

LOUISE: Can you do her job, Ani?

ANI: You mean, cook and take care of the kids and Dad and everything?

LOUISE & ARMINE: Ya.

ANI: Um…

LOUISE: I will cook for your father, Sunday meal: the Beregg, the Sarma, the Tass Kebob. I will cook. You can help.

ANI: OK.

LOUISE: And the Podiatrist, Armine, for Marie, don't forget.

ARMINE: I'll give directions.

LOUISE: Write them down. A map!

ARMINE: Of course, Louise.

LOUISE: And put it on the wall!

ARMINE: Ya. I will, of course.

LOUISE: Do you need a suitcase?

ARMINE: No, no. I have.

LOUISE: A new one! With a handle!

ARMINE: Ya, OK. I'll get.

LOUISE: I have, Armine. I'll give.

ARMINE: Alright.

ANI: Mom? Where are you going?

   (Armine looks at Louise.)

LOUISE: She's going to Armenia.

ARMINE: I.O.

ANI: You're going to Armenia?

ARMINE: I.O…I am going, Ani.

ANI: What will you do there, Mom?

ARMINE: I will sit.

ANI: Sit?

ARMINE: Ya. I will sit.

ANI: Sit?

ARMINE: Ya I will sit with the children in the orphanages.

LOUISE: She will watch.

ARMINE: Ya. I can do that.

ANI: Yes. You can, Mom.

ARMINE: And I will send you letters, Ani.

ANI: And I will save them.

ARMINE: Ya. That's perfect.

LOUISE: Bravo!

   (Non enters.)

NON: John is waiting.

ARMINE: OK, let's go.

NON: Aneen, Keh dae? (Ani knows?)

LOUISE: Ya. She just told her.

NON: Ah. Ani, your Mother is going to Armenia!

ANI: Yes.

LOUISE: She is able, Ani. She knows it. Because of you, dear.

ANI: Me?

NON: She waited for you, Ani. Every minute.

LOUISE: Never stopped.

ARMINE: It's true.

NON: So now, she can go!

LOUISE: Ya!

ARMINE: Ya! Look at me! *(Laughs.)*
   (They all look with pride.)
ANI: Yes, Mom! Look at you!
ARMINE: Aman.
LOUISE: Bravo!
ARMINE: Thank you, Ani.
ANI: You're welcome, Mom.
LOUISE: Who would have thought?
ANI: Does Dad know?
NON, ARMINE, LOUISE: Not yet.
ARMINE: Soon. I'll tell him soon. Next week.
NON: Let me tell him.
ANI: I can tell him!
LOUISE: I'll tell him!
ARMINE: I will tell him!!
LOUISE: OK.
NON: That's best.
   (Car horn.)
JOHN: *(Offstage.)* LET'S GO!
ARMINE: ALRIGHT! *(To Ani.)* Let's go, dear.
LOUISE: Marie, Papa's Grave, it's all white now.
NON: Ya. Lot's of Bird Metzaquartz! (poop)
LOUISE: Ya. Too much!
JOHN: *(Offstage.)* COME ON!
LOUISE: You'll fix?
NON: I'll fix!
LOUISE: OK!
JOHN: *(Offstage.)* COME ON!
ALL: WE'RE COMING!
ARMINE: Let's go!
   (They exit. Lights shift and come up on Ginya and Raffi downstage.)

SCENE XVI

The driveway. Ginya and Raffi are downstage. They are tearing little pieces of Kleenex and making a little pile. John comes out of the house carrying a pan of food wrapped in aluminum foil. He is headed for the car. Ani catches up to him.

GINYA: Raffi, those pieces are too big.

RAFFI: What? No, they're not.

GINYA: Yes! Make them smaller. Tear them smaller. Like this.

(Raffi gives Ginya a "get off my back" look.)

ANI: Want me to take that, Dad?

JOHN: Sure. Thank you. *(He hands the food to her.)*

(Ani and John simultaneously.)

ANI: Shall I put it in the back seat?

JOHN: Put it in the trunk!

ANI: OK.

JOHN: OK. I'll get your mother. What are you kids doing?

GINYA & RAFFI: Nothing.

JOHN: Alright. We're going. Is that for the bird?

GINYA: Yup.

JOHN: You must move your little pile, it is too exposed.

RAFFI: Where should we move it, Dad?

JOHN: The tree. To the tree. Near the tree.

GINYA & RAFFI: OK. *(They don't move.)*

ANI: DAD!

JOHN: What?

ANI: Did you like the Sarma?

JOHN: It was good.

ANI: Thanks.

JOHN: Not so many raisins, perhaps, Ani.

ANI: Raisins.

JOHN: More nuts.

ANI: Nuts.

JOHN: The leaves were tender!

ANI: Mom did that.

JOHN: Ah.

ANI: Oh well.

JOHN: Ya.

ANI: Will you miss her, Dad?

JOHN: Ani.

ANI: Don't you want to go with her to Yerevan?

JOHN: She is going. She is ready.

ANI: She will help.

JOHN: Yes.

ANI: In her way.

JOHN: I must go inside. Ani, I'm going inside.

ANI: OK, Dad.

JOHN: I will miss your Mother, of course.

ANI: That's good, Dad.

JOHN: Aman, Ani.

(From inside the house we hear.)

ARMINE: MANOCK PAROV!

NON: GOOD-BYE, DEAR.

(Armine enters.)

ARMINE: SEE YOU TUESDAY, MA!

JOHN & ARMINE: SHAD SCHNORA GOLLYEM.

(Non enters.)

NON: DON'T FORGET THE TASS KEBOB!

JOHN: I don't think so, Marie.

GINYA: NON! IT'S SPILLING!

NON: VY VY VY.

ARMINE: I'LL GET A SPONGE.

NON: IN THE CUPBOARD! GET THE STOOL.

ARMINE: I KNOW!

JOHN: Oh, boy.

(Armine and Non go into house. John crosses to car. Gets in. Takes out news-paper. Reads. Ani joins Ginya and Raffi who are still downstage with their little pile.)

ANI: This is for the bird with the white nest?

RAFFI & GINYA: Yea.

GINYA: It's browner now.

RAFFI: Beege.

GINYA: Beige! It gets dirty.

ANI: Oh. OK.

RAFFI: Ani, did you take the ashes?

GINYA: We know.

RAFFI: Non told us.

GINYA: Did you take Papa's ashes to Casaria?

RAFFI: Did you?

ANI: No.

RAFFI & GINYA: NO?!?

ANI: SHHHHHHHHHHH!

RAFFI: What did you do with them?

ANI: I lost them.

GINYA: What?

RAFFI: She lost them!

ANI: They inspected my backpack at the airport. I couldn't explain what they were.

RAFFI: Why not?

ANI: They didn't believe me.

GINYA: Did they take them?

ANI: Yes.

GINYA: Does Non know?

ANI: This has to be our secret! You have to promise!

RAFFI & GINYA: OK.

ANI: For LIFE! This is a LIFE promise. No one can know Papa's ashes are in the airport.

GINYA & RAFFI: OK.

JOHN: LET'S GO!

RAFFI: Which airport?

ANI: Yerevan.

RAFFI: At least he's in Armenia.

JOHN: COME ON!

GINYA: What do you think they do with the things they take from people?

ANI: I don't know.

RAFFI: Maybe they bury them.

ANI: Maybe they do.

GINYA: Maybe they toss them to the wind. Or to the sea!

ANI: There is no sea in Armenia. There's a lake! Maybe they toss them to the lake!

GINYA: Yea.

ANI: Yea.

JOHN: WHAT'S GOING ON? WHY IS NO ONE IN THE CAR?
    (Armine enters. Non follows with a pot of food.)

ARMINE: TIME TO GO!

NON: TASS KEBOB!

ANI: It's time to go?

(John gets out of the car.)

JOHN: You know, I remember a time, this will interest you, when I used to open the car door; get in; put the key in the ignition and turn the car on.

ARMINE: I remember that, dear.

JOHN: Then. I would drive.

(Raffi exits. Ginya puts on rollerblades.)

ARMINE: Ma, it spills. The Tass Kebob always spills, Ma.

JOHN: Now. I open the car door ...

GINYA: I'll hold the Tass Kebob, Non.

JOHN: Pick up the newspaper...

NON: BRAVO, darling!

JOHN: Put it across the steering wheel...

ARMINE: It'll spill, Ma!

JOHN: And read, no one's listening.

NON: To what, dear?

(Ginya starts skating.)

GINYA: ANI! Show Non what you learned!

JOHN: Now what?

GINYA: Show Non what you learned.

ANI: Not now.

GINYA: NON! LOOK! *(She points to Ani.)*

NON: Yavroom, I know, darling, wonderful, you're rollaring.

GINYA: Not me, Non! Ani!

NON: What is it, darling?

GINYA: Do it here, Ani. In Non's driveway. This is good.

NON: Ya. This is good.

ANI: Oh, God.

GINYA: Come on!

(Ginya claps her hands and dances on her skates. Then Ani begins to dance an Armenian dance. Non watches, claps her hands. Armine goes into the house. Non joins Ani. They dance.)

JOHN: ARMINE! COME ON! YOU MUST SEE THIS! ARMINE! BETS-GEAH ASEES DESNOTS! (Come see this!)

(Armine appears on steps with her tambourine. She gives it a perfect hit and then, proudly, dances by herself. They applaud her. Then, each of the women, in turn dances some form of an Armenian dance. Ginya does something contemporary on her skates. Each one signals the next to dance. They end up together, dancing with vigor and joy. John plays Armine's tambourine, after she hands it to him. They finish.)

JOHN: BRAVO! BRAVO!

NON: AFAREHIM, DARLING!

ARMINE: GOOD FOR YOU, ANI!

GINYA: Where's Raffi?

ALL: RAFFI!

ANI: OH MY GOD! RAFFI!

ARMINE: WHERE?

ANI: IN THE TREE.

ARMINE: RAFFI! WHAT ARE YOU DOING?

JOHN: JESUS OH JESUS.

NON: Where is he?

ARMINE: RAFFI, WHY ARE YOU IN THE TREE? Virginia, why is Raffi in the tree?

GINYA: I don't know.

RAFFI: I WANTED TO SEE THE BIRD.

GINYA: He wanted to see the bird.

RAFFI: THERE ARE LOTS OF WHITE THINGS IN THE NEST!

JOHN: Oh, for Pete's sake.

RAFFI: IT LOOKS LIKE LACE, NON.

NON: What does, dear?

ARMINE: The nest looks like lace? My goodness. It looks like lace, Mom!

NON: Armine, perhaps the bird is Armenian!

   (They laugh.)

NON: Aman!

ARMINE: ALRIGHT, DARLING, COME DOWN NOW.

RAFFI: I'M A LITTLE STUCK.

ARMINE: You're Stuck?

JOHN: Oh Jesus.

ARMINE: IT'S ALRIGHT, RAFFI. LISTEN TO YOUR FATHER.

JOHN: RAFFI?

RAFFI: WHAT?

JOHN: MOVE YOUR RIGHT FOOT TO THE LEFT. TOWARD THE HOUSE.

RAFFI: I'M STUCK.

ANI: IT'S OK, RAFFI.

JOHN: THE OTHER FOOT. THE RIGHT FOOT! TOWARD THE HOUSE. NOT THE STREET.

RAFFI: WHAT?

ALL: NOT THE STREET.

RAFFI: OK.

JOHN: IS IT LOOSER NOW?

RAFFI: DAD?

JOHN: YES?

RAFFI: IT'S NOT LOOSER

ARMINE: Go up there, John.

JOHN: He can do it, Armine.

GINYA: I'll go up, Ma.

ARMINE: No, no darling.

JOHN: RAFFI, LIFT GENTLY FROM THE KNEE.

RAFFI: OK.

JOHN: THE RIGHT KNEE.

RAFFI: OK.

JOHN: THE RIGHT KNEE!

RAFFI: OK.

ARMINE: RAFFI! THE RIGHT KNEE!

RAFFI: Oh. OK.

ARMINE: COME DOWN NOW, DARLING.

JOHN: Come down now, Raffi.

RAFFI: OK, DAD.

NON: Be careful!

ARMINE: You're ok?

RAFFI: I'M OK!

GINYA: HURRY UP!

RAFFI: OK!

ARMINE: SLOW DOWN!

RAFFI: OK!

JOHN: FOR PETE'S SAKE!

RAFFI: OK!

ARMINE: Alright, now!

RAFFI: I'M HERE!

ALL: YAAAAAAAAAAAY!

JOHN: Alright, come on.

GINYA: Nice going.

RAFFI: Shut up.

GINYA: Duh!

RAFFI: Duh-yourself!

GINYA: Duh-face!

JOHN: OK! Everybody in the car!

RAFFI: Mom, can I take my coat off in the car?

ARMINE: Alright, dear.

RAFFI: AWESOME!

ANI: Non, I have something to tell you.

ARMINE: Come on, Raffi. Get in.

> *(Everyone starts getting in the car except Ani.)*

ANI: *(Whispers.)* Non...

NON: I know, dear.

ANI: You know?

NON: Ya. The airport.

ANI: I'm sorry.

NON: It's alright, Yavroom.

JOHN: ANI SAY GOOD-BYE.

ANI: OK, Dad. *(To Non.)* How did you find out?

NON: My Uncle Herrant, you remember?

ANI: Uncle Herrant...You sat by the Sea of...

NON: Marmara!

ANI: He drank his coffee, you ate your baklava.

NON: Correct!

ANI: Uncle Herrant! He's dead, right?

NON: Ya. His son is Zaven

ANI: Zaven?

NON: The Mayor!

ANI: The Mayor! Zaven! AMAN!

NON: Ya.

JOHN: THIS IS IT!

ANI: Non! Maybe Mom could get Papa's ashes!

NON: No, darling. They are lost.

ARMINE: Come on, Ani!

ANI: Bye, Non.

NON: Yavroom. (Sweet one.)

> *(Hugs, kisses. Ani gets in car. All yell out the windows to Non.)*

ALL: BYYYYYYYYYYYYYEEEEEEEEEEEEEEE!

> *(Louise runs on carrying food.)*

LOUISE: HIIIIIIIIIIIIIIIIIII! *(She waves.)* I JUST WANTED TO BE HERE FOR THE GOOD-BYE!

> *(Everyone waves and yells.)*

EVERYONE: GOOD-BYEEEEEEEEEEEEEEEEEEEEEE!

LOUISE: HUGS! HUGS!

(All doors, except John's, open. They all get out and form a clump around Louise. And again, from the clump we hear:)

ARMINE: GOOD-BYE, DEAR.

LOUISE: I BROUGHT YOU SOME BAKLAVA!

NON: MANOCK PAROV! (Good-bye!)

LOUISE: TAKE THE BAKLAVA!

ARMINE: WE HAVE BEREGG.

JOHN: GET IN THE CAR!

LOUISE: ANI, I BROUGHT YOU A RING!

ARMINE: GO INSIDE, MA!

NON: YOU NEED A RUBBER BAND.

GINYA: IT'S SPILLING!

NON: WHAT IS, DARLING?

JOHN: ARMINE!

ARMINE: LET'S GO.

(Armine, Raffi, Ginya and Ani cross to the car and get in. As they cross:)

LOUISE: CALL WHEN YOU GET HOME!

NON: SEE YOU TUESDAY!

ARMINE: OK.

NON: *(Blows a kiss.)* Bachigs!

LOUISE: YA! BACHIGS, BACHIGS, BACHIGS!

ALL FROM THE CAR: BACHIGS, BACHIGS, BACHIGS!

JOHN: LET'S GO!

(They slam the doors. Lights out. Music.)

END OF PLAY

GLOSSARY

báchigs	kisses
ayoh´	yes
anooshígus	dear one
sahr´kiss	man's name, takes a slightly rolled *r*
tahss kehbob´	lamb stew
yahv´room	darling
ahf´ahreem	excellent, bravo
Ah see inch´ eh?	What is this?
munock´ pahr´ove	good-bye
ahma´hn shehd anooshig	so sweet
turchoo´na	this bird
anoosh´ abour´	sweet pudding
Kehs´ahrya	Casaria
ahsdvahdz´ hogeen´ loosahvoreh´	God rest His soul
Mesrope	father of the Armenian alphabet
Le´vone	man's name
pahsh´ah	sultan
zahv´ahla	pathetic (Turkish)
bah´ ster mah	a form of beef jerky with exotic spices
yer éh vahn	Capital of Armenia
kahr´ khen eh geen´	owner of a whore house (Turkish)
eshahg´ oghlí eshahg´	son of a jackass
anooshíg	dear
bah ´ster mah	Ginya
boregg´	cheese turnover
kehzee´ guh seerehm´	I love you
kah´tah	gourmet rolls
pahrev´	hello
toon gahrtah´ uhsee, my´rig	you read this, Mother
sahr´mah	stuffed grape leaves
oh´dar	connotes non-Armenian
ahmahn´, John, inch´ khent pahn´eh	how silly

shahd kagh tsahtz' em . . . . I am very hungry

shahd on ohteé. . . . . man

inch goozess'? . . . . What do you want?

bahdarmuh hahts. a piece of bread

gurnahss' eenzee ochnell. . . . . Can you help me?

mursoom' mem. . . . . I'm cold

shahd' mursoom' mem . . . . very cold

ockneh'eenz. . . . . help me

shahd shahd shunor hagahl' em . . . . thank you very much

behdk eh uhsee dehsnoss'. . . . . you must see this

PRONUNCIATION

Strive for clarity of diction on all proper nouns, as in names and places:

Armine . . . . Ahr min eh

Sarkiss. . . . . Sahr kiss

Mr. Ararat . . . . Mr. Ah rah raht

Mesrop . . . . Mes rope

Levon . . . . Leh vone

Yerevan . . . . Yeh reh vahn

Hagop. . . . . Han gope

Herant. . . . . Huh rahnt

Zaven . . . . Sah ven

Aman: (Ahmen!) This is an arabic word; translated literally means, "In God's refuge." Can be used as "Oh, my God." Depends on context. Sometimes implies, "Oh, forget it!" The true Armenian equivalent is "Vy, Vy, Vy," (my, my, my,) as appears in other parts of the dialogue.

View of the Dome
by Theresa Rebeck

THE AUTHOR

Spike Heels, Loose Knit, and *The Family of Mann* at Second Stage; *View of the Dome* at New York Theatre Workshop, *Sex with the Censor, Contract* and *What We're Up Against* at Naked Angels, *Does this Woman Have a Name?* at Alice's Fourth Floor and the Double Image One-Act Festival, *Sunday on the Rocks* at the Longwharf. Most of the above published by Samuel French. Other productions include New Georges, TheWorkhouse *InTenCities* project, EST, Westbank Cafe, New York Stage and Film, Actor's Theatre of Louisville, the Source, Victory Gardens, Theatre Geo, Seattle Rep and the International Women in Theatre Festival. Awards include the National Theatre Conference Playwriting Award (1994), Writer's Guild Award for Episodic Drama, and the Mystery Writers of America Edgar Award (1996). Film and television credits include *Harriet the Spy, Brooklyn Bridge,* and *NYPD Blue,* where she was also a producer. *View of the Dome* is the third play she's had anthologized in Smith and Kraus's collections of plays by women.

AUTHOR'S NOTE

I spend a lot of time thinking about America, who we are as a people and a culture and a nation, and I have always felt that the theatre is a truly appropriate place to examine these issues, the way David Hare examines what it means to be British, or brian Friel examines what it means to be Irish. In writing *View of the Dome,* I was trying to consider the cultural idealism that graces our history—the spectacularly beautiful premise that underlies democracy, that all men, and women, are created equal—and how people of power dismiss that ideal. What goes on in Washington, which is clearly power mongering of the highest order, has absolutely nothing to do with who we purport to be historically, which is why I think people are so tired of it all. We are all taught that being an American means striving for justice and equality, and we're offended that so many of our leaders seem more interested in sniping at each other than trying to enact those principles into law.

For years, I have been wallowing in the belief that the world has gotten too weird that social satire and documentary are now the same form. Sometimes when I try this theory out on people, they think I'm kidding. I'm not. When I first wrote *View of the Dome,* three years ago, a few people found it "extreme." In the post–Monica Lewinsky era, it is less possible to take that position. There is something both gratifying and disturbing about finding out how right I actually am.

ORIGINAL PRODUCTION

View of the Dome was originally produced in New York by The New York Theatre Workshop on September 13, 1996. It was directed by Michael Mayer with the following cast:

Senator Geoffrey Maddox	Jim Abele
Tommy	Patrick Breen
Annabeth Gilkey	Candy Buckley
E.T. Black	Tom Riis Farrell
Emma	Julia Gibson
David	Dion Graham
Arthur Woolf	Richard Poe

CHARACTERS

EMMA	TOMMY
ARTHUR	SENATOR
ANNABETH	DAVID
MARJORIE	E.T. BLACK
JUNETTE LARSON	LEONARD LARSON
GOVERNOR	ANCHORMAN
REPORTER 1	REPORTER 2
REPORTER 3	RICHARD RILEY
BELLA	AUGUST
LANCE	SHEILA
RUSH LIMBAUGH	SENATOR A
SENATOR B	SENATOR C

With doubling, the play can be performed with six or seven actors.

SET

A very tasteful restaurant/bar in Washington D.C. A window upstage shows a spectacular view of the capital dome. All of the action takes place in this restaurant, even the action that doesn't.

View of the Dome

A restaurant. Two tables. One seats four people in a lively debate. At the second, Emma, a single woman, sits alone.

ANNABETH: I was mentioning to the senator what an extraordinary coincidence—is this vinaigrette? I don't think this is the vinaigrette.

TOMMY: No, that's it—

ANNABETH: Are you sure?

ARTHUR: Yes, I've got the same thing. It's a raspberry—

ANNABETH: But this looks like it has cream in it.

TOMMY: No, I don't think so—

ANNABETH: In any event, I was telling the senator how extraordinary I thought it was, when I heard Arthur speaking about the call to public service, how close your two positions actually are, and how rare it is to hear politicians, even aspiring politicians, actually speak of civic duty—

SENATOR: Yes, I think the last time someone even said the words up on the hill they were quietly taken aside and stoned.

(They all laugh.)

ANNABETH: Exactly. So I said to Arthur, you have to meet the Senator and tell him your ideas. But when you get to the part about "civic duty"—keep your voice down.

(They all laugh again. The laughter stops suddenly as Emma raises her eyes and speaks to the audience.)

EMMA: Do any of you find this interesting? Some of you must. Every night of the week, all across America, near strangers who want something from each other gather and enact a social ritual involving food which nobody has to pay for because it's being expensed. And then everyone talks about nothing for a couple of hours, somehow sliding into the cracks the mysterious subject of What They Want, and then everybody goes away, pondering the even more mysterious subject of What They Got. It's called a political dinner.

SENATOR: So, Arthur, you're thinking of taking a run at Congress?

ARTHUR: Well, I'm afraid it's gone a little further than that. I declared my candidacy last week.

SENATOR: *(Mock dismay.)* Oh, dear. Then I've come too late.

(They all laugh again.)

EMMA: I happen to think political dinners are a huge crashing bore. Nevertheless, I would give anything to be sitting at that table.

ANNABETH: Oh, the escargot are excellent. Geoffrey—Senator—I think they're even better than the ones we had in Nice.

SENATOR: The ones *you* had. I'm afraid I'm too much of an American to actually consume a garden slug.

(They laugh.)

EMMA: I walked in with those people.

SENATOR: Are you a snail man, Arthur?

EMMA: In fact, I drove them here.

ARTHUR: Well, I'm afraid—

SENATOR: Careful.

ARTHUR: Absolutely not.

ANNABETH: Oh, stop. *(She feeds him a snail.)*

EMMA: You have no idea where this sort of thing can lead. This is what happened. *(She stands and crosses to the table, indicating Arthur.)* Two weeks ago, I received a phone call from this man's wife. Her name is Natalie, she and Arthur and I are old friends, and she wants to know if I will have dinner with them tonight.

ARTHUR: The challenge of any society is balancing the rights of the individual against the rights of the community. America, built on the dream of rugged individualism, is directly challenged by communism, which annihilates the individual and promotes only the dream of the community. But just as communism finally destroyed itself, crumbling under the weight of its singular dream, so shall we fall unless we find a way to support a dynamic interchange between self and society.

EMMA: Now, the fact is, I am a sucker for this kind of shit.

ARTHUR: This is the job of a leader. To protect the individual, and the community, at the same time.

EMMA: Arthur was one of my professors in law school. While everyone else was busy grinding my imagination to smithereens, Arthur spoke of—

ANNABETH: Dreams! Another word you don't hear on the hill…

SENATOR: They stone you for that too, Arthur.

ARTHUR: Mea culpa, mea culpa!

(They all laugh.)

EMMA: So me, Arthur, and Natalie are going to dinner, when Tommy calls to tell us Annabeth Gilkey has arranged for us to meet Senator Geoffrey Maddox in her offices. We planned to hook up with Natalie after, but she gets a head cold and bags the trip.

ANNABETH: He's so delightfully idealistic, isn't he, Geoffrey?

ARTHUR: Oh. I don't—

ANNABETH: No, no, it's charming! Mr. Smith Goes To Washington. It reminds me of you, Geoffrey.

SENATOR: Well, I don't—

ANNABETH: Oh, to a tee! And the time is right for this. Public mood.

SENATOR: You might be—

ANNABETH: Who gives a shit about the presidency, we've gotta take the house back. I mean those fascists on the right are just driving me nuts. Gingrich, and Robertson, those idiot freshmen—oh, my God, that Rush Limbaugh, when is he gonna go away.

SENATOR: The situation is difficult right now.

ANNABETH: I know, it's late; the primary is only a couple months away, but let's face it, we've got *no one* who stands a chance and Geoffrey, I'm telling you, I can *do* something with this. And you know I wouldn't say it if it weren't true. *(She smiles at him.)*

EMMA: Annabeth Gilkey is living proof that it is in fact possible to sleep your way to the top, in any field. She is the kind of person who, if she owned a fur coat, it would be made of puppies.

(The scene changes to Annabeth's office. The Senator leaves.)

EMMA: We arrive at Annabeth's office fifteen minutes early.

ANNABETH: Emma! How lovely to see you again! I didn't know you were coming.

EMMA: Why wouldn't I be coming?

ARTHUR: Is my tie all right?

EMMA: *(Checking it.)* It's fine—

ARTHUR: I'm so nervous—

EMMA: He's gonna love you—

ARTHUR: I just hope I get a chance to explain my ideas to him.

TOMMY: You were great with the governor.

ANNABETH: The governor? Arthur, you *are* moving up quickly.

EMMA: He's a friend of my dad's.

ANNABETH: How darling.

EMMA: Arthur knocked him dead. We're on our way!

ANNABETH: You already have a whole organization, Arthur. What's your title, Emma?

EMMA: *(Fixing tie.)* We haven't gotten to that yet.

ARTHUR: Chief of staff.

(They laugh.)

ANNABETH: How darling.

EMMA: Okay, see you guys at the restaurant. Give my best to the senator.

ANNABETH: Actually, the senator's had to postpone.

(There is an awkward, disappointed pause.)

TOMMY: Oh?

ARTHUR: Oh.

ANNABETH: Oh, stop! Such long faces. He's just running late. He's going to join us. Where were you going?

EMMA: Chardonnay.

ANNABETH: Fabulous. *(She picks up the phone and punches a button.)*

ANNABETH: Jennie? It's Annabeth. The Senator asked me to call and let him know where we'd be having dinner. We're heading over to Chardonnay, can you let him know? Thanks, you're a doll. *(She hangs up, bright.)* Shall we?

(The scene changes back to the restaurant.)

EMMA: *(To audience.)* So all of us get into my car and we drive across town, to a very nice, very discreet French restaurant…

ANNABETH: I *love* this place.

EMMA: where I have made a reservation…

ANNABETH: And I hardly ever get over here

EMMA: to have dinner with my friends and colleagues.

ANNABETH: Now, how do you want to do the seating, Arthur? Four and one?

(Emma looks over as Arthur considers this.)

ARTHUR: *(Quickly.)* Oh, yes. That's exactly right. Four and one.

ANNABETH: David—We'll need a table for four, and a table for one.

DAVID: Right this way.

EMMA: *(To audience.)* I wish I could say that it took me a minute to get this, but unfortunately I understood immediately what was going on.

TOMMY: Wait a minute. There are going to be five of us, aren't there? When the senator gets here—

EMMA: *(To Tommy.)* Apparently, Annabeth and Arthur would prefer that I ate at a separate table.

ANNABETH: We'll set you up at the best single they have. David, can we get her the view of the capital dome?

DAVID: Anything for you, Annabeth.

ARTHUR: Emma, you understand. This is strictly business.

EMMA: Of course!

ARTHUR: The senator—

EMMA: I know.

DAVID: It's a little close to the kitchen and there is a draft, but I think you'll be very pleased with the view.

ARTHUR: *(To Annabeth.)* I can't tell you how much I appreciate your help arranging this, Annabeth—

ANNABETH: I didn't do it for you, Arthur. I did it for all of us. Now, you and Tommy need to fill me in on your campaign strategy before the senator gets here.

ARTHUR: Of course! Tommy—

(They all sit at their respective tables.)

EMMA: *(To audience.)* So, they get to work. I order a drink.

(She does. The waiter delivers it.)

EMMA: The senator arrives.

(He does. The waitress knocks the drink on Emma in her rush to serve the senator.)

EMMA: *(More and more rattled.)* And while they chat, I eat alone. I don't have a book with me because I didn't realize that I would be eating alone. I don't have a newspaper because, same thing. I don't have anyone to talk to because, well, that's obvious. Plus, the service is terrible because everyone in the restaurant is obsessed with "Geoffrey," the senator, once he gets here. So, I sit alone for two hours, wondering why the hell I went along with this, why Arthur went along with it, why Tommy went along with it, and why the fuck the vinaigrette has cream in it!

(Everyone bursts into laughter at the next table. Emma stabs her salad, eating angrily.)

SENATOR: Oh, look at the time! I'm going to miss that fund-raiser altogether.

ANNABETH: Well, maybe you should—

SENATOR: I wish. But I've *got* to put in an appearance. You'll join me, of course.

ARTHUR: That would be delightful—

SENATOR: That's the last time you'll say that, Arthur. If all goes well for you, and I'm sure it will, you will get very tired of fund-raisers.

ARTHUR: That's very kind of you.

SENATOR: We'll have to call a cab, I'm afraid. I sent the car ahead with my wife—

ARTHUR: No, no, that's not a problem. We have a car.

SENATOR: Wonderful!

ARTHUR: Yes, we drove down from Baltimore with my dear friend Emma. Emma— (*He brings the Senator over to Emma's table.*)

EMMA: Hello! Yes—

ARTHUR: The senator is heading over to that DNC fund-raiser. He'd like us to come along.

SENATOR: You came down together? Why didn't you have dinner with us?

EMMA: (*Smiling.*) Apparently, I'm not important enough to sit at your table.

(*She laughs. They laugh. Arthur gives her a hug.*)

SENATOR: Certainly not—

ARTHUR: Oh, no, it wasn't that—

ANNABETH: Aren't we heading over? We'd better go soon, or Geoffrey may just turn into a pumpkin. Think of how *that* would look in the morning papers.

(*They all laugh again. The scene changes.*)

EMMA: What a surprise. The fund-raiser is a huge crashing bore. It's just like a political dinner, except the drinks are watered, everyone stands up and for some reason there's a military band... At times like this, one cannot help but wonder about the rituals of white people.

(*The Senator exits. Music plays. As before, Emma stands off to one side.*)

ANNABETH: (*Waving, working the room.*) Frank, how are you? I *loved* what you said on *Nightline* the other night. I thought Cokie Roberts was going to *hit* you. Paul, meet Arthur Woolf. Maryland's next congressman from District 2.

TOMMY: Al Gore's here.

SENATOR: Emma! Here you are off in a corner again. I've been looking for you.

EMMA: You have?

SENATOR: Would you like to dance?

EMMA: Here? Now?

SENATOR: With me?

EMMA: Maybe the evening won't be a complete disaster after all. I'd love to.

(*The music changes into a tango. Emma and the Senator dance.*)

SENATOR: So what do you do, Emma?

EMMA: I'm a lawyer.

SENATOR: Really? My wife is a lawyer.

EMMA: Yes, we've met. I was opposing council on that Bennington suit.

SENATOR: That was you? You really made her work.

EMMA: Not hard enough. She whipped the pants off me.

(*The senator dips her.*)

SENATOR: Sounds fascinating.

(*Annabeth snaps into action.*)

ANNABETH: Arthur, let's dance.

ARTHUR: Shouldn't I be mingling?

ANNABETH: That depends on what kind of a dancer you are. If you're any good at all, this is a much better way to get people talking about you.
(She whips him around and dips him. Very quickly there are dueling tangos.)

SENATOR: So how do you know Arthur, Emma?

EMMA: He was one of my professors, my first year of law school.

SENATOR: And now you work for him?

EMMA: Unofficially.

SENATOR: Sounds romantic.

EMMA: Arthur? No.

SENATOR: Excellent. *(He dips her again.)*

ARTHUR: Don't you think I should put together a policy statement?

ANNABETH: That's a wonderful point, Arthur. The problem is, no one reads policy statements.

ARTHUR: But everyone says they're sick of the status quo. We have to provide people with options.

ANNABETH: Americans are afraid of ideas.

ARTHUR: Then we have to teach them that there's nothing to be afraid of.

ANNABETH: Oh, Arthur. You are just perfect. I can work with this, I really can.
(Suddenly, flashbulbs go off. Arthur looks up, startled. Annabeth smiles for the camera.)

ANNABETH: Perfect.
(The senator looks terrified and drops Emma on the floor.)

SENATOR: Now, just a minute there. This is perfectly innocent. *(He goes off after the photographers.)*

ANNABETH: I'm telling you, Arthur, my way is easier. We're going to be all over the newspapers by Tuesday.
(She follows the senator offstage. Arthur heads after Annabeth. Tommy helps Emma up.)

TOMMY: I'm sorry, Em. Arthur gets nervous at these things. He just started; he doesn't know what he's doing yet. I mean, that thing in the restaurant…

EMMA: *(Dusting herself off.)* It wasn't his fault. Annabeth set me up.

TOMMY: Still. He shouldn't have let it happen.

EMMA: Look, it's okay.

TOMMY: You sure?

EMMA: Yes!

TOMMY: You are such a sport. I'll talk to him about it, okay?

(The scene changes. The phone rings. The waiter comes in and sets the phone before her. It stops ringing and Arthur steps into the light.)

ARTHUR: Emma, could you call me? I need to talk to you about something.

EMMA: So, not only am I to be humiliated, now I have to listen to people apologize about it. Might as well get it over with.

ARTHUR: Hello?

EMMA: Arthur, Hi. I'm returning your call.

ARTHUR: Listen, Emma. I wanted to talk to you about that evening in the restaurant.

EMMA: You know, Arthur, let's just forget about it, okay? It was just an awkward situation.

ARTHUR: Yes, it was, and I really feel that I need to say something about it. I mean, I appreciate everything you've done to help this campaign get off the ground, the money you've given, the introduction to the governor, bringing Tommy on board, the fund-raisers you've organized, that's been great, but I have to say, I was really upset with you for the way you behaved the other night.

EMMA: What?

ARTHUR: When you said that you weren't important enough to sit at our table, I felt that you were trying to punish me. And I don't appreciate it. I was going to Washington for an extremely important meeting, something you seem to have completely forgotten—

EMMA: I didn't forget—

ARTHUR: It was not appropriate for you to be there!

EMMA: Whoa! Wait a minute—

ARTHUR: Well, now you're upset. I can't talk to you.

EMMA: Yes, I'm upset. You're yelling at me.

ARTHUR: I'm not yelling, I'm making a point!! If you didn't like the seating arrangements, you should have left the restaurant.

EMMA: I was trying not to create a scene—

ARTHUR: Well, you didn't exactly succeed, now did you? You were an embarrassment and I won't have it. Do you understand me? I won't have it.

(Arthur hangs up the phone. Tommy enters.)

TOMMY: You okay?

EMMA: Arthur seems angry.

TOMMY: I'm really sorry, Em. Arthur's just, he's a little crazy right now, and somehow, it all got kind of unloaded on you.

EMMA: Why? I didn't do anything!

TOMMY: Well, you did say that thing to the senator about not being important enough to sit at his table.

EMMA: That was true! I was invited to dinner, I *drove* everybody there, and then you guys made me sit at another table! I can't believe I drove. I don't know, that just makes it worse somehow. I *drove*.

TOMMY: I know, it's crazy.

EMMA: And I was willing to let it go! I mean, when it was over, I was like, okay, that was awful, but now it's over, time to move on, and then *he* called *me*—

TOMMY: I know. When he told me he was going to do that, I thought, I wouldn't, it's just putting salt in the wound, but…

EMMA: He told you? I mean, he told you that he was going to call me and scream at me?

TOMMY: Yeah. And I thought, what a bad idea.

(*Beat.*)

EMMA: But you didn't say that. I mean, you didn't tell him not to. Call me.

(*Beat.*)

TOMMY: Look, let's not blow this out of proportion. These things happen early in a campaign. People are nervous. Things just need to settle out. Let me talk to him.

(*Annabeth and Arthur enter. The scene changes. Emma steps to one side and watches.*)

ANNABETH: I really don't understand why she's making such a big deal about this. I mean, really. She is not the one running for office here.

TOMMY: I just think her feelings were hurt.

ANNABETH: Her *feelings?* What do her feelings have to do with anything?

TOMMY: She's done a lot for us. And she is a friend.

ANNABETH: If she were truly a friend, she would understand what our priorities are here. I mean, Arthur has better things to do than running around apologizing for some girl's hurt feelings.

ARTHUR: Apologize? Now she expects me to apologize?

TOMMY: No, that's not—

ARTHUR: Is she insane?

TOMMY: Arthur, she's given us money, she introduced you to the governor—she introduced you to me, for crying out loud—she took a leave of absence from her job to help us out—

ARTHUR: That doesn't give her the right to try and take over the entire campaign.

TOMMY: Arthur—

ARTHUR: No, you listen to me. I know you're friends with Emma, and that has put you in an awkward position here. I respect that. But I also ask that you respect me. I cannot let her wounded ego interfere with what I'm trying to do. What's happening here is bigger than that. The country is at stake. If she can't learn to make a few compromises, then she doesn't belong. And if you don't understand that, then you don't belong, either.

(Beat.)

TOMMY: No. I do understand.

ARTHUR: Good.

ANNABETH: Look. I think this all just blew out of proportion.

TOMMY: I think that's all I'm really trying to say.

ANNABETH: Of course you are. And Emma has been a big help to you, Arthur, she has! She told me as much.

ARTHUR: Well, yes, but—

ANNABETH: I think we should conserve our resources. The senator seemed quite taken with her. That could be useful in the long run; he can get skittish during a tough campaign. Besides, if she apologizes, there's no reason why she can't come back.

ARTHUR: No. I suppose not…If she apologizes.

ANNABETH: You'll tell her, won't you, Tommy? Come on, Arthur. We don't want to be late for that lunch with 20/20.

(They go. The scene changes.)

EMMA: They want me to what?

TOMMY: Since the senator liked you so much, they think you could be useful. But you have to apologize.

EMMA: And what exactly am I apologizing for?

TOMMY: Well, it's a difficult situation for everyone. You do share responsibility for this, Em. And he's in no position to apologize to you. I want you around. I think you should do it. *(He goes.)*

EMMA: I decide to talk to other people. Be an adult. Get a broader perspective. I call my friends.

(Another woman, Marjorie, sits across from her. They are having lunch. Emma launches in.)

EMMA: It's like, Keats, okay? That negative capability thing? Believing in two completely contradictory ideas at the exact same time, I always thought that was something deeply profound, like the Heisenberg Uncertainty Principle, if you know where that electron is, you cannot know how fast it's going, or, or Kierkegaard, knowing the universe is going to annihilate you and yet embracing the belief in a just God, all of these things, the resonating of opposites, it always seemed so huge to me, and then it turns out it's not that at all. It turns out, it's just a moment in your life, or a person who you thought was one thing who is in fact also its opposite, or not people, maybe, but the things that we yearn for, small tiny things that then make everything else you thought you knew disappear. And I don't know if I can do it. I mean, maybe I did idealize Arthur, but that still doesn't alter the fact that he fell into that whole nasty in-crowd logic so quickly, and I know he wants this badly, but can a dream destroy your ideals? Are integrity and kindness truly the hope of fools? I don't know what to think anymore.

(Marjorie stares at her, takes a piece of bread. Pause.)

MARJORIE: You remember last year when we were playing Pictionary, and you accused me of cheating?

EMMA: What?

MARJORIE: You did, you accused me of cheating. *(Pause. Insistent.)* On New Year's Eve, we were playing Pictionary, and you said, "Come on, come on!"

EMMA: Yes?

MARJORIE: I'm just saying, you know, you're not perfect, either. All this talk about integrity? And *you* accused *me*. Of cheating.

EMMA: Marjorie!

MARJORIE: Look, I have a lot of anger in me, okay? And maybe I should have told you at the time, but this is just not easy for me, and my friends just have to learn to accept my anger because, you know, I have a right to express it. My group feels very strongly about this.

(Pause.)

EMMA: I decide that maybe friends are not who I should turn to at this time. Maybe a total stranger, a chance encounter, a foreign perspective will help me understand the mysterious workings of the human heart. Like Diogenes, I go in search of an honest man.

(She turns to sit at a bar. There is a drunken man there.)

E.T. BLACK: Okay, here's the thing: I'm, like, do you know who I am? I'm E.T. Black. That doesn't mean anything to you, does it? E.T. Black. You've never heard of me. Nobody in this whole place knows who I am. But I'm like, the biggest screenwriter in Hollywood. One of the biggest. Any one of my scripts, I could write anything here, right now, on a napkin, and it would get made. I've got an academy award. You think I'm making this up. But it's because you don't know who I am.

EMMA: Well, I don't go to a lot of movies…

E.T. BLACK: What are you talking about? Everybody goes to movies. What, do you just sit at home and let the television like suck your brains out, is that what you do?

EMMA: No, I'm busy, I'm a busy person.

E.T. BLACK: Oh, little Miss Important, is that who you are? Huh? Too important to go to the movies, is that what you're saying?

EMMA: *(Rising to go.)* You know, maybe I...

E.T. BLACK: No, you talk to me! You said you have a question! Well, I have questions, too! Do you know who I am? I'm E.T. Black! I'm the biggest screenwriter in Hollywood! My movies get made! Nobody reads books anymore! They go to see my movies! If this were the nineteenth century or something I'd be Charles Dickens! *City Slickers?* I wrote that. That thing about starting a stampede with a coffee grinder? That was my idea. *Total Nonsense. Harriet the Spy.* I did the final rewrite on that, most of that is mine. I mean, I'm filthy rich, I'm fuckin'...filthy rich, and nobody asks me what I think about anything. If this were the nineteenth century, I'd be hanging out with Ruskin. Fucking Ruskin would be having lunch with me. Disraeli. Winston Churchill.

EMMA: Winston Churchill was World War II.

E.T. BLACK: What?

EMMA: Well, you said, if this was the nineteenth century, and Winston Churchill didn't live in the nineteenth century, he—

E.T. BLACK: Fuck you! Do you know who I am? You have no idea who I am!

EMMA: Do you think people are good?

E.T. BLACK: Have you been to Hollywood? No. The answer to that is no.

EMMA: Do you think a dream can destroy ideals?

E.T. BLACK: Ideals? What the fuck is an ideal? Who are you, anyway? Ideals are like, nothing. Fucking Plato forgot to tell you that part. I mean, I thought we were talking about reality. Jesus. You are really sad, lady.

EMMA: We're not talking about me.

E.T. BLACK: No? No? I mean, you wanted the truth, you just, now you don't like it, is that it? I mean, I didn't make this shit up. Do you know who I am? I'm a fuckin' world-famous screenwriter, and I'm telling you the way things are. There are things I *know*. Power and money are *it*. Because people aren't just afraid of death, they're *mad* about it, death is what drives us insane, and we think if we collect enough...you know... *(He starts to drift off.)* Maybe...if we have enough...if we're whores...you know, fucking...if we live without meaning...we can beat God at his own fucking game...

(His head is on the table. Emma watches him for a moment.)

EMMA: I don't know why it took Diogenes so long to find an honest man. I got one my first time out. I gotta get away from all this. Far away. Alaska. I'll take a cruise. Those things are great. Everyone takes care of you. All you really have to do is look at the world through binoculars and think. Or not think. Rest. Figure things out. *(She looks at the world through binoculars for a moment.)* Alaska really is spectacular. Oh, look, a whale! *(She continues to look. After a moment.)* Yeah, going to Alaska was a great idea. There's just one thing I forgot. Dinner.

(Leonard and Junette enter, dressed for dinner.)

LEONARD: Leonard Larson, from Minnesota. And this is my wife, Junette. It looks like we're at the same table!

JUNETTE: We'll be eating together all week!

EMMA: It turns out that Leonard's wife has an identical twin sister named June. June was born first, which is why Junette is named Junette.

JUNETTE: *(Bright.)* It's true!

EMMA: You can't make this stuff up.

JUNETTE: So did you see that glacier today? My goodness.

LEONARD: Just great.

JUNETTE: And tomorrow, I guess we're gonna stop in Valdez.

LEONARD: See the pipeline. I been looking forward to that, let me tell you.

JUNETTE: Oh, I don't know…

LEONARD: What?

JUNETTE: That pipeline tour. I just don't know.

LEONARD: *(Disappointed.)* Well, we don't have to. I just thought…

JUNETTE: I don't know.

LEONARD: I was kinda looking forward to it.

JUNETTE: Well.

LEONARD: We don't have to.

EMMA: Instead of seeing the pipeline, Leonard and Junette take a bus tour of the Worthington Glacier Mountain Pass, which carries you through Keystone Canyon, past Bridalveil Falls, three thousand feet up the side of a mountain. There, Leonard, who has a heart condition, goes into arrest.

JUNETTE: It was pretty scary, let me tell you!

LEONARD: It's nothing!

EMMA: He doesn't survive the night.

LEONARD: *(Bright.)* I guess we should've gone to see the pipeline! *(Less bright.)* I woulda liked to see that.

EMMA: Junette, I'm so sorry.

JUNETTE: *(A little confused.)* Oh, well, these things happen. Nice meeting you, Cathy.

(She and Leonard go.)

EMMA: All told, I learn nothing on my cruise, except that Alaska is very far away, and the human race is at best a touching disappointment.

(The scene changes. Tommy enters. He and Emma meet in a restaurant.)

TOMMY: Hey, how's it going?

EMMA: Fine. Just got back from Alaska.

TOMMY: Yeah, I heard. Must've been fantastic.

EMMA: It was very beautiful.

TOMMY: I bet. How was the cruise?

EMMA: Lotta food. Gained a few pounds.

TOMMY: I've heard that about those things.

EMMA: The Love Boat, with lots of old white people. Dutch crew, Nigerian porters. It was an exercise in imperialism with bad night club shows and bingo. They actually had sit-down aerobics.

TOMMY: *(Laughing.)* Oh, no.

(Long pause.)

EMMA & TOMMY: So— *(They laugh.)*

EMMA: Go ahead.

TOMMY: No, you.

EMMA: I was just going to say…that, I did a lot of thinking while I was up there at the ends of the earth, and I got kind of lonely, frankly, and I don't want to lose you. *(Beat.)* There was this old couple on the boat—ship, I mean, the ship—and at first I found them truly annoying, they were from "Minnesota," but they were also so *together,* you know, and then they lost each other, over a mistake, a foolish mistake, and I don't want that to happen to us. I mean, I don't really know what that whole thing in the restaurant was, but it was just a moment, a foolish mistake, and it doesn't matter as long as you and I are okay, because you are so dear to me, Tommy—

TOMMY: Emma. *(Beat.)* Um.

EMMA: What?

TOMMY: This is awkward. *(Beat.)* You should have let me go first.

EMMA: *(Beat.)* Why?

TOMMY: Arthur feels that you have been a destructive influence. He, things aren't going as well on the fund-raising, as he had hoped, the primary is right around the corner and he's very frustrated. He needs an outlet to express that frustration, and you seem to be providing that outlet.

EMMA: I wasn't talking about Arthur.

TOMMY: Yes you were.

EMMA: No. I wasn't. *(Beat.)* Why are you?

TOMMY: Well. I am his campaign manager.

EMMA: And what am I?

TOMMY: You? You're nobody. *(Beat.)* You should have apologized, Em.

EMMA: I didn't do anything. I didn't have anything to apologize for.

TOMMY: Yeah, well, I'm the guy's campaign manager. You can't expect me to side against him.

EMMA: *(Getting mad.)* Side against Arthur, what does that mean?

TOMMY: Emma, come on. You're putting me in an awkward position. You have to at least acknowledge that.

EMMA: No, actually, I don't think I do.

TOMMY: Emma.

EMMA: What? I mean, what are you telling me, that you're cutting me off because Arthur's gone paranoid, that it wasn't enough for him to insult me in a restaurant, now he's got to take away my friends, too?

TOMMY: Look—

EMMA: No, you look! This is ridiculous! Tommy, are you really willing to throw me away over nothing? Can you really just throw people away like that?

TOMMY: I'm sorry. I said what I have to say. I have to go. *(He starts to go.)*

EMMA: Don't you dare walk away from me. I got you this job! No one would hire you! You were a huge drunk, and no one would even talk to you! I practically saved your life!

(He gives her a look.)

EMMA: Well, it's true.

TOMMY: I had some problems. I've worked them out. I hope I haven't disappointed you or Arthur.

EMMA: *(Apologizing.)* No, of course not. You've…you seem to be doing a great job. How would I know? I don't know. Because no one will talk to me, because now, I'm nobody. *(Beat.)* I just want this all to go away. I want it never to have happened. I don't understand it.

TOMMY: Why don't you just let go of this?

EMMA: I've been trying to.

TOMMY: No. You haven't.

EMMA: There's something I have to talk to you about, Tommy—

TOMMY: I am not talking to you anymore! *(Beat.)* Look. I'm not trying to be mean, but you know—there's no big mystery here. You act like what's happened to you was crazy; well, it wasn't. People just love to create a pecking order. It's everybody's favorite pastime, deciding who is more important than whom. This is why communism never worked. Oh, we're all equal.

Yeah, right. It doesn't even work that way biologically. It doesn't work for monkeys, why should it work for us? You just ended up on the bad end of it for once. To Arthur, you were the least dangerous. The most expendable. It made him feel better to insult you so he did it.

EMMA: *(Cold.)* What happened to Mr. Smith Goes to Washington? Democracy? A man of the People?

TOMMY: He's still that. On a profound level, he has not compromised his ideals. I mean, this is just politics. And I have to go. *(He stands.)*

EMMA: Fuck you.

TOMMY: Fine. I did my best.

EMMA: Your best isn't very good. You're weak.

(He looks at her, doesn't answer, and goes. Emma sits alone.)

EMMA: I mean, you think you have something to say, and then you find out that you don't because no one's listening. Is that possible? Like a tree falling in the forest, thoughts and feelings directed at no one don't exist? This is starting to BOTHER ME. ARTHUR! *(She turns, mid-roar, to find Arthur and Annabeth in a big, indiscreet clinch. For a moment, she doesn't put it together.)*

EMMA: Oh, I'm sorry, I was looking for—

(Annabeth and Arthur shriek and pull apart, guiltily shoving their clothes together.)

ARTHUR: This isn't what it looks like. We are both consenting adults, my marriage has been in trouble for many years—

ANNABETH: Arthur. Arthur! It's Emma, Arthur.

EMMA: Hi.

ARTHUR: Oh, my God.

EMMA: What are you doing, Arthur?

ARTHUR: How did you get in here?

EMMA: The kid at the desk said you were free. He said go on in—

ARTHUR: *(To Annabeth.)* He's fired.

ANNABETH: I'm on it.

EMMA: Oh, Arthur. Annabeth? Oh, ick. Oh.

ARTHUR: And get her out of here.

ANNABETH: Gladly.

EMMA: I'm not going anywhere!

ARTHUR: I'm calling security.

EMMA: Fine, call security. I'd love a scene. So would the press, I'm sure!

(Pause.)

ANNABETH: Just hold off for a second, Arthur. I'm sure that won't be necessary. What do you want, Emma?

EMMA: *(Beat.)* I want my money back.

ARTHUR: What?

EMMA: I gave you five thousand dollars for your campaign because I thought you were something that it turns out you're really not. I want my money back.

ARTHUR: *(To Annabeth.)* She's insane.

ANNABETH: Arthur, could you go into the next room please? I'll handle this. Just wash your face; we have to be at the Rotary Club in fifteen minutes. *(Firm.)* Arthur. I'm handling this.

(Arthur goes. Annabeth considers Emma.)

EMMA: Wow. He walks, he talks, and you can't even see the wires.

ANNABETH: Emma, you're sounding like a bad soap opera. What you're doing here, I don't know, but I find it tacky.

EMMA: *I'm* tacky?

ANNABETH: You're embarrassing yourself. Your obsession with Arthur is abnormal. He told me you were in love with him. I didn't believe him. But this? Clearly, he was not imagining things. I'd think about that before I started babbling nasty little rumors to the press. Your motives aren't exactly pristine.

EMMA: My motives are fine. I'm not in love with Arthur. I'm mad at him because he squashed my ideals.

ANNABETH: *(Laughing a little.)* What?

EMMA: Oh, never mind. *(Mouths: Why do I even bother?)*

ANNABETH: You know, just for the record, I wanted you back. Geof Maddox was really taken with you and that sort of thing works with him. If you actually cared about Arthur, that might have occurred to you.

EMMA: What are you saying?

ANNABETH: I'm saying if you wanted to help, you had your chance. All this talk about broken ideals. This is nobody's fault but your own.

EMMA: I can't follow this. Just give me my money, and I'll go.

ANNABETH: That is not going to happen.

ARTHUR: Give her the money. *(Arthur stands in the doorway.)*

ANNABETH: I don't think that's wise, Arthur.

ARTHUR: If it will get her out of here, give her the money.

(Annabeth shrugs, reaches into her jacket and pulls out a checkbook. She writes a check and hands it to Emma.)

ANNABETH: Don't come back, Emma. It's embarrassing.

(She goes. Emma looks at the check, at the audience as Arthur brings the podium downstage. Emma listens.)

ARTHUR: Without question, America has fallen into a crisis of imagination. This great, troubled country, still the strongest force for freedom on this earth, seems to be slipping from our grasp. The two-party system has collapsed upon itself, imploding every issue into a middling sameness. Our leaders have shrunk into mere politicians, squabbling endlessly over nothing. And the most powerful voice now heard in our land is the shrill shriek of the hate monger, claiming our airwaves, our heartland, claiming the highest legislative body of our nation. But we can tolerate this crippling cynicism no longer. We must build a bridge from our past to our future, and embrace the spirit of those democratic ideals, our own, which for the past two hundred years have provided a beacon for our suffering planet. "We hold these truths to be self-evident: that all men are created equal, that they are endowed by their Creator with certain inalienable rights, that among these are Life, Liberty and the Pursuit of Happiness." There is no quibbling here. There is only vision. Hope. The conviction that the human spirit can and will transcend its own pettiness. Only that conviction will save us now.

EMMA: I keep going back over that night. What I could have done to stop it.

(The restaurant comes together around her again. The others take their places as she speaks.)

ANNABETH: Now, how do you want to do the seating, Arthur? Four and one?

(Emma looks over as Arthur considers this.)

ARTHUR: *(Quickly.)* Oh, yes. That's exactly right. Four and one.

ANNABETH: David— *(She waves the waiter on.)*

EMMA: And it always seems inexorable, in an odd way.

ANNABETH: We'll need a table for four, and a table for one.

DAVID: Right this way.

EMMA: The whole thing was so smooth. Like they'd practiced it.

TOMMY: Wait a minute. There are going to be five of us, aren't there? When the senator gets here—

EMMA: *(To Tommy.)* Apparently Annabeth and Arthur would prefer that I ate at a separate table.

ANNABETH: We'll set you up at the best single they have. David, can we get her the view of the capital dome?

DAVID: Anything for you, Annabeth.

EMMA: Like a secret handshake.

ARTHUR: Emma, you understand. This is strictly business.

DAVID: It's a little close to the kitchen and there is a draft…

EMMA: And the only reason it was even this gracious was because graciousness is our excuse.

ANNABETH: Now, you and Tommy need to fill me in on your campaign strategy before the senator gets here.

EMMA: I'm just lucky we don't live in Rwanda.

ANNABETH: Arthur, this is awkward. Should I shoot her?

ARTHUR: Oh, yes. That's exactly right. Go ahead and shoot her.

(Annabeth draws a gun and shoots Emma, who goes down. Annabeth then turns and pockets it.)

TOMMY & ARTHUR: Good shot! Good shot, Gilkey!!

EMMA: I'm lucky this isn't the Vatican.

TOMMY: Arturo, why are these women talking?

ARTHUR: Good point. Guards! ANNO. DOMINI PATRI CHRISTO. NINA, PINTA, SANTA MARIA. AMEN.

(The waiter grabs Emma, Tommy grabs Annabeth; they force them down as Arthur dismisses them with a cross.)

EMMA: I'm lucky this is America. Where democracy is a goal to which we, and our leaders, aspire.

ANNABETH: Now how do you want to do the seating. Arthur? Four and one?

(Emma looks over as Arthur considers this.)

ARTHUR: *(Quickly.)* Oh, yes. That's exactly right. Four and one.

ANNABETH: David— *(She waves the waiter on.)* We'll need a table for four, and a table for one.

DAVID: Right this way. *(The waiter starts to move a place setting to the separate table.)*

EMMA: So why should I go along with this nonsense?

TOMMY: There are going to be five of us, aren't there?

EMMA: I mean, if they want to play this game, I can play too, right?

ARTHUR: Emma, you understand.

EMMA: No, I don't, actually. I'm sitting here.

(She sits at the table. They all stare at her.)

ANNABETH: *(Horrified.)* What is she doing?

EMMA: You invited me to dinner.

TOMMY: What are you *doing?*

ARTHUR: WHAT ARE YOU DOING?

EMMA: I want to meet the senator.

(They all scream. Arthur has a heart attack. Emma leaps up from the table. Annabeth goes to Arthur's dead body. She glares at Emma.)

ANNABETH: He's dead. You killed him.

DAVID & TOMMY: MURDERER!

SENATOR: ASSASSIN!

EMMA: I'm sorry.

ARTHUR: You are an embarrassment.

EMMA: I'm sorry.

TOMMY: You're nobody.

EMMA: But, I drove.

ANNABETH: David, can we get her the view of the capital dome?

DAVID: Anything for you, Annabeth.

EMMA: Because finally there was nothing to be done.

DAVID: Anything for you, Annabeth.

EMMA: Somehow, it was a moment that would not be denied.

DAVID: Anything for you, Annabeth.

ARTHUR: *(Again speaking.)* We must reclaim that idealistic heritage which was, at one time, our birthright. With the courage of our forebears we will reshape ourselves as a country and people of discipline, wisdom, and compassion.

(Loud cheers and applause, as if at a convention. Arthur acknowledges.)

EMMA: I know it's vague, I know it's just rhetoric. But this is my problem. When people say things like that, I believe them. Or, I used to.

(The governor enters. The others exit as they take a seat in a restaurant.)

GOVERNOR: Emma!

EMMA: Hello Governor!

GOVERNOR: Emma, I warned you.

EMMA: Oh, come on.

GOVERNOR: I mean it!

EMMA: I am not calling you "Uncle Jack." Everyone will think you're my sugar daddy.

GOVERNOR: If that's the way you feel about it… *(He turns to go.)*

EMMA: *(Protesting.)* Uncle Jack…

GOVERNOR: *(Sitting.)* Much better. How's your dad?

EMMA: Oh, you know. The same. Lots of gardening, golfing, fighting with Mom.

GOVERNOR: Your mother is a saint.

EMMA: She knows.

GOVERNOR: And your friend Arthur won the primary. This must be a very exciting time for you.

EMMA: Actually, I'm not involved in his campaign anymore.

GOVERNOR: No? You were so high on him.

EMMA: I found some things out. It's complicated.

(*The waiter brings tea. She sips it.*)

GOVERNOR: *(Worried.)* Oh?

EMMA: I just had to put some distance there. It's nothing.

GOVERNOR: If it's nothing, then why don't you tell me?

EMMA: Because you're the governor.

GOVERNOR: It's sounding more and more like something you should tell the governor.

EMMA: I don't want to get anybody in trouble.

GOVERNOR: Emma, you introduced me to this man. I endorsed him. If there's something there that could come back and bite me, I need to know about it.

EMMA: No. There's nothing. Really.

(*The governor thinks about this, seems satisfied, and goes for his tea.*)

EMMA: Just a little bit of erratic behavior. I'm sure it's nothing that you need to worry about.

GOVERNOR: What kind of erratic behavior?

EMMA: I don't want to damage Arthur! But the stress of the campaign seems to be making him increasingly unstable. He kind of lashed out at me at a dinner, recently. It was very humiliating. And then when I tried to patch things up, he just became enraged. It got worse and worse until finally I just had to disengage myself from the whole thing.

GOVERNOR: Well, what set him off?

EMMA: Honestly, Uncle Jack, I don't know. Nothing, as far as I can tell. It was actually kind of psychotic. I mean, not psychotic. Psychotic is too strong. I'm sure it's just stress! But maybe you should keep an eye out. Just in case it happens again with, you know. Someone important, God forbid.

GOVERNOR: You're important, Emma.

EMMA: Thanks, Uncle Jack. Do we have to talk about this? I hardly ever get to see you. Let's talk about something else.

GOVERNOR: *(Paternal.)* Of course. Let me just make a phone call.

(*He goes. Emma watches, then sips her tea. Beat.*)

EMMA: *(Musing.)* Wow. That was easy. I didn't even have to lie.

SENATOR: Emma?

(*The Senator approaches, delighted.*)

SENATOR: Well, this is a pleasure. I haven't seen you since...

EMMA: That fund-raiser.

SENATOR: With your friend, Arthur. I see he's doing well in the polls.

EMMA: Actually, I think he's slipping.

SENATOR: Surely not. Annabeth tells me he's a huge hit.

EMMA: You don't think his rhetoric is sounding a little empty these days?

SENATOR: Well, whose isn't?

(*He laughs. She laughs with him.*)

EMMA: So true. They're throwing that big lunch for him today. You're probably on your way in, huh.

SENATOR: As a matter of fact, I am. Are you at my table?

EMMA: That would be novel, wouldn't it? Actually, I was going to skip it.

SENATOR: (*Disappointed.*) Oh.

EMMA: Well, you don't have to go, do you? As I recall, you hate these things.

SENATOR: Annabeth has me down for the keynote address.

EMMA: Cause I was hoping we could sneak off. Go get some seafood or something.

SENATOR: (*Suggestive.*) Lobster bisque?

EMMA: Lobster bisque.

SENATOR: Tuna tartare?

EMMA: Tuna tartare.

SENATOR: Creme brulée?

EMMA: Senator!

SENATOR: You're right, it's too risky. Well. (*He starts to go.*)

EMMA: Then again, I've always liked creme brulée.

SENATOR: Emma. You're not talking about lunch.

EMMA: I'm not?

SENATOR: You're talking about politics.

EMMA: I'm very interested in politics. (*Listening intently, she steers him to the other side of the stage.*)

SENATOR: It is a fascinating subject. You want to know what my life is like?

EMMA: Yes, I do.

SENATOR: I'm a prominent man. People are out to get me.

EMMA: It's so unfair, the system these days.

SENATOR: My home life is a mess. I never see my family.

EMMA: That's awful.

SENATOR: I don't make a lot of money. I go to battle every day up there on the hill, my work is murderously dull and the electorate I serve hates me. Why would anyone live this life?

(*He casually drapes his arm around her. She sees where this is going but doesn't want to stop it.*)

EMMA: Service?

SENATOR: Power! When I walk into a room, people applaud. My picture is in the newspapers, which quote the things I say. I eat delicious food. And women want me. Why should I give that up? It's the only reward I get. *(He is undressing her.)* Without the danger, I'm a petty bureaucrat. With it, I'm a senator!

(They fall into bed. Across the stage, Annabeth, Tommy, and Arthur look about. Tommy, Annabeth, and Arthur enter. Tommy is on cellphone.)

TOMMY: We can't find the senator.

ARTHUR: *(Panicking.)* What do you mean, you can't find him? He's giving the keynote speech!

ANNABETH: *(Overlap.)* Goddammit!

TOMMY: *(Reporting from phone.)* He's not backstage. He's not on the floor.

ARTHUR: Annabeth, you take care of this.

TOMMY: He's not picking up his cellphone.

ANNABETH: I hate it when he does this!

ARTHUR: You said put yourself in my hands! You said I'll take care of everything!

TOMMY: *(Reporting.)* There's a chance he's still in subcommittee—

ANNABETH: Get real. He's off screwing some campaign worker. The man is positively led around by his dick.

ANNABETH: Arthur, get Leon Panetta. He's always available. Tommy, call Jimmy Carville, he owes me big-time. And somebody see if John-John's in town. *(They go.)*

EMMA: Make no mistake, the senator and I had a wonderful time. I needed it. It made me feel better. And there was an element of poetic justice that frankly added a certain zing to it all. Hey!

(The half-naked senator takes her picture with a Polaroid camera. They playfully fight over it and take pictures of each other. They romp.)

SENATOR: I want to be able to see you whenever I want.

EMMA: In subcommittee hearings? I always wanted to be in politics. *(She's snapped a picture of him.)*

SENATOR: Just be careful who you show that to. Emma…

(She keeps snapping pictures as he stands.)

EMMA: You look delicious…

(He checks his watch.)

SENATOR: Oh my God. Look at the time. I gotta get to that dinner.

(The mood changes immediately. Emma watches him dress.)

EMMA: What dinner? The one for Arthur?

SENATOR: *(Beat.)* Yeah.

EMMA: I thought you weren't going to that.

SENATOR: Annabeth gave me such a hard time. I've missed the last three because of you, young lady. I can't skip another one.

EMMA: Did you tell her about us?

SENATOR: No. She may have guessed, though. Did you two have a fight or something?

EMMA: What makes you say that?

SENATOR: Just a vibe I get.

EMMA: Don't go. Come on, don't go. Please?

SENATOR: Emma. I have to.

EMMA: Because Annabeth says so.

SENATOR: Emma. Don't be a child.

EMMA: Don't treat me like one.

SENATOR: Oh, brother.

EMMA: What does she have on you?

SENATOR: Nothing.

EMMA: If she told you to dump me, would you?

SENATOR: You and I are having a wonderful time, Emma. Don't get like this.

EMMA: What would you do if she told you to dump me?

SENATOR: You're being ridiculous.

EMMA: Answer the question.

SENATOR: *(Point blank.)* I'd want to know her reasons. And if they were good, I'd follow her advice. But it's not going to come to that, okay?

EMMA: No, not okay. For almost six weeks now, you and I—

SENATOR: Wait a minute. There's no "you and I here." What is—I knew this was going to happen. You girls, you always think you have rights. Well, you don't, okay? I'm a public figure, for God's sake. You know what you're doing? You're trying to control policy. You think you have the right to do that just because you're a good lay?

EMMA: I'm a what?

SENATOR: Look. You started this.

EMMA: That's not precisely how it happened.

SENATOR: Well, Annabeth never did this. She understands, this is business.

EMMA: And what business is that?

SENATOR: *(Beat.)* You shouldn't have pushed.

(He grabs the photos and splits. She takes this in for a moment.)

EMMA: I do think there are moments in life when you realize that everything you thought about yourself and the world were just never true. And that knowledge brings with it, frankly, great temptation.

(She reaches into a pocket and pulls out one last Polaroid. An anchorman appears in a spotlight.)

ANCHORMAN: And the hotly contested race for Maryland's second district just got hotter. In an already scandal-ridden electoral season, a new star has appeared on the horizon as a young campaign worker has stepped forward to accuse congressional candidate Arthur Woolf and his sponsor, Senator Geoffrey Maddox of some rather exceptional forms of sexual misconduct. On the basis of rumor and innuendo alone, the polls are already fluctuating wildly. And while few facts are as yet available, pundits are leaping to comparisons with Donna Rice, Paula Jones, Jennifer Flowers, Fannie Fox, Kristine Keeler, Camila Parker Bowles, Lucy Mercer, Jessica Hahn, Rita Jenrette, every woman who's ever *met* Bob Packwood, Judith Exner, Kim Novak, Sherry Rowlands, and Marilyn Monroe. We take you live to Baltimore. Maryland.

(Emma turns and speaks. Flashbulbs pop.)

EMMA: Three months ago, I accompanied the candidate and his campaign manager to a dinner and a fund-raiser. At the time, I was not an important part of the campaign—they even sat me at a different table in the restaurant—but as soon as the senator showed interest in me, things changed. Arthur made it clear that I should be…"nice" to the senator. He really needed his endorsement, so I was basically told to do whatever had to be done. If I cooperated, he said, I would be rewarded.

ANCHORMAN: And you took that to mean sexual favors?

EMMA: That is what it meant, yes.

ANCHORMAN: And were you compensated for these favors?

EMMA: Only recently. The senator and I met for the last time a week ago, and I told him I was pregnant. At that time, he decided he wanted nothing more to do with me. When I told Arthur, he gave me a check for five thousand dollars and told me to get an abortion. I realized then that I could no longer participate in their sick, twisted morality.

ANCHORMAN: You realize that both the candidate and the senator have denied your allegations.

EMMA: Well, that doesn't surprise me. They're both pretty heavily into denial. Anyway, I have the check, and some pictures of myself with the senator. *(She shows these things to the anchorman.)* Oh. And here's my doctor's report. I'm just starting my second trimester. *(She shows it to the anchorman.)*

ANCHORMAN: *(Clears his throat, to audience.)* As I said, the offices of both the candidate and the senator have issued denials at this time. However, several supporters of opposing candidate Oliver Riley have hailed this young

woman as a heroine and a prophet for the new morality. They are calling
for a senate investigation into this matter.

(He nods, and exits. Emma looks at the audience.)

EMMA: This town is about spin. They spun the story one way, I spun it another.
Oh. Did I tell you I was pregnant?

(Flashbulbs pop. A crowd of reporters descend.)

REPORTER 1: Emma—

REPORTER 2: Over here, Emma—

REPORTER 3: Emma, could we have a statement?

EMMA: I made a mistake. I didn't stand up for myself. I'm doing that now.

REPORTER 1: Is there anything you want to say to Senator Maddox?

EMMA: I'm sorry he's going to be hurt by this, but frankly he should've kept it
in his pants.

(They laugh.)

REPORTER 2: And, why have you decided to come forward with this story now?
By your own admission, you were quite happy with this arrangement for
months. What made you change your mind?

EMMA: I just realized that men who could behave like this had no business
serving in the highest legislative body of our land. I mean, I talk to people,
and there's this sense that we can do better, we can be a better people, but
we need leaders who will understand our hunger of spirit. Our yearning.
Our hope that humanity is not merely degraded.

REPORTER 3: We're living in the gutter but looking at the stars, huh?

REPORTERS 1,2 & 3: Yeah, yeah, yeah, yeah. *(They go.)*

EMMA: I can't believe it took me so long to figure this out. When you're good,
everybody stomps on you. When you're bad, you end up in the newspaper.
I'm going to be in the newspaper!

RICHARD: Can I speak with you?

*(Emma looks over. Richard, a carefully dressed party organizer smiles at her
politely.)*

EMMA: Actually, I'm kind of tired. The press conference went longer than I
thought.

RICHARD: Yes, I saw. I'm Richard Riley. People in my organization were impressed
with what you did. You're a brave woman.

EMMA: Thank you.

RICHARD: Well, I'm afraid what you're doing is going to lead you into a lot of
very difficult, very frightening situations. You are aware of that, aren't you?

EMMA: Actually, I hadn't really thought about what happens next—

RICHARD: Of course not. You were just trying to do what was right. Let the world know who these men are.

EMMA: Yes.

RICHARD: Unfortunately, Washington is not a town that respects someone with a really pure motive. People here don't seem to understand that once in a while, maybe someone just wants to do what's right.

EMMA: No. They don't.

RICHARD: Why don't you let us help you?

EMMA: Well—who are you?

RICHARD: We are the Keepers of the American Promise.

(Bella and August enter, bustling about Emma, making her comfortable.)

BELLA: She's pregnant, Richard! Would you offer her a seat?

(August gives her a chair.)

AUGUST: Congratulations. I know that might be hard for you to hear, under these circumstances—

EMMA: Well—

BELLA: But babies are great. You're going to have a great time.

EMMA: I hope so. I'm a little—

AUGUST: We think you're very brave.

BELLA: Very.

AUGUST: Aren't politicians awful?

BELLA: Just terrible. What they did to you.

EMMA: It was pretty—

AUGUST: It's certainly time for a change. Washington just doesn't understand what people want any more.

BELLA: What *good* people want.

EMMA: Who are you again?

BELLA: Emma. Some of the fine points of our philosophies are not going to match up. But we want you to know that you are not alone. The system doesn't work anymore. A lot of people realize that. And we're trying to organize, on a grassroots level, to rebuild the country from the bottom up. Our schools. Our cities. Our communities. These are the things we're concerned about. I think that's what you're concerned about, too.

RICHARD: Besides, they fucked you over. Forgive me, for such language, but they did.

AUGUST: Richard, I really think—

RICHARD: Look. Unless we spell things out, they're going to crucify her. Emma. This is the hill. No one gives a shit about women here. And no one cares about the truth. Remember Tailhook? Remember Anita Hill? That's what's

going to happen to you. You are about to become the biggest lesbian fanta-
sizing lovesick crazy bitch the world has ever seen. Unless you let us help you.

EMMA: Help me how?

(Lance, a flaming costume designer, approaches, carrying sweaters and skirts.)

LANCE: God, no. Absolutely not. Everything has to go. SHEILA! I'm going to
need the rack of Laura Ashley. *(Fingering Emma's jacket.)* Oh, this is *fabu*-
lous. Rayon and wool, right? These new blends are unbe*liev*able. What size
are you? Six? And you can eat anything, right? I hate you, I really do. *(He
holds up a hideous pink sweater.)*

EMMA: I'm not wearing this.

LANCE: Sweetheart, you can't go out there as a fallen woman, it's completely
unsympathetic. Even Ingrid Bergman couldn't pull it off. *Notorious?*

EMMA: That's my favorite movie!

LANCE: *(Impersonating Ingrid Bergman.)* Why won't you believe in me, Dev? Just
a little bit.

LANCE & EMMA: Oh, Dev! Dev! Dev!

LANCE: She's fabulous, of course, but people just didn't want to see it. And with
all due respect, dear, your story is wretched enough. You don't want to look
the part. We have to go much more midwest…

EMMA: Nobody wears this stuff. Even in the midwest.

LANCE: I wouldn't lie about clothes this ugly. Isn't this hideous? I love it!
SHEILA!

*(Sheila enters, pushing a rack of Laura Ashley dresses as Lance continues to
dress a resisting Emma.)*

SHEILA: *(Frazzled.)* I don't know, Lance. This is all I could find and I was sure
we had just a mess of them from that Junior League tag sale…

LANCE: Those whores. They promised me a lot of at least twenty. Oh, this is just
pathetic…

EMMA: I'm not wearing this!

SHEILA: That's not my battle, honey. You and I are gonna accessorize. Some
pretty earrings. A little something at the neck. I love your hair. Is that your
real color? Wait a minute, what happened to that little gold rosary?

EMMA: I don't know…

SHEILA: I'm telling you, this stuff will make all the difference. Cause when you
look good, you feel good. And when you feel good, you do good. That's
what I say. It's not strictly true, but what the hell.

*(She drapes it on her arm as Richard enters, businesslike, and oversees the final
touches.)*

RICHARD: Here's the new statement. The rosary's too much.

SHEILA: I like it…

RICHARD: It's too Catholic. We need a broader appeal.

(Sheila goes after her with a hairbrush. Richard hands Emma some pages.)

EMMA: I can't say this. These people used to be friends of mine.

RICHARD: Wait until you hear what they say about you.

(Annabeth, Arthur, and Tommy enter as the others leave.)

ANNABETH: That fucking *cunt*.

TOMMY: Has anyone tried to talk to her? I mean, maybe if we just tried to have one conversation. She can't be completely crazy—

ANNABETH: Have you read the newspapers?

TOMMY: I'm just saying—

ANNABETH: Fuck her, I'm not talking to that bitch. I'm taking out a fucking contract on her life. I told you, Arthur, I told you not to give her the money—

ARTHUR: If you didn't want to give it to her, you shouldn't have given it to her! You were the one who made out the check!

ANNABETH: Only because you told me to!

ARTHUR: I said, call security! I said, she's insane!

ANNABETH: That's my point! How the hell did you ever even let her into this fucking campaign?

TOMMY: Things were fine when she was involved. The whole mistake was kicking her out in the first place—

ANNABETH: I'm sunk. I'm fucking dead meat in this town. Geoffrey Maddox won't return my fucking phone calls, did you know that? Has anyone thought about that? You introduced her to a major fucking senator and she fucked us both, Arthur, that's not the sort of thing people forget around here—

ARTHUR: You take care of this, Annabeth. You said, put yourself in my hands, I'll take care of everything—

ANNABETH: I swear, if it was legal I'd take out a fucking contract on her life. I'd rip that baby out of her womb with my bare hands if the press wouldn't be so shitty about it.

TOMMY: You think she's really pregnant, then?

ANNABETH: Of course she's fucking pregnant! It was the first thing I checked!

TOMMY: So, who's the father? I mean, we don't really think it's Senator Maddox, do we?

(Silence. Arthur and Annabeth look at him, exhausted.)

ANNABETH: We don't know, Tommy. He won't return my phone calls. He has distanced himself from our campaign. *(Beat.)* I'm fucking sunk in this town.

TOMMY: So what do we do?

ANNABETH: I'll spread some money around her firm, see who I can get to smear her.

TOMMY: You're not going to come up with anything.

ANNABETH: Don't be smug. There's always somebody who got passed over for a promotion, or got turned down for a date. Arthur, what about law school?

ARTHUR: What about it?

ANNABETH: She fuck any of her professors? Cheat on a test? Plagiarize anything?

ARTHUR: I'll come up with something.

ANNABETH: Tommy, you'll make the statement.

ARTHUR: *I'll* make the statement.

ANNABETH: Arthur, you have to stay above this.

ARTHUR: They're not above it.

ANNABETH: Of course they're not, they're *republicans*.

(Richard stands at a podium and reads a statement.)

RICHARD: We insist that this matter be given the fullest scrutiny.

(Tommy approaches the other podium.)

TOMMY: This woman was only peripherally involved in Mr. Woolf's campaign, for a very short period of time.

RICHARD: This man was running a prostitution ring out of his campaign headquarters!

TOMMY: The candidate was aware that she had a history of mental illness dating back to when she was a student in law school, but it was our understanding that those problems had been resolved.

RICHARD: If, as Mr. Woolf claims, this young woman is emotionally disturbed, that makes their behavior even more reprehensible!

TOMMY: We have documentation from several psychiatrists and ex-boyfriends. She is a nymphomaniac and a pathological liar.

RICHARD: We have also uncovered evidence that the campaign funds used to pay this woman off may have come from an illegal foreign bank account connected to several failed Savings and Loans. I wouldn't be surprised if this conspiracy reached all the way to the presidency.

TOMMY: Oh, for heaven's sake!

(The two men's arguments start to overlap.)

RICHARD: You are not going to sweep this under the rug. Your candidate and Senator Maddox were incapable of controlling their penises, well, you can just reap the rewards of that, because you're in the big leagues now, buster, and the rules of the game have been made pretty damn clear these past few years, so—

TOMMY: *(Overlap.)* I'm sick to death of you and your little troop of fanatics, ranting on and on about what's right and true and godly when none of you give a shit about truth, or God for that matter, all you care about is winning and you'll stoop to absolutely any kind of lie you Bible-thumping CONTROL FREAK!

(Richard and Tommy square off. Emma enters, watching. She has been transformed into a modern-day virgin type.)

RICHARD: FORNICATOR!

TOMMY: HYPOCRITE!

RICHARD: HOMOSEXUAL!

TOMMY: NEO-NAZI!

RICHARD: LIBERAL!

TOMMY: Oh, fuck you, you fascist scum.

RICHARD: Yeah, fuck you, too.

(They reach across the divide and shake hands, congratulating each other as after a debate. Emma changes channels. Rush Limbaugh comes on.)

RUSH: I'm sure I should be surprised, but I'm not. The new way to get elected, according to the democrats, is to pimp your campaign workers for political favors. Have you heard about this one? A candidate for congress told one of his campaign workers to sleep with a well-known senator in order to get an endorsement. And you thought you had seen it all. Not yet! Now, this woman is apparently some sort of ex-feminazi, and it's hard to have sympathy for her because out of party loyalty, I guess, she actually went along with this sick arrangement for at least three months. Yeah, she's a real prize. Scratch a feminist, find a prostitute. And it turns out she's pregnant! And I for one am not sanguine about her shall we say "maternal instincts," are you? The chances of this little tyke running afoul of the law are just a little too rich for my blood. More police, more court costs, more prisons— more of your tax dollars being spent to address the misdeeds of the liberal elite! Not to mention the cost to the victims of this whore's demon seed! It's a good thing we have the death penalty, that's all I have to say! I mean, if it were up to me, I'd say we should just drown the kid at birth!

EMMA: Oh, my God!

RUSH: Oh, what did you expect, a baby shower? *(He goes. Lance enters.)*

LANCE: Doll, you do know how to stir things up.

EMMA: I just don't know about this. Why do I have to look like the Virgin Mary? Everybody knows I'm *not* the Virgin Mary.

LANCE: Hey, you're getting a little bit of a pooch here.

EMMA: I am not.

LANCE: Oh my God. Isn't that the most beautiful thing you've ever seen? *(Calling.)* Sheila, get the baby clothes.

EMMA: *Baby* clothes. I'm only twenty weeks!

LANCE: Oh come on, aren't you getting excited? Little shoes and socks and those tiny baby overalls, hats, little tiny baseball caps—

EMMA: It is kind of great. I felt the baby move the other day.

LANCE: OhmyGod. Can I? *(He holds his hand over her stomach.)*

EMMA: Well, sure, but you probably won't feel anything. It doesn't happen all that...

(He starts, holds up his hand. She falls silent as he feels the baby move.)

LANCE: Is that it?

EMMA: That's it.

LANCE: Just that little flutter?

EMMA: Wait a minute.

(They pause.)

LANCE: *(Laughing.)* Isn't that something?

(They smile at each other.)

LANCE: You're so lucky. I can't wait to have children.

EMMA: You want children?

LANCE: I love children. You should have seen me in my heyday. I was the babysitting queen of America.

EMMA: Really?

LANCE: Oh honey, I'm telling you, they were lining up around the block. My dance card was *full.* Some nights I had four or five of 'em in my mother's living room crawling all over me, crawling all over each other, diapers everywhere—I was in pig heaven.

EMMA: It sounds awful.

LANCE: I'll tell you this much, there's nothing better than putting a baby to sleep. Children are life's holy blessing.

EMMA: Yeah, it's what they grow into that worries me.

LANCE: I think I could be satisfied with maybe seven or eight. Course, I have to find the right woman first.

(He goes back to work. Emma looks at him.)

EMMA: It must be hard.

LANCE: What's that?

EMMA: Well, you know. Being a gay man who wants kids.

LANCE: *(Beat.)* What makes you say that?

EMMA: Well—I don't know. It's hard for gay men to have kids, isn't it? It just seems to me there'd be a lot to work out. Logistically.

LANCE: And what makes you think I'm a homosexual?

EMMA: *(Beat.)* Well, gee, Lance, I mean—Oh. You're kidding, right?

LANCE: You think this is funny?

EMMA: Well—No. I'm sorry. Let's forget I said it.

LANCE: I don't want to forget it. What you've accused me of is very serious. I don't see how you can ask me to forget this!

EMMA: I'm not accusing you of anything! I just thought—I mean, come on, you're so—flaming. Lance—

LANCE: Homosexuality is a sin. It is a perversion of nature. The Bible is very clear about this.

EMMA: The Bible?

LANCE: You don't believe in the Bible?

EMMA: Well, I don't know. I mean, some of it seems okay, but—

LANCE: You can't pick and choose among the word of God, Emma. Do you know what you're saying?

EMMA: I didn't, I just—look. I don't think there's anything wrong with, you know. Being gay. So, I'm sorry. I misunderstood.

LANCE: Yes. You did.

EMMA: So I'm sorry.

(Beat.)

LANCE: It's all right. But you should read your Bible. It—what you're talking about—is disgusting to God.

EMMA: I'm sorry to hear that.

LANCE: It's just that I've been accused of this before. This is why—for years people trusted me with their children, and I loved every one of them. You would've had to strike me dead before I let anyone hurt those children.

EMMA: I know that.

LANCE: Then someone decided it was unnatural. I was unnatural. I never had a girlfriend, it just didn't happen, all of a sudden, people started thinking— well, I don't have to tell you, you thought the same thing. And they decided their children were not safe. I just, I can't take this lightly, Emma.

EMMA: I'm sorry.

(Lance exits.)

SHEILA: Emma! You're on in five minutes.

(Emma turns, confused. The lights come on her.)

EMMA: Oh, I'm sorry—I'm just so confused about all this—

SHEILA: Honey, no. Confusion's bad. They'll just eat you up.

EMMA: Oh! I don't know.

SHEILA: Now, you can do this! I know you can! The world wants to hear from you. All those normal people out there, they're sick of these politicians. They want to hear someone real talk about the way things are. They want to hear the truth. Come on now. Tell us who you are.

EMMA: I'm a concerned citizen.

SHEILA: That's right.

EMMA: I am not insane.

SHEILA: We know you're not. Emma, just tell the truth.

SENATOR A: You are not on trial here. This is a simple investigatory hearing which should allow us to gather the facts.

SENATOR B: The senate is grateful to you for bringing these matters to our attention. And may I just take a minute to assure the public, I knew *nothing* about this prostitution ring. I was in no way involved.

(He laughs, uneasy. The other senators look at him as they set up before her.)

SENATOR C: I'd like to begin by asking the witness to provide us with a short synopsis of events beginning I think with the evening you first met Senator Maddox. According to your statement, the meeting took place in a restaurant here in Washington.

EMMA: Yes.

SENATOR C: *(Reading off his copy of her statement.)* You came with the candidate and his party with the intention of meeting the Senator, but you ended up sitting at another table. Is that correct?

EMMA: Yes.

SENATOR C: Why was that?

EMMA: I never was entirely clear about that.

SENATOR A: You came together?

EMMA: Yes. I drove.

SENATOR A: You drove! And then the candidate, who I believe is a friend of yours—

EMMA: Was a friend of mine, yes.

SENATOR A: He asked you to sit at another table?

EMMA: Yes.

SENATOR B: Not very good manners.

(The senators concur.)

SENATOR A: Not good manners? It was downright rude! Didn't that hurt your feelings?

EMMA: Yes, actually it did—

SENATOR A: I should think so! Did he ever apologize?

EMMA: No, in fact, he became angry with me.

SENATOR B: He became angry with you? Why?

EMMA: You know, I never could really figure that out, either.

SENATOR C: Now, wait a minute. I just want to make sure I've got this straight. He completely humiliates you by asking you to sit at another table, and then *he* gets mad at you.

SENATOR A: That takes some nerve! I mean, she *drove*.

SENATOR C: So what did you do?

EMMA: Well, then I tried to suggest we just put it behind us, but he was more and more angry—

SENATOR A: Unbelievable!

EMMA: It just seemed to keep going, no matter what I did—

SENATOR C: It became a point of pride? He decided he was too important to deal with it, and you got left in the dust?

EMMA: I guess.

SENATOR A: I hate it when men do that. You give them a little bit of power, and their manners go right out the widow.

SENATOR B: But he wasn't even elected yet!

SENATOR A: Well, it's a good thing. Can you imagine how insufferable he'd be if he actually got in Congress?

SENATOR B: Oh, my God.

SENATOR A: We've all missed a speeding bullet if you ask me.

EMMA: He's really not that bad.

SENATOR A: Oh, no. Don't defend him. There's no excuse for this kind of nonsense.

EMMA: But the guy he's running against is no saint, either.

SENATOR C: Why? What did he do?

SENATOR A: Did he do this?

(*He bonks Senator B on the head with a gavel. Senator C stands up and pulls his nose. For a brief, hysterical moment, they whack each other crazily and then sit down.*)

SENATOR A: Is that what he did? Because we won't stand for that!

SENATOR B: The idea!

SENATOR C: This is the senate! We insist that people BEHAVE!

(*Senator A bonks him on the head. Senator C glares at him.*)

SENATOR C: Why, I oughta…

(*And they all go at each other again, in a fast, furious slapstick fight.*)

EMMA: Hey! HEY!

(*They all stop and stare at her.*)

EMMA: What are you doing?

SENATOR A: We were just making a point. If your friend wants to be in Congress, that means you have to behave better, not worse, than everyone else.

SENATOR C: Well put.

SENATOR B: I couldn't agree more.

SENATOR C: I have everything I need.

SENATOR A: Same here.

SENATOR B: *(To Emma.)* Thank you for your time. The country needs people as civic-minded as you are.

(They start to exit.)

EMMA: Wait a minute! I mean—don't you want to talk about this prostitution ring?

SENATOR C: What about it?

SENATOR B: I knew *nothing* about it. I just want to make sure everyone knows that.

EMMA: Well, of course you didn't, you moron, it didn't exist! I made it up!

(She stops herself. Pause.)

SENATOR C: What are you trying to tell us, Emma?

EMMA: All right, look. The men I was working for disappointed me greatly. I did feel the need to let people know, and this was a way I thought I could do it. I mean, if I just told my real story, no one would care, petty acts of meanness and cruelty don't seem to make an impression on people anymore. To get anybody's attention, you need a big, vulgar scandal, even though, if you asked me, what actually happened was worse than this stupid story I made up. But no one would understand that, and I was angry, so… I'm sorry. I never meant—

SENATOR C: No need to apologize.

SENATOR B: I couldn't agree more.

SENATOR C: I have everything I need.

SENATOR A: Same here.

SENATOR B: *(To Emma.)* Thank you for your time. The country needs people as civic-minded as you are.

(They exit. Sheila enters.)

SHEILA: Emma! You're on in five minutes.

(Emma turns, confused.)

EMMA: Oh, I'm sorry—I'm just so confused about all of this—

SHEILA: Now, what I'd tell you about confusion!

EMMA: Oh—I don't know…

SHEILA: The world wants to hear from you! All those people out there! Someone real's gotta tell the truth! ! Normal people are sick of this shit! The truth will set you free! Hallelujah! Praise Jesus! *(She starts to sing in tongues.)*

EMMA: Sheila?

SHEILA: *(Fast switch back to reality.)* Emma. Just tell the truth.

(She goes. Emma looks at the audience.)

SENATOR C: *(Voice over.)* WHY DON'T YOU TELL US WHAT HAPPENED THAT NIGHT?

EMMA: I was introduced to Senator Maddox. He seemed interested in me. It was suggested that I should be nice to him because it might help Arthur's campaign. *(Beat.)* That is what I did.

(The lights change. The senators leave. Emma sits alone on stage. Lance enters.)

LANCE: Hey. How you doing?

EMMA: Oh. Lance. Hi.

LANCE: I thought it went good. The hearing.

EMMA: Yeah, it went fine.

LANCE: I mean, you seemed a little nervous at first.

EMMA: Did I?

LANCE: But you looked fabulous.

EMMA: Thanks.

LANCE: Richard really thought it went well. And I thought—to tell you the truth, I think you're the bravest person I've ever met.

EMMA: Oh. No.

LANCE: To stand there and admit to the whole country what you've done wrong—

EMMA: Yeah, well—

LANCE: And then to do whatever you have to, to set it right, no matter what the cost—

EMMA: It's really not what you think, Lance.

LANCE: It's meant a lot to me. I've learned a lot from you.

(Pause. Emma sighs.)

LANCE: I'm sorry I took your head off the other day.

EMMA: It's okay. I shouldn't have said anything.

LANCE: No. You were right. *(Pause.)* When you said, that you thought I was— that way. You were right.

EMMA: *(Beat.)* I was.

LANCE: I've tried to fight it. I've prayed a lot. I see a counselor. But I just don't seem to be able to overcome it.

EMMA: Well, Lance, maybe that's because there's really nothing wrong with it. Have you thought about that?

LANCE: That's what the devil would like me to believe.

EMMA: Oh. The devil.

LANCE: Anyway. You don't need to hear about my problems. I just wanted you to know. You were so brave about admitting your sins. I thought I should do the same.

EMMA: Lance, you're fine—

(Richard enters.)

RICHARD: You were wonderful, Emma! Your testimony means a great deal, not just to us, but to the entire country.

LANCE: I was just telling her.

RICHARD: Lance, do you think that tomorrow we could go for a slightly more sophisticated look? I think we've erred too much on the side of caution. She looked like a perverse school girl out there.

LANCE: Maybe a blazer—

RICHARD: And lose the headband. Emma, we've made some revisions in your testimony. We came up with some evidence that implicates the first lady, and it would be good if you could lay some groundwork for that. *(He hands her pages.)*

EMMA: No, no, no. I'm not doing this anymore. This is bullshit. I'm not going back there. I'm not testifying anymore. *(There is a terrible, awkward pause at this.)*

RICHARD: I think you are. Lance, I'd like to speak with Emma alone, please.

LANCE: I'll be praying for you, Emma. *(Lance exits.)*

EMMA: You know, this whole thing is a lie. You know I made it up. Don't you?

RICHARD: Of course.

EMMA: And that doesn't matter to you.

RICHARD: Not one bit. Sit down, Emma.

EMMA: I'm not doing what you tell me anymore, Richard. You're a bunch of fucking hypocrites, couching all this bile and hate in terms of righteousness—

(Beat.)

RICHARD: Now, I'm not going to have a conversation with you about hypocrisy, Emma. With all due respect, you could teach a class. I said, sit down. *(She does.)*

RICHARD: I mean, what do you think this is? What do you think is going on here? Do you honestly think you can just do whatever you want and there will be no consequences? For God's sake, we could take your child from you. We could send you to jail. And if you cross me, we'll do it. Do you understand that?

EMMA: *(Beat.)* You can't take my baby.

RICHARD: Well, it's wonderful to hear that that concerns you. I wasn't sure. So, you want this baby. You care about this baby.

EMMA: Yes.

RICHARD: Then you listen to me. You've perpetrated a fraud on the entire nation! You've tried to interfere with the workings of the senate! You're clearly mentally unstable. So if we want that kid, we're not going to have any trouble getting it. And then we're going to give it to some nice, Christian family to raise. Am I getting through to you? *(Pause.)* Look. There's no need to throw threats at each other. You came here because you belonged here. You didn't like the way people were behaving, so you decided to punish them. No one held a gun to your head. You did it because it made sense to you. You're just like us. You understand right-eousness, and anger, and retribution. You understand the human condition. So stop whining, and play by the rules. Don't ever talk back to me again.
(He goes. Beat.)

EMMA: *(To audience.)* All right. I admit it. I've made some mistakes. But, you know, I didn't start this. You saw what happened. You were with me every step of the way. And it all made sense to you, I mean, I didn't hear anyone trying to stop me, now did I? YOU'RE IN THIS EVERY BIT AS DEEP AS I AM. I'm sorry. Once again, it seems that I am in need of a little per-spective.
(Marjorie enters as the stage changes into a bar. A drunk sits at another table.)

EMMA: *(To Marjorie, ranting.)* It was, somebody said this, I remember, but I can't remember who, said this thing about culture and objectivity, that when a culture values objectivity and, you know, *reason,* then that's good, because that means we're all in this together, we're trying to find this col-lective objective *thing,* right? But that doesn't always happen, sometimes whole cultures, whole, like, America, slide toward subjectivity, everything is me me me, and then, all hell breaks loose, no one is talking to each other anymore, it's like we've all got these reflector sunglasses on only the reflector part is on the inside, so we just keep looking at ourselves until we're completely blind and then there's nothing holding us together any-more, and I didn't mean to do it, but I got angry, and I thought anger was a good thing, because it helps you fight for change, but it's also dangerous because it's so sub*jec*tive, you think you're helping the world, and you're the problem, that's just it, isn't it, the lesson is, there's nothing you can do. I'm sorry. I've just, I've done terrible things and I don't know how to set it right.

(She drinks. Marjorie smiles at her, happy.)

MARJORIE: Hey, I saw you on TV today.

EMMA: What?

MARJORIE: I thought you looked great. That dress you had on was adorable. That's a good look for you. Kind of young.

EMMA: Marjorie—

MARJORIE: Oh, come on, cheer up! I mean, this is very exciting. They were talking about you on the news, too. And I was like, wow. I know her.

EMMA: What were they saying?

MARJORIE: Oh, you know. I don't know. But you should be having a great time. Everyone is paying all this attention to you. You get to meet all these famous people.

EMMA: I'm in the middle of a terrible scandal.

MARJORIE: Yeah, but you're on TV! I mean, this stuff doesn't happen every day. I think you should enjoy it, is all I'm saying.

EMMA: Well, you're in a good mood.

MARJORIE: Oh, yeah. I feel great. I'm on Prozac, did I tell you?

EMMA: No, actually, you didn't.

MARJORIE: Oh, yeah. I love it. You should try it. I mean, with all due respect, Emma, you're getting a little negative these days.

EMMA: I realize that. I was counting on you to be negative too. That's sort of why I called you.

MARJORIE: Well, yeah, but I'm on drugs now.

EMMA: So you said.

MARJORIE: OK. I love you.

EMMA: *(Sour.)* I love you, too.

(Marjorie goes. The drunk at the next table calls at her as she leaves.)

E.T. BLACK: Hey! Do you know who I am?

MARJORIE: Oh, of course! Hi! How's it going?

E.T. BLACK: You know me?

MARJORIE: Oh! No. I thought you were someone else. I'm sorry. *(She smiles and goes.)*

E.T. BLACK: *(To his drink.)* Well, fuck you, I don't know who you are, either. *(He drinks. After a pause, Emma calls from her table.)*

EMMA: Hey, E.T.

E.T. BLACK: What?

EMMA: I know who you are.

E.T. BLACK: You do?

EMMA: You're E.T. Black. You're a famous screenwriter.

E.T. BLACK: You know who I am? Wait a minute. You know who I am? *(The drunk stares at her, stands and slowly staggers over to her table.)*

EMMA: Yeah, you're E.T. Black. I met you here a couple months ago.

E.T. BLACK: Fuck. Did I sleep with you?

EMMA: No.

E.T. BLACK: I can't remember anything anymore… Wait a minute. I know who you are.

EMMA: Yeah, we met a couple months ago.

E.T. BLACK: You're the girl from the senate hearings. Not Anita Hill, the other one. With the weird story. I know all about you.

EMMA: *(Cold.)* Good.

E.T. BLACK: Yeah, Hollywood is all over you. You got everything—sex, money, politics, a good part for a woman. They want me to write a movie about you.

EMMA: They do?

E.T. BLACK: Nobody's called you yet? Well, isn't that a fucking kick. They're pitching your story to me, and they don't even own the rights. Assholes. Listen, when they come after you, first thing they're gonna do is try and rob you blind. Don't be stupid. Hire a lawyer and hold out for seven figures.

EMMA: Thanks for the tip.

E.T. BLACK: Yeah, like you need to be warned about how the world works.

EMMA: And you'll write the screenplay?

E.T. BLACK: Oh, fuck, no. I passed. I'm not getting involved with this. I mean, with all due respect, sweetheart, that story you told is a complete whopper.

EMMA: *(Beat.)* Is that so?

E.T. BLACK: Oh, come on. I may be a drunk, but I'm still a writer. I can tell when something's made up.

EMMA: I don't know what you're talking about.

E.T. BLACK: Yeah, of course you have to take that position. And most of them will fall for it. I said to these guys, these producers, she's *lying,* and they all stared at me like I was insane, of course, they all tell so many lies per second they can't tell the difference anymore, but what am I supposed to do? You can't fictionalize a piece of fiction, where would that fucking put you? You keep building on something fake and the next thing you know, you got just some psychic no man's land, the American government, or Hollywood, some weird fucking place where nothing has to make sense anymore, it just has to move or make money. Everyone keeps acting like two lies make a fucking truth, when that isn't exactly how it works, hasn't that *occurred* to anybody? How long do they expect me to go along with this? That's all I'm saying! I'm E.T. Black, I'm a *writer*, for God's sake, if this were the nineteenth century I'd be having lunch with *Disraeli* and these guys just keep paying me to lie, but there are limits, all right? There are fucking limits!

EMMA: You won't write my story.

E.T. BLACK: No I will not.

EMMA: Because you have too much integrity. Is that what you're saying?

E.T. BLACK: Sweetie, it shows up at the oddest times. *(He stands to go.)*

EMMA: I just put a spin on things. Everybody does it.

E.T. BLACK: Yeah. That's the first one you tell yourself. You know—you're gonna have a kid. You should be thinking about these things.

EMMA: Oh, I am.

E.T. BLACK: And you shouldn't be drinking. It's not good for the baby.

DAVID: It's apple juice.

E.T. BLACK: Well, that's good. Don't start drinking, okay? It doesn't help. You think it does, but it doesn't.

EMMA: Thanks for the tip.

(He goes.)

EMMA: *(To audience.)* So, it turns out I have less integrity than a Hollywood screenwriter.

DAVID: Hey, are you E.T. Black?

E.T. BLACK: You know I am. I drink in here all the time.

DAVID: I love your work, man.

E.T. BLACK: You're just saying that.

DAVID: No, I'm not. You're the best writer in America.

E.T. BLACK: Really?.

DAVID: Ever since you started drinking in here, I went out and rented all your movies. You're a fucking genius, man.

E.T. BLACK: You watched my movies?

DAVID: Yeah. Look, I got this killer idea for a screenplay. Takes place in Washington. All these white people are just like they're fucking nuts, okay, and there's this brother who sees everything, he's around all the time but nobody figures out that he's watching, and going, man, the country is fucked up, people suffering and dying on the street, children with guns, it's like a war out there, and none of these fuckers see any of it, they're totally lost in this nonreality and it's like Anacostia or South East, different country man, they could give a shit, and every night this guy he's out there serving escargot, Puilly Fuisse, and Coque whatever to these people who are talking about taking food out of the mouths of children—like it's good *policy,* it's good *politics.* And he's gotta be polite to these idiots. What do you think that does to somebody's *heart?* What do you *think? (Beat.)* Anyway, this brother, the one watching them, he finally says fuck you, fuck you all, do your own fucking dishes, and then he blows up the White House.

E.T. BLACK: It's been done. *(Beat.)* If you blew up the dome, that would work.

BARTENDER: Yeah, it could be the dome.

E.T. BLACK: Let's talk about this.

(He staggers off with the bartender. Emma calls after them.)

EMMA: But that's not how we started! It's not!

(Arthur enters, hopeful and excited.)

ARTHUR: I don't know. It's such a huge undertaking—

EMMA: Arthur, don't do this to me! It's taken me months to talk you into this, you can't back out now!

ARTHUR: I just think we should be realistic! I don't have a chance of winning—

EMMA: Come on, this is America. All sorts of idiots get elected to Congress. If they can do it, you can too. Arthur! You've been talking about running as long as I've known you, and you're never going to get a better opportunity. I talked to my friend Tommy about you, he's been managing campaigns for a long time, not this high profile, but he knows the ropes. He says you have a shot. At least talk to him. Tommy!

ARTHUR: Tommy? Is this your young man?

EMMA: Sort of.

ARTHUR: "Sort of?"

EMMA: It's still early. But it's going well.

(Tommy enters.)

TOMMY: So, is he going to do it?

EMMA: He's going to do it.

TOMMY: Excellent.

(Emma and Tommy kiss.)

ARTHUR: I didn't say that!

TOMMY: The party's in complete disarray, sir. The old standbys are terrified and well they should be. Everybody's looking for a dark horse. If you want to run, there's never going to be a better time.

ARTHUR: *(Considering.)* And you can help me?

TOMMY: Yes. I can.

EMMA: Come on, Arthur. Wouldn't it be worse not to try? What's the worst that can happen?

(Beat.)

ARTHUR: I'll do it.

EMMA: Yes!

> *(She and Tommy kiss again. There is a brief celebratory moment as they all hug and congratulate each other.)*

ARTHUR: *(To Tommy, joking.)* Now I have to call Natalie and tell her the bad news. *(He heads off. Tommy calls after him.)*

TOMMY: Get her down here! We can use all the help we can get!

> *(He goes. The mood changes. Emma watches him as a bartender crosses, pours him a drink, and hands him the bottle.)*

TOMMY: *(Cool, drinking.)* Hello, Emma.

EMMA: Tommy.

TOMMY: I thought that was you.

EMMA: Hi.

TOMMY: Hi. *(Beat.)* You're looking good.

EMMA: Thanks.

TOMMY: I mean, you look good. You just had a baby, right? I heard you had your baby.

EMMA: Six weeks ago.

TOMMY: Well, you look great.

EMMA: Thank you.

TOMMY: So, what'd you have?

> *(He pours himself a drink. She watches.)*

EMMA: A boy.

TOMMY: Wow. That's great.

EMMA: Yes. It is.

TOMMY: So. Is it mine?

> *(Beat.)*

EMMA: No, actually. "It" is mine.

TOMMY: Yeah, that virgin birth stuff may have worked with your friends over in Christian la la land, but I happen to know better. *(He pours himself another drink.)*

EMMA: You're drinking again.

TOMMY: How very observant of you. Yes. I have, for the moment, fallen off the wagon. It's temporary.

EMMA: It won't solve anything.

TOMMY: What would you know about it?

EMMA: Nothing. It's just, someone told me that.

TOMMY: Drinking doesn't solve anything. There's a news flash. I don't expect it to solve anything. I'm more interested in the way it blots things out.

EMMA: How's Arthur?

TOMMY: A little depressed. Losing kind of does that to you.

EMMA: He'll be fine.

TOMMY: Oh yeah. He was a newcomer; no one expected him to win. In fact, to tell you the truth, most people thought it was pretty impressive that he got as far as he did. A major scandal his first time out. The party boys took note. They want him to try again.

EMMA: Is that right?

TOMMY: *(Nodding.)* Hoping for a liberal backlash. If the religious right hates him so much, he can't be all that bad, something like that. Annabeth thinks he's got a shot. Politicians, every last one of them, they're like this special breed of human beings made out of cork and teflon...

(He reaches for the bottle. Emma tries to stop him.)

EMMA: Come on, Tommy—

(He moves it away from her.)

TOMMY: You could have returned my phone calls.

EMMA: I didn't see the point.

TOMMY: The baby is the point, Emma. The baby is the point.

EMMA: I just told you. It's not your kid.

TOMMY: Yeah, and I'm telling you. You're a big liar. I never thought you were. But then you got up, in front of the whole country and told the most spectacular set of fibs I ever heard. So I wouldn't stand there and act like just because words come out of your mouth we all have to believe them. I want to see the baby.

EMMA: That is not going to happen.

TOMMY: *(Furious.)* I have a right. That is *my* son.

EMMA: *(Warning.)* Tommy.

TOMMY: HE'S MY SON.

EMMA: Listen to me. He is not your son.

TOMMY: You just can't keep lying about this, Emma. Not about this.

EMMA: Like you're so honest. If you were so sure about this, why didn't you say something during the hearings? You had plenty of opportunities. You could have just slid it in between all those stories about how deranged I am.

TOMMY: I wasn't sure then. I'm sure now.

EMMA: That's convenient.

TOMMY: I didn't want to be involved!

EMMA: So, you got your wish.

TOMMY: You can't stop me. I'll demand a court order. I'll get paternity tests.

EMMA: *(Impatient.)* No one is going to grant you parental rights. You come forward now, and everyone's going to think you collaborated in this elaborate fraud waged on the U.S. Senate. Plus you're a big old alcoholic. I'm not afraid of you.

TOMMY: *(Beat.)* You're a cold bitch.

EMMA: Fine.

(She stands to go. Tommy grabs her arm to stop her. There is a very brief struggle. Embarrassed, he lets her go.)

TOMMY: I'm sorry.

(He sits. She watches him.)

TOMMY: I guess none of us are who we thought we were, huh?

EMMA: I guess not.

TOMMY: Emma, please. What happened that one stupid night, it was so small, why can't you just let it go?

EMMA: Look, you're the one who dumped me. Over nothing, over Arthur being a prick about seating arrangements. And now my child has no father. So don't tell me how small that evening was. That evening was not small.

TOMMY: You should have told me about the baby—

EMMA: I tried! But you could barely speak to me, remember? Arthur said to get rid of me, so you did. You didn't think twice. You didn't flinch.

TOMMY: That's not how it was.

EMMA: You couldn't throw me away fast enough.

TOMMY: We all made mistakes.

EMMA: Forget it. I got one good thing out of this whole mess, and I'm not going to screw it up. None of you people are coming near that kid. He is not your kid.

TOMMY: You can't keep away the whole human race.

EMMA: There are good people somewhere. I'll find them.

TOMMY: You thought Arthur was good. You thought you were good. *(Beat.)* Please. Let me see the baby.

EMMA: No.

TOMMY: You can't protect him.

EMMA: I have to go. *(She goes.)*

TOMMY: YOU CAN'T PROTECT HIM!

(He slumps in his chair. Emma looks at the audience.)

EMMA: You should see my boy. He's quite beautiful; he is, in fact, the most beautiful thing I've ever seen. My doctor tells me that the reason babies are so adorable is that if they weren't, we'd leave them by the side of the road. Which, I think, says more about us than it does about them. So how do you raise a child in a world that has people in it? How can I teach him to be good when I know that goodness will not protect him? I don't actually want to raise a little idealist, they turn into the most God-awful cynics. And I don't particularly want to watch his heart break when he learns what people are really like. But I look at him, and he is so clearly good, I don't know if I can bear to teach him anything else.

ANNABETH: Now, how do you want to do the seating, Arthur? Four and one?

(Arthur, Annabeth, and Tommy enter, taking their seats. Emma looks over as Arthur considers this.)

ARTHUR: *(Quickly.)* Oh, yes. That's exactly right. Four and one.

EMMA: And yet I fear the anger of the righteous.

ANNABETH: David— *(She waves the waiter on.)* We'll need a table for four, and a table for one.

DAVID: Right this way.

(The waiter starts to move a place setting.)

TOMMY: Wait a minute. There are going to be five of us, aren't there? When the senator gets here—

EMMA: What's that quote about those small unremembered acts of meanness that make up a man's life?

WAITER: Kindness. Small, unremembered acts of kindness.

EMMA: Are you sure?

ANNABETH: We'll set you up at the best single they have.

EMMA: I suppose the best I can do is to teach him to watch carefully. To struggle for objectivity. To believe always that the human spirit can and will transcend its own pettiness.

ANNABETH: David, can we get her the view of the capital dome?

DAVID: Anything for you, Annabeth.

EMMA: So when someone asks him to sit at another table…

ARTHUR: Emma, you understand.

EMMA: He can go peacefully. Whole unto himself, without surrender.

ARTHUR: This is strictly business.

EMMA: *(To Arthur.)* It's all right, Arthur. I prefer it over here.

(David hands her a paperback.)

EMMA: Thanks.

END OF PLAY

Windshook
by Mary Gallagher

FOR CRAIG SLAIGHT

THE AUTHOR

Mary Gallagher's plays, including *Father Dreams, Little Bird, Chocolate Cake, Buddies, Dog Eat Dog, Love Minus, How to Say Good-bye, De Donde?* and *Windshook* have been published by Dramatists Play Service and produced at such theatres as the American Conservatory Theatre, Actors Theatre of Louisville, Hartford Stage Company, the Alley Theatre, the Main Street Theatre the Ensemble Studio Theatre, the Women's Project, HOME, the Provincetown Playhouse and the New York Shakespeare Festival; and in many other countries.

Screenplays include movies for Paramount, MGM, HBO, NBC, Lifetime and Showtime, including *Nobody's Child* (NBC, 1986), cowritten by Ara Watson and directed by Lee Grant (Writers Guild Award, Luminas Award from Women In Film, Emmy for Marlo Thomas); *Bonds of Love* (CBS, 1993), starring Treat Williams, Kelly McGilliss and Hal Holbrook (Best TV Movie of the Year, International Television Festival); and *The Passion of Ayn Rand,* starring Helen Mirren, Peter Fonda, and Eric Stoltz (Showtime and European theatrical distribution), shooting as of January 1998. Gallagher will produce and direct her next film, *Hard-Headed Women,* as an independent feature.

Grants, fellowships, and prizes include the Guggenheim, the Rockefeller, the NEA (two fellowships), the New York Foundation for the Arts, through the Dutchess County Arts Council, the Susan Smith Blackburn Prize, the Rosenthal New Play Prize, and a 1997–8 NEA/TCG Residency Grant to develop a new mask theatre piece at Capital Repertory Theatre in Albany in collaboration with three Hudson Valley companies: GYPSY, MaskWork Unltd. and Compost West. These three small companies, under artistic directors Gallagher, Shelley Wyant and Greta Baker, have previously cocreated two large-cast, site-specific mask-and-music theatre pieces in the Hudson Valley, *Premanjali and the Seven Geese Brothers* (1994) and *Ama.* Their next project is *The Scottish Play,* a mask deconstruction of *Macbeth,* in collaboration with Capital Rep.

Gallagher is a member of the Alumni Coordinating Committee of new Dramatists, where she produces and moderates the series, "You Can Make a Life: Conversations with Playwrights."

HISTORY OF THE PLAY

Windshook was commissioned by the Young Conservatory of the American Conservatory Theatre in San Francisco, where it received two workshop productions, one with students from the Young Conservatory in 1991, and another with professional actors and students in 1996. My love and thanks to Craig Slaight, Director of the Young Conservatory and the New Plays Program, and to Edward Hastings and Carey Perloff, past and present Artistic Directors of ACT, for their faith in the play and commitment to my work.

In the first workshop in 1991, Dad, Mom, and Brooks were played by the same young actors playing younger roles, who put on masks to assume the personalities of the adults. It was directed by Craig Slaight, assisted by Svetlana Litvinenko. The musical direction was by Maureen McKibben. The cast was as follows:

Darlene/Mom	Tyson Sheedy
Ruby	Rainbow Rachel Underhill
Dylan/Dad	Andrew Irons
Rafe	Devon Angus
Julie	Shona Mitchell
Jackie/Brooks	Pavlos Politopoulos
Lance/Dad	Jon Lucchese

By the second workshop, I had done a great deal of rewriting, and we took out the mask convention. The adults were played by professional actors in the company. The young people were played by students in the Adult Training Program and the Young Conservatory. There was no doubling. The cast was as follows:

Darlene	Chelsea Peretti
Mom	Christianne Hauber
Ruby	Katherine Foster
Dylan	Kevin Crook
Rafe	Robert Oliver
Julie	Marcelle Rice
Lance	Michael Smith
Dad	Warren David Keith
Brooks	Michael Fitzpatrick

Over the period of rewriting the play, I did a number of readings at New Dramatists in New York City. As always, my love and thanks to New Dramatists, putting faith in playwrights since 1949.

THE STORY

The play began with an old folk song, one of the Child Ballads, called "The Mill o' Tifty's Annie." But as I wrote it, the story in the play took a different path from the story in the song. "The Mill o' Tifty's Annie" is sung by Jean Redpath on her "Song of the Seals" album. The melody of the song is sung by Ruby in the last scene of the play.

PLACE AND TIME

The language of the play is that of the old families in the Catskill Mountains, only two hours' drive from New York City. This language is as deeply rooted and specific as the language of the African-American inner city. The people who speak it have learned to speak differently at school. But among their own, or when they're making a point, they revert to it.

The time is the present, in summer and fall. Scenes happen in and out of doors in various locations, with few set pieces or props.

The play has no intermission and runs about an hour and forty minutes.

THE MASKS

Windshook was originally commissioned to be played by high school age conservatory students. I decided that the young people were telling the story to the audience and they would put on character masks to play the adults—Mom, Dad, and Brooks—whom they saw as the powerful mythic figures who controlled their lives. So Darlene put on a Mom mask to become Mom, and took it off again to become Darlene again. The actors who played Lance and Dylan took turns playing Dad, depending on who else was in the scene with Dad.

I found that this works very well with a cast of young people. But when there are adult actors cast as the adults, the play becomes more "real" and the relationships more complex. Masks, which convey a heightened sense of reality, are no longer appropriate.

CHARACTERS

DARLENE: 17. Ruby's friend. A good-natured fatalist. Married to Dale, a loser, and mother of a toddler, Ashley. Neither of these are seen.

CEELIE CARROLL (MOM): 40s. A faded beauty, living with disillusionment. But she has a hidden energy, a secret dream.

RUBY CARROLL: 17. The prettiest girl in town, and the stubbornest. Her goal is to get out and keep on going.

DYLAN: 25. A drifter, till he finds a home. Lives on his charm, but he's wearing out.

RAFE: 20. As idealistic and stubborn as death.

JULIE: 20. Loves Rafe desperately, but is determined to have a different life.

LANCE: 20. Rafe's friend and Ruby's sometime boyfriend. Wildly driven, frustrated. A talented dirt-track racer.

MARLIN CARROLL (DAD): 40s. Bright, charming, trapped, angry. A drunk, who still has control most of the time.

EVAN BROOKS: 30. The man with the money who changes everything without thinking of the consequences. Smart, charming, cold.

Windshook

Lights up on Darlene. To the audience.

DARLENE: After it happened, I just couldn't even go over to their house or nothing, not for weeks. I wouldn't even walk past it when I was wheeling Ashley, I'd go around by the back road past the old fire house. It's way out of the way, and we was having heavy rains, that back road was awash, just about…but I just felt so bad…But when I did go see her mom, finally, go by just to see did they need anything or what…her mom said the saddest thing to me. She said, "I was the one who started it all up, Darlene. I seen him on the road, first day he was in town here, and I pointed him out to her. That's where it all begun."

(Lights up on Mom, in old gardening clothes. Her hands are grimy with dirt. She carries a trowel, stands upstage, gazing out toward the house. Ruby enters behind her, in jeans and dirt-caked garden gloves, her hair raked back.)

RUBY: Mom, you want me to spray the tomatoes too?

MOM: 'Course I do, wadaya think? Ruby, look at this boy that's passing.

(Dylan, with a backpack and a bedroll, enters downstage, strolling down the road, looking with interest and pleasure at the countryside.)

MOM: Don't he look like Dirk, who used to be on my soap?

RUBY: *(Looks; impressed, but not showing it.)* Don't look like much to me.

MOM: Choosy, ain't ya?…You don't know him?

RUBY: No.

(Dylan stops, dumps his pack and sits.)

MOM: What's he doing out so far from town?—Oh, look, he's sitting down there by the creek—go on and wander by.

RUBY: *(Laughs.)* Get out!

MOM: Go on! He's cute!

RUBY: He'd know why I was doing it.

MOM: Well, ain't that terrible, for him to know.

RUBY: You go and wander by.

MOM: I'll tell you, if I was your age, I'd be after him.

RUBY: If he's around, I'll meet him soon enough.

MOM: Must be nice to be so cocky.

(Beat; all three women stare at Dylan. Then.)

DARLENE: *(To the audience.)* That's where it all begun.

(Crossfade as Darlene, Mom, Ruby, and Dylan exit. Rafe enters. He speaks to the audience.)

RAFE: I knew what I wanted. Since I was a little kid, I always had that dream. But my dad always said, "You can't eat bread you haven't earned." And ain't no way he'd ever go beyond that, not for me. So I had to earn it, had to show what I could do. Now how it is around here, you get outa high school and there's only two places to go—the army or the prison. And working at the prison, that's good security. Them guards, they got their pensions in their minds first day they walk inside them gates. How I see it, they're lifers, worse'n cons are. I wanted more than that…So I went for the army. Give it two years. If I liked it, I could save my money up. I could make a plan.

(Julie enters, wearing a yellow bow corsage and carrying a small yellow bow. She goes to Rafe, smiling, starts to pin the ribbon on him.)

RAFE: *(To Julie, flatly.)* But the army didn't work for me.

(Very disappointed, Julie pins the ribbon on him anyway, then turns away, but stays near Rafe. The others enter: Ruby, with a cheap folding lawn chair which she places at center; Dad, in jeans and a worn feed cap, with a six-pack of cheap beer; Lance, Rafe's friend and Ruby's sometime boyfriend; Mom, with a yellow bow corsage and a can of Coke, which she gives to Rafe. As the talk continues, Dad hands out beers to everyone but Rafe and then sits in the lawn chair. This is the lawn outside the Carroll house, and Rafe's coming home party. Ruby goes back offstage.)

DAD: Hell, no. You work for the army. That's how *we* did it.

RAFE: I done it too. But I ain't signing up again.

MOM: You'd have a real good life in there. They help their own.

RAFE: That ain't all they do. You make a mistake and three guys rub your nose in it, like you're a dog that shit indoors.

LANCE: But what about the action, man? Did you kick some ass?

RAFE: Hell, no. We just sat and sweated. Or drilled and sweated and passed out. One guy in our outfit died 'cause he was drilling in his gas mask and protective suit, got too hot in there and panicked, had a heart attack.

MOM: But still, you boys went over there and you were ready. People appreciate that.

RAFE: Oh, yeah. Before we even got there, we had packages from strangers waiting for us to come. Boxes full of cookies and candy bars and lollipops, all melted down and beat to shit. And razor blades and toilet paper, like the army hadn't thought of stuff like that. And little gift-type stuff, Pocahontas key chains and Rush Limbaugh coffee mugs. And stuff they made, little knitted stuff…and all these letters from strangers, thanking us and praising us…

DAD: When we was in Viet Nam, we didn't get no letters. Nobody gave a damn.

RAFE: The worst part was just sitting. You go over there all rared up to show what you can do…and then you gotta sit on it…

DAD: Yeah, you do. Like hunting. Main thing you gotta do is wait. I taught you that.

RAFE: You did. But waiting for the deer…out in the woods, all by yourself…it ain't the same as waiting with a thousand other guys. We took it out on each other some.

DAD: Sure you did. It's human. Sure.

RAFE: Then come to find out, we was going home. And we hadn't done nothing.

DAD: Well, I'll just say one thing and then I'll shut up. When we was in Viet Nam, we knew why we was there and we knew what to do about it. And when we come home, we didn't sit around and cry-baby.

RAFE: …I ain't saying nothing against having a job to do.

DAD: Oh, well, good, that eases my mind. Where's that girl got to?
(Dad drinks his beer as Ruby enters with an open fifth of whiskey and a shot glass, comes to Dad.)

MOM: *(To Rafe.)* Did you see all them little yellow bows along the fence? Julie and me did that. Took the best part of the afternoon.

RAFE: Looks nice, Mom.

DAD: *(Hits Ruby on the butt.)* Just pour that out for your old man.
(Ruby pours the shot and Dad takes it as Mom says to Rafe.)

MOM: Julie come around to see me quite a bit while you was gone. She helped me out more than your sister. With the garden and the farmstand too.

DAD: *(A toast.)* Here's hoping all you good people live forever and I sit right beside ya.
(They all drink. Dad slaps his knee.)

DAD: Come on, Rube, sit with your old man once before you get too big.

RUBY: *(Sits on his lap.)* I'm too big already.

DAD: Oh, you ain't too big to spank.

LANCE: I'll spank her for you.
(Ruby ignores this.)

DAD: I wouldn't put money on ya. *(Laughs, slaps Lance's back. To Ruby.)* Don't be so stingy with that bottle, Rube.

(Ruby pours him a shot.)

LANCE: *(To Rafe.)* Hey, you want to go up to hunting camp on Sunday, shoot a mess of turkeys? I been cleaning house up there.

RAFE: *(Looks at Julie.)* Maybe. Hafta see.

(Dad gives Lance the shot. Lance drains it.)

JULIE: *(To Rafe.)* My stepdad says they need people up to the prison.

RAFE: You know I ain't doing that.

DAD: *(To Lance.)* How's that now? Is that smooth?

JULIE: It ain't like you know the prisoners. They're all from the city. My stepdad says they're animals, some of 'em.

RAFE: They're men. And keeping other men locked up—I can't see my way to living my whole life like that.

JULIE: …Well, what *are* you gonna do?

RUBY: *(Takes the shot glass from Lance.)* My turn.

DAD: Listen to this, now…you will, will ya?

RUBY: Can I?

DAD: *(Proud of her.)* Aw hell, just don't say who give it to ya.

(Ruby holds the glass as Dad pours.)

MOM: Marlin, she's too young for that.

(Dad and Ruby ignore her. Feeling the old wound of her exclusion, Mom watches.)

RAFE: *(To Julie.)* What you been doing since I left?

JULIE: *(Letting him wonder.)* Not too much.

RAFE: How much is too much?

(Julie has to smile. Rafe smiles back: contact.)

DAD: Watch this here, now.

(Everyone looks as Ruby nonchalantly drains the shot. Dad and Lance laugh.)

DAD: Now where d'ya think she gets that from?

MOM: And where's it gonna take her?

DAD: *(Gives Mom a cool glance, then.)* Yes, dear. *(To the others.)* My uncle Percy always told me, "Only two words a married man's gotta know—'Yes, dear.' Keep saying 'em, you'll be all right."

RAFE: Uncle Percy had three wives. Kept leaving 'em. Has seven kids in three states and he never sees 'em.

(Brief pause.)

RUBY: He musta kept saying, 'Yes, dear,' right up till he left.

(Dad laughs. Relieved laughter from all but Rafe—he's partly relieved, partly disappointed. Dad abruptly shoves Ruby off his knee. Indicating Rafe.)

DAD: This one's left the army. Guess he's got a better idea how to make a living around here than the rest of us.

RAFE: No. But I know what I want.

MOM: You hear that, Ruby? Somebody around here knows. Ruby don't know *what* she wants, she just knows she ain't got it.

RUBY: *(Coolly.)* I'll know when I see it.

DAD: That's my girl.

RAFE: *(Plowing on.)* And now I got a plan.

DAD: Holy Jesus, Rafe, how'd I know it was you if you didn't have a plan?
(Laughter, sympathetic to Rafe but giving Dad what he wants.)

RAFE: I want to get Granddad's farm going again. I thought it through this time. I got a little money saved, and I'm a veteran, I can get a loan and give you a down payment on the land and the old farmhouse—and I'm gonna buy a team of draft horses and use 'em to farm, and do farmwork for other folks, haul timber and plow and do their haying—

DAD: We work with machines around here—

RAFE: Week ends and summers, I'll give hayrides, and teach kids about the old times. And I'll do odd jobs too, work up to the lumberyard, deliver stuff, whatever needs doing to bring a little money in—

DAD: Aw hell, why don't you make barrel hoops and sell 'em from a wagon?— that's the way you're talking.

RAFE: It ain't just me—you oughta read *The Small Farmer's Journal.* There are folks all over the country who've gone back to farming the old way—

DAD: Yeah, and they all got their heads up their asses. They think chickens are cute, 'cause they never had to get to know no chickens, and find out they're the dumbest, meanest critters out in nature. There ain't one of them fools that grew up on a farm like I did, where you had to get up every goddamn morning of your life before it was even light, to milk them goddamn cows—and if I overslept, my dad just come and threw me out of bed, and he was right to do it—'cause winter, summer, Sundays, Christmas, it wasn't no different, it was the same chores to be done. And you had more chores *off* the farm—'cause even if your whole family worked till your guts ached, you couldn't make your ends meet unless you had a couple of you working off the farm. You grow up on a farm, you got no *ro*-mance about farming. You shoulda stuck it out in the army, boy.

RAFE: Sell me the farm.

DAD: I told you to quit thinking of that years ago.

JULIE: *(Defiantly speaking up.)* He sold it off, Rafe.

(*Silence. Rafe looks at his father, who won't look at him, takes another shot.*)

RAFE: You sold off Granddad's farm while I was in the army?

JULIE: The house too. All of it.

DAD: *(To Julie.)* When did you join this family? *(To Rafe.)* I don't answer to you, boy. But I'll tell you this—all my life, I never had two nickels to rub together, no more'n my dad did, till I give up on farming. When I went to work for the propane company, that's when we started paying bills regular around here. Aw hell, ain't nobody even offered to farm that land in twenty years—

RAFE: I offered! You knew I always wanted it—

DAD: Ruby, talk some sense into your brother—

RAFE: Who'd you sell it to?

(*Dad makes a disgusted gesture, starts to exit with the whiskey bottle.*)

RAFE: *Who was it?*

DAD: I'm going to bed. Some of us gotta work tomorrow.

(*Dad exits. Rafe looks at Mom. She's helpless, torn.*)

RAFE: All my life…

JULIE: I know.

MOM: I know. But your dad…he sees it different…

RAFE: You coulda talked to him—

MOM: I talked to him—

RAFE: You coulda written me about it—

MOM: It wouldn'ta helped none. *(Beat.)* Rafe…that old-style farming, I always liked your idea of that. But when it comes to push and shove…

LANCE: Yeah, pretty tough row to hoe, Rafe—

RAFE: Nobody believed me.

JULIE: I believed you. *(Under his gaze, she weakens.)* I mean…I knew you always really wanted it…

RAFE: Did you think I could *do* it?

JULIE: *(Weaker.)* …If your dad woulda let you.

(*Rafe turns away. Mom gives up, exits, leaving Rafe with Julie, Ruby, and Lance.*)

RUBY: It's a guy from the city. Evan Brooks, his name is. Not too old either—maybe thirty. Kinda good-looking, in a way.

LANCE: Oh, yeah?

(*Lance tries to drop an arm on Ruby's shoulder. She shrugs it off, goes on.*)

RUBY: I only seen him twice, he hardly ever comes up here. Don't know why he bought it. *(Beat.)* You gonna do something?

RAFE: I ain't gonna let it go.

RUBY: You better be careful, Rafe.

RAFE: You against me too?

RUBY: No, I don't care. But I'm just saying… Dad could still hurt you if he wanted to—

RAFE: Not no more, he can't.

(*Crossfade as they exit, Rafe in one direction, the others in another. Mom re-enters, stands by the empty lawn chair, addresses the audience.*)

MOM: He talks like he hates farming, but you notice we still got the biggest garden on the road, with the farmstand out front, where we sell off what we don't eat or put up for the winter. The garden and the stand, that's my work, mostly—and Ruby, when I can catch ahold of her—but he acts like he hates all that. Every fall he says, "Aw, hell, let's not even plow up the field next year." But then come spring, he says, "Aw, hell, might's well put something in the ground." See, he can change his mind. If that Brooks from the city hadn't made his offer when he did, right after the tax bill come…or if Marlin hadn't heard about the Harrises up in the vly* selling off their pastureland for fifty thousand dollars… (*Brief pause.*) But see, Rafe wanted him to keep the land for *Rafe*…to have that be his reason. And he never woulda done that. He don't see life that way. Life is hard. Mostly you don't get what you want. But you take it and you keep your mouth shut and you do the best you can. Mostly he's been a good husband to me. And when he ain't…mostly I don't hold them times against him. (*Hesitates, then.*) But one time comes back up on me. I was sick, and the kids was sick, and it was hard winter. Marlin was out there following the county snowplows fourteen hours a day, trying to get the propane up to the folks who needed it, and coming home when he could and taking care of us. He didn't say nothing about it, that ain't his way. But one night when he finally laid down to sleep, the cat was sick right there under our bed. And Marlin, he got right up and cleaned up the cat-sick, and then he got dressed again. He took that cat, Alice her name was, and he drove off with her into the snow. When he come back, he didn't have no cat. (*Brief pause.*) I didn't say nothing…I could see how he come to do it…but she was *my* cat. (*Beat.*) If she'da been Rafe's cat, it woulda been the same. Now, Ruby's cat, I don't believe he woulda done that way.

(*Crossfade. Dylan enters, shirt off, pushing a wheelbarrow of fireplace wood. Mom watches him for a moment; drops her gaze to Dad's chair. She folds the chair and takes it as she exits. Ruby enters with a big shoulder bag, walking*)

*"Vly" (rhymes with fly) is an old usage for "valley."

along the road downstage of Dylan. The farmhouse would be upstage; the meadow is in the audience. Ruby keeps sauntering till indicated. Dylan sees her.)

DYLAN: Hey.

RUBY: *(Glances.)* Hey.

DYLAN: Hey, hold on a minute.

RUBY: Why?

DYLAN: Why not?

RUBY: Gotta go to work.

DYLAN: Where?

RUBY: *(Smiling.)* Why?

DYLAN: *(Smiling.)* Why not?

(Ruby has passed him. Now she turns, whisks a McDonald's cap out of her bag, puts it on her head, walking backward.)

DYLAN: McDonald's? That's way out in Lindaville.

RUBY: I know it is. I gotta catch my ride.

DYLAN: I've got a truck, I'll take you.

(Ruby stops walking at last, considers this.)

RUBY: You're not from around here.

DYLAN: Nope. Caretaking this place for the guy who owns it. He can vouch for me.

RUBY: He ain't around much.

DYLAN: *(Grins.)* No, it works out great.

(Ruby smiles back, but still considers. Dylan continues, low-key, charming.)

DYLAN: Beautiful land, isn't it? Especially this meadow across the road. You just picture horses in it. And this old house is pretty beat-up, but it's got style. I'll be sorry if he tears it down.

RUBY: *(Thrown by that idea.)* …My granddad was born in it.

DYLAN: *(Even more intrigued.)* …I'll go get my truck.

(Ruby watches him exit. Crossfade as Darlene enters with a grocery bag. She and Ruby take their McDonald's uniforms out of their bags and put them on as they talk. They're in the restroom.)

DARLENE: Where'd you go last night? I thought you was coming out to the dirt track.

RUBY: Didn't feel like it.

DARLENE: Lance was looking for you. He looked good too, got his ear pierced in three places! Had little gold rings in, he looked so cool.

RUBY: *(Amused.)* That ain't gonna go over too good at the lumberyard.

DARLENE: Lisa was hanging on him, I'm serious. He won all his races too.

RUBY: *(Dismissive gesture like her father's.)* Aw hell, he always wins the quarter-mile, since he was twelve or something. Why don't he move up to the half-mile and go for it?

DARLENE: Why do you give him such a bad time? I wish Dale ever treated me half as nice as Lance treats you.

RUBY: I wouldn't take the shit you take from Dale, Darlene. And you don't have to either.

DARLENE: Well…I got Ashley to think of now…

RUBY: You always took shit from him.

DARLENE: …He don't mean it…

RUBY: What *does* he mean?

DARLENE: He don't mean nothing. You know Dale. He don't think that much.

RUBY: One of these days, he's gonna run you down in the V.I.P Lounge parking lot in that stupid high-wheeler he went and bought.

DARLENE: Well, see there, aren't you lucky, how nice Lance is to you? Lance'd do anything for you, if you'd just not spit on him.

RUBY: He likes it when I spit on him.

DARLENE: Do you want Lance or not?

(Beat; Ruby starts playing with Darlene's hair, twisting it around various ways as they look into an invisible mirror. Darlene lights a cigarette.)

RUBY: You ever read the wedding announcements in the *Banner?*

DARLENE: You know we don't take a paper regular—

RUBY: *(Affectionate.)* Yeah, you only read the *Star.*

DARLENE: Hey, when I buy the *Star,* you read the whole thing—

RUBY: Yeah, but you believe it.

DARLENE: Well, it's right there in black and white, why wouldn't it be true?

RUBY: Darlene…

DARLENE: Well, I spose you don't believe the wedding announcements either.

RUBY: I believe 'em. That's what's wrong with 'em. "The bride is a medical receptionist. The bridegroom is a shipping clerk at Sears. After a honeymoon in Florida, they are living in Lindaville."

DARLENE: I wish Dale was a shipping clerk at Sears.

RUBY: "The bridegroom is a plumber's assistant. The bride is a clerk at the Crawley Laundromat. After a honeymoon in the Poconos, they are living in Crawley."

DARLENE: I bet I'll never in my whole life see the Poconos.

RUBY: You're missing the point, Darlene! Is that all they're gonna get? Prob'ly get pregnant on their stupid boring honeymoon, if they ain't already, and forever after they'll be "living in Crawley"! Don't that depress you?

DARLENE: Yeah, they depress me 'cause they're so much better off than me.

RUBY: I give up.

DARLENE: You're just spoiled is all.

> *(Ruby looks at her in the mirror. Darlene nods wisely. Ruby slowly smiles.)*

RUBY: ...Maybe.

DARLENE: Are you seeing somebody besides Lance?

RUBY: I ain't seeing Lance.

DARLENE: *Are* you?

> *(Beat; Ruby drops Darlene's hair, picks up her shoulder bag. Darlene ponytails her hair.)*

RUBY: ...I don't know what I'm doing yet...

DARLENE: Well, you seem all wired up to me.

RUBY: That's 'cause everyone around here is dead, and I'm alive.

> *(Ruby exits with her bag. Darlene grabs her bag and follows Ruby out. Crossfade to Rafe at a workbench, trying to rebuild the carburetor of an old pick-up truck, using small wrenches and screwdrivers to replace the jets— painstaking, greasy work. Dad enters with a sack lunch and thermos, stops a short distance from Rafe.)*

DAD: What are you doing there?

RAFE: Gonna get that truck going.

DAD: Well, I hope Jesus Christ and Moses and all the twelve apostles is gonna come down and piss on that truck, 'cause that's what it'll take to get her going again.

RAFE: *(Eyes on his work.)* I'll get her going.

> *(Dad makes his disgusted gesture, but keeps watching another moment. Then.)*

DAD: Well, you don't give up easy, I'll say that for ya.

> *(No response. Brief pause.)*

RAFE: I'm moving out.

DAD: Good. What kept ya?

RAFE: *(Beat.)* You can still cut me deep, you old son of a bitch.

DAD: *(Regrets his words but can't say so.)* Who you calling old? *(Beat; no response.)* I ain't saying I know how to talk to you or ever did.

RAFE: That's for damn sure.

DAD: Aw, shut up. *(Brief pause.)* I gotta go to work. And you better get your tail out and find yourself a job.

RAFE: I told you what I'm gonna do, I'm gonna get that land back—

DAD: Now just don't talk so goddamn stupid, Rafe. Do what you *can* do in this world, and don't go getting tangled up in fairy stories. *(No response. Approaching the bench, Dad sets down the sack, opens the thermos.)* You want a little pick-me-up?

RAFE: No, thanks.

DAD: There's coffee in it too, for all you know. *(Pours coffee-whiskey mix into the thermos cup, drinks, then.)* I'm gonna give you some of Granddad's land.

RAFE: *(Stunned. Beat; then.)* I thought you sold it all.

DAD: The farmland and the pastureland, I did. But there's all that timberland leading up to hunting camp. Close to fifty acres. I'll give you ten.

RAFE: I couldn't farm that land.

DAD: *(Laughs.)* Hell, no. Your Granddad used to say, "It's so steep back there, you'd have to harness the thunder and lightning to haul 'em up top."

RAFE: What good is it?

DAD: ...It's family land. Build a cabin, where our old hunting cabin used to be...before they burned it down, whoever them bastards was...

RAFE: I'm gonna farm.

DAD: ...He's gonna farm. Well, goodness to mercy, you go right on and do that. You break your back cutting down and hauling trees, and hauling boulders, and clearing out the poison ivy and the nettles and the skunks and snakes...it's your land, you have yourself a time, suffering all over it. *(Starts to exit.)*

RAFE: I ain't gonna farm it. But I'll take it.

(Dad stops, looks at him, maybe hoping for some connection. Rafe regards him stonily.)

DAD: "Never give nothing." That's you, ain't it?

RAFE: It is now.

(Crossfade as Dad and Rafe exit; the bench is cleared. Dylan enters with a spade. He's been digging holes for trees, flops on the ground, sweaty and exhausted. Rafe reenters, wary but drawn.)

RAFE: 'Lo.

DYLAN: ...Hey, how you doing?

RAFE: I see you're planting trees here.

DYLAN: Right. Man, it's a bitch.

RAFE: My family's been clearing this land for a hundred years. Now you're planting trees on it.

DYLAN: Oh, you're Ruby's brother? I'm Dylan. *(Offers his hand. They shake.)* They aren't my idea. The trees. I just work for him.

RAFE: What's he want more trees for?

DYLAN: Sell 'em later. Christmas trees. I think it's a tax thing...I dunno. Like I said—

RAFE: We're sitting in the middle of a forest.

DYLAN: Guess the tax guys don't know that. Or don't care.

RAFE: What else is he gonna do?

DYLAN: Well…he wants to make a pond or something over in the meadow. *(Indicates the meadow area in the house.)*

RAFE: A pond? What for?

DYLAN: *(Shrugs.)* Swim in it?

RAFE: We got swimming holes all around here.

DYLAN: Maybe that's a tax thing too. Or else it'll increase the resale value—

RAFE: Resale?

DYLAN: I'm just guessing. He doesn't tell me stuff like that. But there's a bunch of turtles that hang out in the pond. I don't know what'll happen to them if it goes.

RAFE: Them mud turtles. I seen 'em since I was a kid. *(Brief pause. Abruptly.)* That meadow oughta have horses in it.

DYLAN: That's what I think too. But this guy I work for, Brooks…seems like an okay guy, you know…but he hardly ever comes up here. And when he does, he gets the backhoe itch.

RAFE: Them city guys. They'd move Slide Mountain, put it on the other side of Hightop.

DYLAN: *(Laughs.)* That's it. Me, I like it around here. Like it the way it *is.*

RAFE: *(Warming to Dylan.)* If I had my way, none of the crap that come in since I was a kid'd be here. I'd like to see trees growing up through the Walmart parking lot.

DYLAN: *(Laughs.)* Right…yeah, that'd be great, wouldn't it?

RAFE: I gotta talk to him before he starts bringing them backhoes in…you know Ruby?

DYLAN: …Yeah, uh-huh…

RAFE: *(Looks at him a beat; abruptly.)* See that ridge up there above the stand of pine trees?

DYLAN: …Yeah…

RAFE: That's where I'm living now. You can find me there and let me know when he comes up again.

DYLAN: Okay.

RAFE: I'm gonna buy that meadow back, keep my horses in it.

DYLAN: Great! What kind of horses have you got?

RAFE: Ain't got 'em yet.

DYLAN: Oh.

RAFE: Not yet. But I will.

(Rafe exits, leaving Dylan puzzled and amused. Crossfade to Rafe's camp, night. Rafe and Julie enter, Rafe using a flashlight to lead the way along a path.

He wears a pack. Julie wears a cute outfit and highheeled sandals, carries a tote bag. She's being bitten by mosquitoes and stumbling over rocks and roots.)

JULIE: *(Trips.)* Shit!

RAFE: Well, why'dya want to wear them shoes?

JULIE: How'd *I* know it'd be this rough? There's hardly a trail, even.

RAFE: That's why my dad give me this land. He can't sell it 'cause it's on the back side of a mountain. Nobody in his right mind'd trouble to build on it.

JULIE: *(Rueful.)* But that ain't stopping you.

RAFE: I ain't building here. I'm just squatting, temporary. You know where I'm gonna build.

JULIE: In the meadow.

RAFE: Sure. Well, on the rise…looking down on the meadow. I wanta be able to see that big old rock and them two little branches of the creek from my bedroom window. *(Pause.)* You want something to drink?

JULIE: Okay.

(Julie slaps a mosquito.)

RAFE: Got Coke and 7-Up in the stream there, keeps it nice and cold. Got a watermelon too.

JULIE: You hauled a watermelon up here? *(Looks at him; no response, so:)* How 'bout a beer?

RAFE: Don't keep it around.

JULIE: One beer ain't gonna hurt you, Rafe.

RAFE: You know my dad, you know why I'd rather not get into it.

JULIE: I'll take a Coke. *(Slaps a mosquito.)*

RAFE: Put some of that bug stuff on, it's in my pack.

JULIE: I don't want to smell like that tonight…

RAFE: Okay, get bit.

(Rafe exits. Crossfade. In moonlight, Ruby and Dylan sit on the floor of an otherwise empty attic in the old farmhouse.)

RUBY: Tell me some more about your travels. Like about that old hotel in Mexico with all the birds.

DYLAN: I'm going to run out of stories pretty soon.

RUBY: You better not.

DYLAN: Oh, that's all you're coming around for, huh?

RUBY: *(Looks at him, letting him wonder, then.)* What's your favorite place you've ever been?

DYLAN: *(Beat; saying what she wants to hear.)* The next place.

RUBY: *(Delighted.)* Yeah? Where'll that be?

DYLAN: Won't know till I get there.

RUBY: That's it! That's what *I* want!

DYLAN: Why not?

    (He holds her gaze: a powerful connection. Brief pause. Ruby breaks it, turns away.)

RUBY: Funny, being up here in the attic. I used to play in here when I was little. And my dad talks about it sometimes...how it was when he was growing up in this house, and even what it musta been like way back in the old days, when my great-great-grandparents homesteaded here. They had twenty-two kids in this house. Don't know where they put 'em all...well, a lot of 'em died, though.

DYLAN: Maybe they're still around.

RUBY: Where, here?

DYLAN: Perfect place for 'em. Their old home sold off to a stranger. They're gonna hang around till the one true rightful family is living in the house again.

RUBY: They're gonna get tired of waiting.

DYLAN: Ssshhhhh...you'll get 'em all riled up. *(Leans close, makes ghostlike noises.)*

RUBY: *(Laughs.)* Quit that, you!

DYLAN: Doesn't it bother you?

RUBY: *(Scornfully.)* What, ghosts?

DYLAN: Losing your family's house and land. It sure bothers your brother.

RUBY: ...A little bit, I guess. But my dad's right, land that don't make money is just a stone around your neck. Let somebody else pay the taxes. Anyway, who wants to farm? You can't never get away! My dad says when this whole county was nothing but farmers, and a killing frost was coming, the church bills would ring in the middle of the night, and people would get out of bed and gather all the blankets and clothes in the whole house to cover up the crops, so they wouldn't all die that same night.

DYLAN: ...Wow...that's *real*, you know?

RUBY: But, Dylan! Farmers gotta be around *all the time* for stuff like that! I ain't gonna get stuck like that, nowhere, no how, no way. I'm gonna go everywhere, see everything, like you.

DYLAN: Well, don't leave just yet, okay?

RUBY: Same to you.

    (She holds his gaze, challenging him. Abruptly, she kisses him passionately. Crossfade to Rafe and Julie. Rafe returns with a bottle of Coke and firewood, gives the Coke to Julie.)

RAFE: Gonna make a fire. Keep the bugs off.

JULIE: That'd be nice. *(Slaps a mosquito on her thigh.)*

RAFE: Here, put this on your legs.

> *(He hands her his jacket. She wraps it around her legs. Rafe builds a fire. Julie watches. Brief pause, then.)*

JULIE: I got promoted.

RAFE: Good for you.

JULIE: My boss says I've got a real good future there. Says he's lucky to have me.

RAFE: Smart guy.

JULIE: So I asked him would he pay for me to take some courses at the CC—

RAFE: At the what?

JULIE: The community college.

RAFE: Oh. Right…

JULIE: And he said he would. So in the fall I'm gonna go to school three nights a week. I'm gonna take advanced computer science and French.

RAFE: You're on your way, sounds like.

JULIE: That's right, I am. I don't want to live in a trailer all my life.

RAFE: Your folks done the best they could.

JULIE: People ain't meant to live in trailers, Rafe. Not in America.

RAFE: Well, you're doing what you gotta do for yourself, just like I am. I respect you, you know that.

JULIE: *(Beat.)* I brought you some stuff, here. *(Opens her tote bag.)*

RAFE: *(Teasing.)* Uh-oh. It ain't candy and cookies and razor blades, is it?

JULIE: Shut up. It's food, though. I just thought…you roughing it up here… maybe I'd bring you something special…

> *(Julie spreads a cloth, lays out pretty paper plates, matching napkins, grapes, a little cheese knife, a box of French crackers and two slabs of cheese. Meanwhile.)*

RAFE: This ain't so rough. Had it a whole lot rougher when I hunted with my dad. Up here, I got a latrine, even. Dug it myself. Only thing they taught me in the army that come in handy. Had to dig it twice, though. Spent all day digging an eight-foot hole and then I didn't cover it and it rained all night. Filled up the whole damn hole in one damn night. Had to dig another one just to get even.

> *(As Julie laughs.)*

RAFE: Now don't you never tell that story on me. If my dad come to hear about it, he'd tell it on me every day till the day he died.

> *(Rafe kneels to light the fire: Lighting effect. He looks at the food, picks up the cracker box.)*

RAFE: What're they getting at here?

JULIE: It's in French. They're French crackers.

RAFE: …Uh-huh… *(Picks up a slab of brie.)*

JULIE: That's French cheese too. Brie, that one is. It's real good.

RAFE: Looks pretty well cooked down, here, Julie.

JULIE: That's how it's supposed to be. "Runny," that's the way they like it.

RAFE: …Well, at least it ain't presliced in them little envelopes.

JULIE: This is the classy stuff! I would've brought some wine, they always have wine with their meals in France, but I figured you wouldn't drink it.

RAFE: You figured right. Where'd you get wine anyway? You ain't twenty-one.

JULIE: …I can get it when I want to.

RAFE: From your boss, or who? *(No response. Picking up the other cheese.)* This one must be a reject—it ain't runny.

JULIE: It ain't the runny type—it's chevre.

RAFE: "Shevrah?"… *(Opens the wrapper to sniff the cheese.)* What's that mean?

JULIE: *(Reluctantly.)* …Goat cheese—but it's good, go on and try it—

RAFE: *(Laughs.)* Goat cheese! Hell, my grandma used to make that stuff and us kids wouldn't eat it. We played with them goats, we knew 'em. They'd eat anything from poison ivy to chicken shit—

JULIE: Well, fine! You can spend the rest of your life living in a tent and eating Ritz Crackers!

RAFE: Nothing wrong with Ritz Crackers. Charlton Heston eats 'em. You're the one who told me that—

JULIE: Well, I can't live my life on 'em! I gotta go to work in an office every day, and I gotta look my best! I gotta wear nice stockings that don't have ladders in 'em, not to mention twigs and burrs, and I gotta shower and shampoo my hair every day and mousse it and blow-dry it and put my makeup on—

RAFE: All for this boss of yours? Lotta trouble, seems to me—

JULIE: It's for him and me and everyone who's living out there in the world—it's how we live now, Rafe! And I can't do all the stuff I gotta do to get ahead, if I hafta live in a tent and piss in a latrine and hike a two-mile trail just to get to my car, can I?

RAFE: Who asked you to?

(Julie starts to cry. Shocked, Rafe doesn't know what to do. Awkwardly, touching her.)

RAFE: …Julie, I'm just teasing you…

JULIE: …I thought…I thought you…

RAFE: …What?

JULIE: You know!…I thought you wanted me around.

RAFE: …I do…

JULIE: ...All the time, I mean...

RAFE: ...Well...I got things to do, I got a hard row to hoe, and—

JULIE: You're *making* it a hard row! You don't have to do all this—you could do *anything!* Rafe, all's we gotta do is get on the same road together. We can have a real good life—'cause the opportunities are out there, I just know it! *(Rafe can't answer—he doesn't want the life she wants. He keeps stroking her back. She quiets, knowing argument is futile, but she's deeply unhappy. Still stroking her back.)*

RAFE: D'I tell you I bought a team of draft horses?

JULIE: ...You told me. *(Beat.)* I shouldn'ta waited for you.

RAFE: Don't say that. I'm glad you waited.

(Gently, he embraces her, kisses her. She responds. Crossfade to the porch of the old farmhouse: a couple of wicker chairs, a small table, a screen door leading off into the house. Evan Brooks enters the porch, arriving from the city, with an expensive briefcase and a paper deli bag. Dylan hurries out to meet him, flustered, striving for his usual easy charm.)

DYLAN: Hi, Mr. Brooks, good to see you—

BROOKS: Hey, Dylan, I see you got those trees in.

DYLAN: Yeah, they look real nice too. Can I help you, have you got some other stuff—?

BROOKS: Nah, this is it, I'm just here overnight. Got a van coming up with some furniture tomorrow. Can you be around for that?

DYLAN: Oh sure, no problem.

(Brooks sets the deli bag on a small table and the briefcase on the floor.)

BROOKS: Great. You know, we never talked about your hours when I'm up here.

DYLAN: Oh, well...fine, whatever...

BROOKS: *(Taking a wrapped sandwich out of the bag.)* Well, usually I'd say you can take off most of the time I'm here, go visit friends, stay all night, have fun...I'd like the privacy too, frankly...

DYLAN: *(Uneasy: where would he go?)* ...oh...oh, sure...

BROOKS: ...but this van is coming pretty early in the morning. *(Sees his sandwich is shedding.)* Oops, I'm making kind of a mess, here...

DYLAN: You want a plate or something? And napkins? I could—

BROOKS: No, I'll get it—I think I left some beer here too—

(Brooks starts for the screen door. Dylan gets in his path, eager to intercept him.)

DYLAN: Yeah, you did—no, really, let me get it—I gotta admit, I got a few dishes piled up in there—

(Ruby comes out of the house, looking tousled, like she just got out of bed. She's embarrassed, but has decided to carry it off.)

RUBY: Hi, Mr. Brooks. I'm here too.

BROOKS: *(Amused, impressed with Ruby.)* Oh…oh, okay…hello *(Juggles sandwich, shakes hands with her.)* …Evan Brooks.

RUBY: Ruby Carroll. My dad sold you this house.

BROOKS: I've seen you, but we haven't met. Well, nice to meet you, Ruby.

DYLAN: Ruby wanted to look around the old place—

BROOKS: Sure, sure. Any time.

RUBY: I ain't been inside here in a lot of years. When my granddad got sick, he moved in with us and my dad closed this place up. Glad somebody bought it…maybe even have kids playing in it again.

BROOKS: Not mine. I mean, I'm not married…Well, I'm going to get a beer… Ruby, would you like—?

RUBY: Oh sure.

BROOKS: Dylan…?

DYLAN: Uh, sure, thanks a lot…

(Brooks goes into the house. Dylan and Ruby give each other "Oh my God!" looks, laughing silently.)

DYLAN: *(Whispering.)* I don't believe this! You've got him waiting on you!

RUBY: *(Playfully airy.)* Why don't you believe it?

(Dylan laughs, proud of her, reaches for her. She smiles, evades him teasingly, sits demurely.)

RUBY: *(Playing "casual.")* I coulda combed my hair, I guess…

(Dylan loves this. Brooks comes back out with three expensive imported beers. Dylan quickly takes two of them and hands one to Ruby.)

DYLAN: Thanks a lot. Want me to get that plate for you—?

BROOKS: No, I'll eat later—I need to relax.

RUBY: Well, you come to the right place. It's so relaxing around here, you're like to fall asleep.

BROOKS: *(Amused.)* Tired of country life?

RUBY: What life? There's the mall and the dirt track. And skinny-dipping in the summer—that's the *real* big thrill.

BROOKS: …But it's beautiful country.

RUBY: Yeah, well, trees is trees.

BROOKS: Sounds like you're a city girl. Get down there much?

RUBY: Couple times on high school trips is all. My dad thinks it's the hell-and-damnationville.

BROOKS: He's not far wrong.

RUBY: I bet things are changing every minute down there.

BROOKS: Sometimes it kind of wears you out.

RUBY: Ain't nothing ever changes here, unless somebody's house burns down. I'll get to the city one of these days, and I ain't coming back.

BROOKS: You should check it out first.

RUBY: …Yeah, I guess…

BROOKS: If you decide to come down for a visit, call me. I could show you around a little.

RUBY: *(Hiding her amazement.)* Oh…well…thanks…

BROOKS: Here, I'll give you my card.

(Stunned silence as he takes out his wallet, opens it. Ruby and Dylan try not to stare at the money and credit cards as Brooks extracts a card, hands it to Ruby.)

BROOKS: Give me a few weeks notice, things are always hectic. But sure…the city seems pretty grim to me these days. It might be nice to see it through your eyes…

(Dylan wills Ruby to look at him. She stares into space and drinks beer. A moment of silence, then.)

BROOKS: Well. I've got more phone calls to make tonight. *(Hands Dylan his empty bottle, takes the deli food, and starts to exit.)* See you in the morning, Dylan—bright and early, right?

DYLAN: Right.

BROOKS: *(To Ruby.)* Will I see you, too?

DYLAN: Oh, no, no, she's not living here or anything…

(Ruby gives Dylan a cool look. Both men pick up on it.)

RUBY: *(To Brooks.)* No, I'm not living here or *anything.*

BROOKS: Ah. Well, see you, then.

(Brooks exits. Ruby swigs the dregs of beer, not meeting Dylan's look. He listens, makes sure Brooks is really gone, then.)

DYLAN: *(Softly.)* What was that?

RUBY: What was what?

DYLAN: "I'm not living here or *anything.*"

RUBY: Well, how 'bout you? Apologizing for me—

DYLAN: I was not apologizing, I was—

RUBY: Kissing his ass—

DYLAN: Like hell! I just, I need this job—

RUBY: Thought you was passing through.

(Brief pause.)

DYLAN: You're not gonna take him up on it, are you?

RUBY: Why not?

DYLAN: …What would you want to do that for?

RUBY: Why not?

(Dylan looks at her a beat, starts to turn away toward the house, holding the two bottles.)

RUBY: Dylan?

(He turns back. She hands him her empty bottle as if he's a servant. He takes it automatically, then has an uprush of anger—she laughs: Gotcha! Furious, he wheels to go out. She's on her feet, wraps her arms around him from behind, presses herself against him. Dylan freezes, then mimes a fierce over-the-shoulder movement of braining her with a beer bottle.)

RUBY: *(Laughing joyously.)* I don't know as I'd blame you.

DYLAN: ...Nobody'd blame me.

RUBY: *(Softly, nuzzling him.)* I just don't want you to go thinking this is easy.

DYLAN: No danger of that.

RUBY: Don't be mad. I chose you.

(Beat; Dylan slowly turns in her arms as she clings to him. Face to face.)

DYLAN: Ruby, what do you want from me?

RUBY: *(Passionately, full of hope.)* Take me with you! Get me out!

(He drops the bottles, kisses her wildly. She pulls him down to the floor, responding passionately.)

DYLAN: *(Making crazy love but still protesting.)* We can't—not here—he's right upstairs—

RUBY: *(Pulling his shirt off.)* ...I love you, Dylan...

(Dylan loses control, is making love to her with all his frustration and need. Crossfade to the Carrolls' yard. Mom and Julie stand at a small table with a big bowl of whole peaches on it. They're cutting up the peaches for a pie.)

JULIE: *(Hoping for reassurance.)* It ain't like Rafe has another girl. It ain't...it isn't like he doesn't care about me...I don't think...

MOM: Oh, no...

JULIE: But he doesn't listen. He doesn't even think about what I say.

MOM: I know it. That's just how they are. When I was a girl, and Marlin come looking out for me, he wouldn't do *nothing* I wanted. Wouldn't change his shoes for me. He'd come see me in his workboots, all gunked up with manure and mud...and he *wanted* me.

JULIE: *Yeah...so...how...?*

MOM: He was a handsome boy.

JULIE: He still is. Damn him anyway.

MOM: Marlin.

JULIE: ...Oh...

MOM: You don't see it now. But he was. And men around here, mostly they don't talk. But Marlin, he told stories good as I ever heard. And quick—he had a way of turning what you said around on you…but it wasn't mean then, it was…we had good times in them days. He built our house at night while he was working full days on the propane truck. He'd come home dog-tired and eat some supper and then start to work again, pouring cement or laying joists. Come dark, I'd hold the flashlight for him so he could see to work. Sometimes we'd be real close like that and he'd say, "Ceelie, put that flashlight down…"

(Julie is embarrassed—a parent talking about sex! Mom is away for a moment. Then.)

MOM: But stubborn. Stubborn. Wouldn't go out of his way…wouldn't take nothing back…not for me or nobody…till Ruby come along.

JULIE: Ruby…yeah.

MOM: Right from the first, she owned him. Making him go here and there, like she was driving team.*

JULIE: Wish I could do that even once—

MOM: You can't. You gotta be like Ruby and her dad. And we ain't like them.

(Crossfade to the yard of the old farmhouse. Dylan enters, carrying a heavy piece of furniture. He stops just onstage, sets it down, and rests. Julie exits. Mom enters the farmhouse area, watching Dylan from a little distance. She struggles against a violent impulse, loses, blurts.)

MOM: Hey, you.

DYLAN: *(Surprised.)* Oh, hi.

MOM: …What you doing?

DYLAN: Just hauling some furniture.

(Mom moves closer to Dylan, slowly, as if drawn.)

MOM: Looks like thirsty work.

DYLAN: Yeah…kinda hot already.

MOM: *(Can't help herself.)* Come on up to the house and have a cold drink.

DYLAN: *(Beat.)* The house?

MOM: Right up the road, there.

DYLAN: …You're Ruby's mom? Nice to meet you, Mrs. Carroll.

(He extends a hand. Mom slowly takes it.)

MOM: I'm Ceelie.

DYLAN: I'm Dylan.

MOM: I know. Pretty name.

(Mom stares down at their clasped hands, shyly, but can't let go. Dylan starts to feel that something else is going on here, and he's thrown. Gently, he extricates his hand as.)

---

* "Driving team" is an old country expression.

DYLAN: *(Delicately.)* Is Ruby…? Is she home or…?

MOM: *(Shy but tenacious.)* No. She's at work. So's her dad. It's real quiet up there. And cool, I keep the house dark when it's hot like this, so it stays nice and cool inside. I got cold things to drink.

(As always, Dylan is pulled toward giving someone what she wants. But he can't screw things up with Ruby and Brooks. As he hesitates, Brooks enters from the house with a mug of coffee. Mom instantly moves away from Dylan, who's relieved.)

DYLAN: *(To Mom.)* Well, thanks, but my boss needs me to help him out.

(Mom exits, in turmoil, relieved and disappointed.)

DYLAN: But really, thanks…sometime I'd really like that… *(Starts to pick up the piece of furniture.)*

BROOKS: Hold on a sec, I'll finish my coffee and give you a hand…who was that?

DYLAN: Ruby's mom.

BROOKS: Ah…sure didn't take you long to find the prettiest girl around. Ruby seems so sure of herself too…for someone that young…

DYLAN: …Yeah…

BROOKS: How old is she, do you know?

DYLAN: …She just got out of high school. Eighteen, seventeen, in there…

BROOKS: Eighteen? She'll be dangerous in a few years.

DYLAN: Dangerous?

BROOKS: But she's too young yet, and…well…rough around the edges.

DYLAN: *(Relieved.)* Oh, well, sure…

BROOKS: *(Abruptly.)* So if she does call me, I think I'll meet her in the city. Can't hurt, right?

DYLAN: *(Very thrown.)* …Sure…right…

BROOKS: I should probably talk to her parents about it. Let them know it's all highly respectable…I bet they watch her like a hawk.

DYLAN: I bet.

BROOKS: Do they?

DYLAN: Well…I don't know, really.

BROOKS: They'd be crazy not to.

(Dylan is afraid to assert his rights to Ruby, but he makes an effort.)

DYLAN: She's…we're seeing each other, you know…but…she'd make up her own mind anyway…..

BROOKS: She made that clear. Let's lug that thing inside.

(Brooks sets down his mug to help move the furniture as Rafe enters, intercepting Dylan.)

RAFE: *(Softly.)* You said you was gonna come and tell me when he showed up here.

DYLAN: *(Softly.)* He got in late last night. You didn't expect me to climb up there in the dark, did you?

RAFE: I do it all the time.

DYLAN: Well, look, don't…just take it easy, okay?

(Brooks joins Dylan. Rafe extends his hand to Brooks, they shake.)

RAFE: Rafe Carroll.

BROOKS: Evan Brooks. You're Ruby's brother?

RAFE: *(Looks at Dylan, back at Brooks.)* That's right, Mr. Brooks, and I'll get right to the point. Nothing against you, but I can't go along with my dad selling out the family land.

BROOKS: *(Beat.)* Your name's not on the title…?

RAFE: I don't have no legal rights. It goes beyond that.

BROOKS: …Oh. Well, I can see that you might feel—

RAFE: It ain't how I feel. It's what I'm gonna do. I'm gonna buy my own land back from you.

BROOKS: *(Beat.)* Do you know what I paid your father for this property?

RAFE: No, but it's gotta be more than I can raise just all at once. So I wanta start by buying this here meadow. I got a team of draft horses, big beautiful animals, I wanta turn 'em out to graze right here where they belong. So how much would you take for it?

BROOKS: For the meadow?

RAFE: Yeah. Clear up to the treeline.

BROOKS: I really couldn't sell it for less than a hundred thousand.

RAFE: *(Speechless. Finally.)* It ain't even twelve acres.

BROOKS: Right. But I haven't decided whether I'm going to live on this property or develop it—

RAFE: Develop it?

BROOKS: There's great potential. If I had a big pond dug, built three, four at the most, houses around the pond…upscale housing, cedar decks, local bluestone chimneys…

RAFE: You can't sell houses now. Every highway and back road is nothing but "For Sale" signs!

BROOKS: In the long run, land values only rise. You just have to wait the rough times out. Your dad sold at a bad time. But I couldn't make the same mistake.

RAFE: So you're gonna stick to that. A hundred thousand.

BROOKS: That would be rock-bottom. And I'd have to be sure that however *you* develop it, it would increase the value of the rest of my property—

RAFE: I ain't gonna develop beans. I'm gonna leave it whole.

BROOKS: Well, you'll use it for something, won't you?

(Rafe can't believe he has to explain to this stranger. He looks at Dylan, meets a blank wall. Long beat; then.)

RAFE: Graze my horses.

BROOKS: So you'd have to fence it.

RAFE: ...Sure...tall, stout fence...water trough...little stable, for the weather. Outside the fence, prob'ly put a garden in. Out toward the rise there...maybe in a couple years, put a house up there...

BROOKS: Well, all that might be charming, or it might be an eyesore, depends on how you do it. As I said, I'm sympathetic, but this is what I do, and I can't do it badly just to make you feel better. I'm sure *you* understand *that*.

RAFE: *(Beat.)* To a point, I do.

BROOKS: Sorry, Rafe. Look, I'll make you a deal. You raise the money and draw up a specific proposal of how you'd use the land, and we'll talk about it. Okay? *(Claps Rafe on the back. To Dylan.)* Let's go. Heave-ho.

(Brooks and Dylan exit with the furniture. Crossfade to Ruby and Darlene, walking toward McDonald's across a parking lot. They carry their bags, wear their caps at rakish angles. Darlene is fervently smoking in the last moments before she'll have to stub it out. Ruby is thinking of Dylan and half-listening to Darlene.)

RUBY: ...You shoulda called the cops on him.

DARLENE: Oh, sure! Then how'd I raise the money to bail him out? Go around all begging to everybody who don't have no money anyway...or not for Dale, they don't...I know I oughta dump him, I know you're gonna say that, but...

RUBY: ...You gotta do what you gotta do.

(Puzzled, Darlene looks at her. Hoping to hook her interest.)

DARLENE: You shoulda seen Lisa last night at the Lounge. She's got some french-fried nerve. Had her big old butt squeezed into them tight, shiny bicycle pants. And her hair looked like a rat sucked it.

RUBY: ...Lisa ain't so bad.

DARLENE: Since when? Since you got tired of Lance?

(Lance appears, following Ruby and drinking a beer in a paper bag.)

RUBY: *(Indifferent.)* They'll prob'ly be real good together. "Lance and Lisa," I can see it on the matchbooks.

DARLENE: Ruby, what the hell? Where *are* you?

(Ruby's smile gives her away. Lance slowly comes nearer. He wants her to see him.)

RUBY: I just feel good is all.

DARLENE: My ass! It's that whoever-whatsit you been seeing without admitting nothing lately—what's his name? When do I get to meet him?

(Ruby is laughing, shushing her. She looks around, sees Lance, squeezes Darlene's arm.)

DARLENE: Ow! Shit! What—? *(Sees Lance.)*

RUBY:	DARLENE:
Hi, Lance.	Hey, Lance, how's it hangin'?

LANCE: So what's his name?

RUBY: ...Say what?

LANCE: Don't bother. I seen you in the woods with him.

(Ruby is embarrassed, but clings to her cool.)

DARLENE: Lance, we gotta get into work—

LANCE: So git.

(Darlene hesitates. Ruby shrugs. Darlene stubs out her cigarette. To Ruby but warning Lance.)

DARLENE: The manager's prob'ly watching through the window there, you better hurry up.

(Darlene exits. Beat.)

RUBY: So you've seen me with him. So?

LANCE: You can't treat me like shit—

RUBY: I don't owe you nothing.

LANCE: Bullshit!...You was damn glad to be with me till he came along. And I ain't no different. I'm still kicking ass at the dirt track every Saturday and taking home that prize money—

RUBY: It ain't just him. I grew up, that's all.

(Lance has a violent impulse to sock her. She sees it and flinches. They both glance toward the McDonald's windows.)

RUBY: The manager sees you drinking, he'll come out and run you off—

LANCE: Just let him try, I'll kick his fucking head in. *(Brief pause. Almost an appeal.)* I got a sponsor, Ruby.

RUBY: Who?

LANCE: Quincy's Tavern. They're gonna back me to move up to the half-mile track. And if I make it there, I can go out on the circuit! No more dragging some old wreck outa the woods and building her from the ground up, just so's I could race...knowing I never had no chance at the half-mile track, 'cause the high-dollar cars'd win it even if them guys couldn't drive a nail...A custom-built car, Ruby! Gonna go to driving school and learn all them techniques I can't learn on my own, 'cause nobody I ever seen up close knows shit...now I can show what I can do!

RUBY: *(Impressed.)* Well, that's great.

LANCE: And you're the one kept telling me I had to move up or die. Well, now I'm moving up. And you can come along. You can travel with me. Go down to Florida in the winter for the nationals—

RUBY: You sure about this, Lance? You seen their money yet?

LANCE: …We shook on it. They can't go back on me.

RUBY: Well…I mean, Quincy's Tavern, they ain't much. How they gonna come up with enough money for all that stuff? You're hanging your hat on a small peg if you think—

LANCE: Shut up, now!…That's your old man talking in your mouth, that ain't you talking, Ruby. *(Touching her gently.)* …If you stood by me…Ruby…I think about you—

RUBY: *(Shrugging him off.)* Don't. Just don't think about me. Any day now, I'll be outa here. And Lisa, she'll be good for you.

LANCE: You ain't going nowhere.

RUBY: *(Beat; coolly.)* I ain't afraid of you.

(She turns to go. He grabs her arm, hurting her. She gasps, is motionless as Lance, behind her, moves in close.)

LANCE: What if I had my gun?

(Darlene races out, in uniform, screaming.)

DARLENE: LANCE, YOU GET ON OUTA HERE, THE MANAGER'S CALLING THE COPS! *(Tries to pry Lance's hand off Ruby's arm.)* Come on, I ain't kidding, the cops're coming—

(Lance shoves Darlene away, scaring her. Still holding Ruby, he kisses the back of her neck, lets go of her, and exits.)

DARLENE: Jesus! Did he hurt you?

RUBY: *(Shaken, shakes her head no.)* …Was everybody watching?

DARLENE: Are you kidding? Them golden-agers like to fall outa their chairs! You're gonna have a bruise—I know. Listen, you need a drink, and I got that peach schnapps hid in by the frying vats—

RUBY: *(Shakes her head no.)* …Let's get on in.

(They head offstage. Crossfade to Rafe's camp, night. Rafe and Dylan are sitting by the fire.)

RAFE: First time my dad took me hunting, I was twelve years old. We come up here to camp, the two of us, and we took our guns and went deep into the woods. Dad sat on a big rock, so I sat beside him. And we sat there, holding our guns, and ready. Seemed like hours. Dad didn't move a muscle, so I didn't either. Got real hungry, had to piss bad—but I didn't move. *(Beat.)* Then I seen her, a big pretty doe, maybe thirty yards away.

She was coming through the brush and walking straight at us, with that almost floating look they got on them twiggy legs, but you can see the strength in 'em too...Dad, he didn't move. And then I seen another doe behind her, and another, and another, coming toward us in a line, like we'd called 'em to us. But Dad still didn't move. *(Beat.)* I was getting wild inside, sweating through my clothes—wild to get a clear shot while I had at least a chance of getting my first deer, showing Dad what I could do. But he was so still, I couldn't even feel his breathing, up close against him like I was, and I couldn't do nothing but what he would do...till there was thirteen doe coming toward us, and the closest one I swore was gonna come right up to me and nuzzle me for sugar...and Dad still didn't move. *(Beat.)* And then he moved so quick, I hadn't hardly felt him move 'fore I heard his gun crack out and seen that big buck fall—that big six-pointer coming at the end of the line of doe, like Dad knowed he would do. He got him. I seen him fall. Them doe were scattering everywhere, and we just watched 'em go. I said, "You got him, Dad!" And my dad said, "Well, I did, didn't I?" *(Long beat; then.)* After that...I was wild to go hunting... hunting with my dad.
  (Brief pause.)
DYLAN: Yeah, that's...I never looked at it that way...that's cool...
RAFE: *(Beat.)* 'Preciate you coming up to see me. Mostly folks don't bother.
DYLAN: Oh, no, hey, I can really see this. I love being in the woods.
RAFE: Me too. I like the sounds. That's why I ain't got a radio. Or a clock nei-
  ther. Tell time by the sun. Close enough. *(Brief pause.)* Want some more of
  that brie cheese?
DYLAN: No, thanks. It's good, though.
RAFE: It ain't too bad with Ritz Crackers.
  (Pause.)
DYLAN: Ruby said you've got a girlfriend.
RAFE: Well, she don't come up here if she's got her stockings on...She's going
  out, some. Playing the field.
  (Brief pause.)
DYLAN: So what do you guys do at night around here? Besides this, I mean.
  Ruby says there's nothing, but there's gotta be *something*, right?
RAFE: If you drink...you drink.
DYLAN: ...Uh-huh...
RAFE: Go to the V.I.P. Lounge...play pool...or there's the dirt track...
DYLAN: Yeah, I'd like to check that out.
RAFE: It's loud.

(Pause. Dylan waits. That's it.)

DYLAN: I was kind of wondering…the nights are getting cold already. Are you going to try to stay up here in winter…or…?

RAFE: *(Long beat; then.)* My dad told me about one time my granddad drove a team up here when the snow was so deep, it took him half a day to make it to the cabin. And it was deep cold too. But Granddad come ahead, 'cause he was gonna meet his crew and help 'em do some logging. And my dad come along. He was just a kid. He said it was so durn cold, he was afraid he'd freeze to death sitting in the wagon, but he knew my granddad and he never said a word. When they made it up here, wasn't nobody around logging. Come to find out, the crew was all huddled up inside the cabin, burning all the wood. Said it was too durn cold to work. Granddad was so disgusted, he took and threw a load of wood up on the wagon, told my dad to climb aboard, and they went right straight back.

(Pause. Blam! Sound offstage of a high-powered rifle shot. Rafe hits the ground.)

RAFE: Get down!

(Dylan hits the ground. Another shot.)

RAFE: *(Yells toward the sounds.)* HEY, THERE'S FOLKS UP HERE, QUIT SHOOTING!

(Silence. Pause. Rafe starts to rise. Another shot, closer. He hits the ground again.)

RAFE: HEY, GET THE FUCK OUTA HERE!!!

(They listen. Sound of branches breaking underfoot.)

DYLAN: He's not going away.

RAFE: Some asshole trying to prove something…

(Rafe pulls himself along the ground to his gear, unearths his rifle. Another shot, closer yet.)

DYLAN: Jesus, who *is* that guy? Think maybe some psycho escaped from the prison?…Or has someone got a grudge against you…?

RAFE: Just my dad.

(Dylan laughs nervously, then screams as Lance roars into camp, wildly drunk, whooping and waving his high-powered hunting rifle. He falls over Rafe and Dylan, gets entangled with them. His rifle smacks the ground hard and goes off—a deafening Blam! Stunned silence, then.)

LANCE: *(Laughing.)* …Whoa, shit…

RAFE: *(Grabs the gun.)* "Shit?!"…You…you…shit-for-brains!! What the fuck are you doing here?!

LANCE: I just miscounted, I thought it was empty—chill out, you ain't hurt none...

(Rafe checks—now the gun is empty. He throws it on the ground, grabs Lance, enraged.)

RAFE: Don't you never...don't you never in your life...come around my camp again with a loaded gun...!

LANCE: Let go of me, don't fucking tell me—gimme back my gun—

RAFE: *(Violently shaking Lance.)* Don't you never...you hear me? You hear me? You hear me?

LANCE: *(Shocked and too drunk to fight.)* Okay, shit, let go...

(Rafe hurls him away. Lance staggers, almost falls, stares at Rafe. So does Dylan. Long moment as Rafe fights for control, then.)

RAFE: This is *my* place. Don't you *never*...Get outa here.

(Lance stares at Rafe, disbelieving, then looks at Dylan, recognizes him. Dylan doesn't know Lance, meets his look, surprised.)

RAFE: *Get out!*...And don't come back till I ask you.

LANCE: Fuck you. And fuck your sister too.

(Rafe jumps him—they go down. Rafe savagely pummels Lance. Dylan leaps on them, tries to pull Rafe off.)

DYLAN: Rafe! Rafe, he's drunk, he didn't mean it, come on, stop now...!

(Dylan wrestles Rafe off Lance—they roll away. Lance doesn't move...finally stirs and shakily sits up. Dylan goes over and tries to help Lance up. Lance shoves him away, unsteadily gets to his feet, picks up his gun, almost falling over, and looks at Rafe, who is still struggling to control his rage.)

LANCE: Some fucking friend.

RAFE: Not no more.

LANCE: ...Fine by me. Fucking head case. *(Starts woozily out.)*

RAFE: I've got a gun too, Lance. You come up here again with a loaded gun, I'll shoot you.

LANCE: *(Stops.)* You're alone, asshole. Ask Ruby. You're alone.

(Lance exits. Crossfade as Rafe and Dylan exit and Dad enters with his chair and a can of beer. He sits, drinks beer. To the audience.)

DAD: Now I'll just say one thing and then I'll shut up. There are some folks in this world, if they wake up in the morning and they can see dollar signs, it's a good day. And if they can't, it ain't.

(Dad drinks. Lights up on Ruby and Dylan, wearing jackets and sitting on a blanket in the woods, wrapped up in each other.)

RUBY: You can smell the winter coming out here in the woods.

DYLAN: ...Yeah.

DAD: Now you take Rafe and Evan Brooks…there's a pair to draw to. Them two were at loggerheads, and they were bound to be. 'Cause when it come to dollar signs, them two were day and night.

RUBY: Well, ain't it time?

DYLAN: …We got it pretty good here.

RUBY: *(Stunned.)* …What?…

DYLAN: …Winter is a lousy time to be on the road. We can stay nice and warm right here… *(Tries to cuddle her.)*

RUBY: Dylan, I ain't gonna sit around for another winter!

DAD: But, you know, at basics, them two were the same. Neither of 'em could sit still, put their feet up, have a drink—leave it for a while. Hell, no. One of 'em was busy doing nothing, and the other one was busy doing nothing yet.

DYLAN: Okay, look, I don't see moving on when we've got a great opportunity right here—

RUBY: Like what!

DYLAN: Evan Brooks. He's got a lot of money—all these properties, investments, he's partners in all kinds of things—your family's land is nothing compared to what he's got.

(Ruby is upset, off-center: Where's this leading them?)

DAD: Rafe, now…he was out there every day, sunup to sundown, with them draft horses, training 'em to do the chores like in Granddad's day. He took and bought a sawmill, one of them that's movable, you sit it on a flatbed and bring the sawmill to the logs. I seen him hauling it with his team of horses, right down the two-lane highway that's the onliest main road from here to anywhere, and stuck behind him was a whole long train of trucks and high-wheelers and rice-burners and macaroni-burners and krautmo-biles them city folks like to drive up here. And do you think that boy would turn out, let them folks go by? Hell, no! He was holding up the whole parade and he liked it that way! Now, Brooks would do that too. Far as them two are concerned, they *are* the whole parade.

DYLAN: So we've got to wait, Ruby. We've got to play this out.

RUBY: But we don't need his money if we get outa here!

DYLAN: With what? Do you have any money?

RUBY: …What I've been saving up lately…a couple hundred dollars.

DYLAN: I don't even have that.

(She stares at him, devastated.)

DAD: But here's the difference, and you listen to what I'm telling ya. Every day's a good day for Brooks, 'cause all's he sees is dollar signs every blessed day. But Rafe…you could put them dollar signs in his food, he'd spit 'em out and rinse his mouth out. *(Calls Offstage.)* CEELIE, COME ON OUT HERE AND BRING THAT WHISKEY!

(As Ruby and Dylan continue, Mom enters with the whiskey bottle and shot glass, moves slowly toward Dad. Lights dim on them, leaving them in silhouette, as Mom gives Dad the glass and bottle, stands behind his chair.)

RUBY: You tricked me! You never meant to travel with me—

DYLAN: No, I did, I thought that's what we'd do, at first...but...

RUBY: Have you ever even been to any of those places?

DYLAN: *(Sadly.)* Oh, yeah...you don't know...

RUBY: That town in Mexico with the old hotel and the birds...did you make that up?

DYLAN: ...No...there is a town...there is an old hotel...

(Both try to reconnect, language as love-making.)

RUBY: ...this old hotel in the square, with a marble fountain...

DYLAN: ...and the birds, flying south in winter...

RUBY: ...when they come to fly through this little town in Mexico...

DYLAN: ...the old hotel is in their path...

RUBY: ...and they fly right in through the open windows...

DYLAN: ...this stream of birds with beating wings...

RUBY: ...and out the other side again...oh, I want to be there! If we go now, maybe we could see them—

DYLAN: *(Pulling her close.)* Ruby, listen, please, please...I'm so tired of hitchhiking. It's so much effort, talking to strangers all day long...letting them think you're anybody they want you to be. I'm sick of starting over...begging for jobs that turn my stomach...sleeping anywhere a stranger'll let me have a bed, a floor—

RUBY: A bed...alone?

DYLAN: ...Sometimes.

(Brief pause.)

RUBY: I would never do that with somebody I didn't love.

DYLAN: *(Simply.)* You don't know what you'll do. *(A moment, then.)* I can't go back to that. I love living here. It's beautiful... it's clean...I feel so happy here, like I'm finally home...like I'm part of the family that built this house and cared for it and filled it for so many years—

RUBY: *(Bewildered.)* But that's my family—

DYLAN: It was. But your family didn't value it. They gave it up. And Brooks— he doesn't give a damn—I'm the one who holds the house together, who works the land—look at my hands, look at the cuts and callouses and bruises, and you can see *I am* this place! We belong here, Ruby. If we just give Brooks what he wants, he'll—

RUBY: "What he wants?" You mean say yes to everything, like you do?

DYLAN: …Not everything.

RUBY: Like when you hitchhike, Dylan? Is that what you want me to do?

DYLAN: *(Afraid of what he might have meant.)* No! I'm just saying—

RUBY: I won't be beholden to Brooks or nobody! He can ask *me* for favors, I ain't asking him!

DYLAN: Oh, Jesus, Ruby, please don't mess this up for me…

RUBY: *(Attacks him, pounding on him.)* You stop all this! You stop! You stop!

(Dylan grabs her, holds her. She struggles, then starts to cry, lets him hold her. Crossfade down to silhouette: Ruby and Dylan, Mom and Dad. Spot on Rafe. To the audience.)

RAFE: When you go inside the gate, they lock the gate behind you. And when you go inside a door, they lock the door behind you. Pretty soon you're locked so far inside, it's like being underground. And you can't get out. *(Brief pause.)* You think about the air a lot. Feels like there ain't enough. Thousands of men inside them walls, and it's all sealed up. Locked windows with bars on 'em, and all them tight-locked doors. And the ceiling's pressing down on you. Feels like it's hard to breathe. *(Brief pause.)* When your shift's over, they let you free for that little while. But the whole time you're outside, sucking in the clean air and looking at the sky, you got this tightness in your chest and this pressure above your eyes like something pressing down on you, 'cause you gotta go back. You don't want to go to sleep, 'cause that'll bring the time closer when you'll walk through them gates again. And you do, you got to. *(Brief pause.)* Every time you hear them locks start to turn behind you, you want to scream out something and hurl them doors open and run. But you can't. You're in there, you're living in there, like the cons. Only difference is, they know when they're getting out. 'Cause you gotta stay in there long enough to buy your land. And ain't no way of knowing yet how long that'll be.

(The silhouettes have slowly faded to black. Lights up on Dad at center, wearing a light jacket and raising a full shot glass.)

DAD: Here's to all you lovely people. "As good as you are, I'm as bad as I am. And as bad as I am, I'm as good as you are."

(Dad tosses off the shot as Mom, Rafe, Julie, Ruby, and Dylan enter, in jackets or sweaters, with beers and a Coke for Rafe and a few lawn chairs, Dad's placed at center.)

DAD: *(Notes Rafe's Coke can. To Rafe.)* Come on now, I hardly ever see ya, have a real drink, for Chrissakes.

RAFE: I'll stick with this.

MOM: *(To Dad.)* You told me if I had him over, you wouldn't get at him—

DAD: *(Mildly.)* Aw, hush up, woman. *(To Rafe.)* Your ma tells me you're working up to the prison now.

RAFE: That's right.

DAD: Well, that's a man's job, I respect that.

RAFE: I'm just doing it 'cause I got to.

DAD: Well, that's what I'm saying.

RAFE: Gotta have a steady job to get a mortgage.

DAD: ...What the hell you doing now?

RAFE: I ain't changed.

DAD: ...Boy, are you telling me you're gonna pay a bloodsucker's interest on land that this family owned free and clear six months ago?

RAFE: If that's what it takes.

DAD: You just ain't gonna face it that that land is lost to you.

RAFE: It ain't till I say it is.

DAD: ...You...are the orneriest, pigheadedest, dug-in-deepest son of a bitch that I ever heard of.

RAFE: Prob'ly so.

DAD: *(Breaks into a smile.)* Well, good for you, boy! You want it, you go after it!

RAFE: *(Stony.)* That's what I'm doing.

(Mom has been covertly drifting toward Dylan.)

MOM: Dylan, you like that pie? There's more.

DYLAN: Oh, no, thanks—it was great, though, thanks.

DAD: *(Abruptly, to Dylan.)* Where you from, boy?

DYLAN: ...No place special.

DAD: Where's your kinfolks?

DYLAN: ...Spread around.

DAD: Don't see 'em?

DYLAN: No, sir.

DAD: So you don't call no place home?

DYLAN: ...This is home for now.

RUBY: We're gonna travel.

(Dylan looks at Ruby. They're still fighting over this—why is she bringing it up now?)

DAD: Oh, you are. Using what for money?

RUBY: You and me gotta talk about that private.

DAD: Oh you say so, do you? *(Slaps his knee.)* Come on over here and sit.

    (Everyone is stunned by the implications. Ruby sits on Dad's lap, picks up the bottle, and pours him a stiff shot. Mom takes Ruby's seat by Dylan, who is watching Ruby.)

DAD: *(To Dylan.)* What you got to offer, boy?

DYLAN: …I'm a hard worker, sir.

DAD: Rafe here is the hardest goddamn worker in the county. What's it got him?

RAFE: I can stand to look in the mirror every morning.

DAD: Aw hell, you ain't even got a mirror. *(To Dylan.)* Rafe here is my boy, and pigheaded as he is, I stand by him because he's mine. But I never made nothing easy for him in his life, no more'n my dad did for me.

DYLAN: I'm not asking for help from you.

DAD: Well, good. Then who is.

    (Brooks enters. Everyone is flustered. Ruby jumps up, Dad rises.)

DAD: Well, looky here! Come on in, neighbor—

BROOKS:	DAD:
Hello, everybody—didn't know I was interrupting a party—call me Evan, please —I can't stay, I—I'm not much for drinking—	Ruby, get a beer for Mr. Brooks—or would you have a *real* drink with me?

DAD: Beer ain't drinking, Evan. Had your supper yet?

    (Ruby hands Brooks a beer. He smiles at her, takes it, and glances at Dad.)

BROOKS: Uh, well, enough that…really, I just had an impulse…I'm driving back to the city in about an hour, and I wondered if Ruby…if you wouldn't mind if Ruby came along for a visit.

    (Dead silence. Everyone looks at Ruby, who tries to seem nonchalant. Mom murmurs in Dylan's ear.)

MOM: You see how she is?

DAD: *(Speechless for once.)* …What…you…what?

BROOKS: Ruby was telling me a while back that she'd like to see the city. And I have a big place. Guest rooms and all that. Comforts of home, you know. I thought you might feel safer with somebody you know looking after her.

DAD: *(Instantly.)* Oh, no question. *(Beat; trying to assess this.)* Well…Ruby…?

    (Ruby won't look at Dylan. She loves this high drama. Suddenly she smiles at Brooks.)

RUBY: Why not?

DYLAN: What about your job?

DAD: Oh, we'll take care of that.

BROOKS: Well, fine, then I'll swing by for you in about an hour… *(Smiles at her, catches himself; to Dad.)* Thanks for the beer. *(To Mom as he goes.)* Bye-bye.

MOM: *(Quietly.)* Bye-bye.

(Brooks goes out. When he's out of earshot, Ruby starts out, passing Dad.)

RUBY: Well, I better figure out what clothes to take—

DAD: Private talks, eh? I *guess* you've been having some private talks. *(To Dylan.)* You better have another beer, son. Ain't no keeping up with her.

(Dylan bolts offstage. Ruby's scared, but too stubborn to go after him.)

RUBY: *(To Dad.)* I'm not changing. I'm just making sure.

DAD: Listen. My girl deserves the best. Didn't I always say so? Just don't get pig-headed like your brother. If you really got a chance…you're a smart girl. Be smart.

(Ruby looks at Mom.)

MOM: If I was your age, I'd go after him. And I'd get him, too.

(Dad laughs, enjoying this sexy side of Mom. Ruby looks at Rafe.)

RAFE: *(Simply.)* He could change everything for me.

RUBY: We don't even know what he wants yet.

DAD: *(Slaps her on the butt.)* Well, go find out, girl!

(Ruby laughs, trying for bravado, exits. Dad looks at Mom, who avoids his look and exits. Dad follows, leaving Rafe with Julie.)

JULIE: She's gonna get it all, ain't she? I'd like to kill her.

RAFE: Easy now.

JULIE: You're crazy if you think she'll help you.

RAFE: Maybe…maybe not.

(Rafe and Julie exit. Crossfade to the sunny Carroll kitchen. Mom sits on a chair beside a laundry basket, folding laundry on her lap. Dylan enters. He's showing the strain since Ruby left with Brooks.)

DYLAN: Hi, Mrs. Carroll—Ceelie.

(Shaken, Mom can't speak.)

DYLAN: Sorry to bother you…I just, you know, came by to see if—

MOM: *(Rises, overlapping.)* You ain't bothering…come on in, come in.

DYLAN: Oh, thanks. I just was wondering if Ruby's back yet—

MOM: You want to sit down? *(Puts the folded laundry in the basket.)*

DYLAN: …Oh…well, that's okay…

MOM: You look tired. Sit down.

DYLAN: *(Sits.)* …I guess I kind of…

MOM: Look like you need a good night's sleep.

DYLAN: …Yeah, I'm not…

MOM: And a good meal. What you been eating over there?

DYLAN: …Oh, you know…

MOM: I'll fix you a plate. *(Starts out.)*

DYLAN: Oh no, don't bother—

MOM: It won't take a minute. We got a microwave. I'll fix you something, then we'll talk— *(Starts out again.)*

DYLAN: No! I mean, it's really nice of you but I…I've gotta get back to work…

MOM: You work too hard. Time he gets back, Brooks won't even notice all you done.

DYLAN: Did Ruby call? Do you know when they're getting back?

MOM: No. She'll do how she wants. And we all gotta step in line.

DYLAN: *(Beat.)* Don't you like her?

MOM: …She's mine. I got a pride in her. But she always done like that. *(Cautiously lays her hand on his back, "comforting" him. Quietly.)* She done it with her father, with every man she come upon. And when I seen her looking at you on the road, first day you was up this way, I knew what she'd do. She'd make you follow in her path. And she'd be careless of you. *(Pause.)*

DYLAN: *(Very upset, rises.)* I gotta go. Could you let me know if she calls?

MOM: *(Gently.)* Sure. But she won't. That ain't Ruby.

DYLAN: *(Not knowing what else to say.)* …Well…thanks…

(He exits. Mom watches him with longing. Crossfade to Rafe's campsite, night. It's cold. Rafe and Julie sit by the fire on a sleeping bag. Rafe's rifle is nearby, broken open for safety. Rafe is coaxing Julie to make love.)

JULIE: Rafe…

RAFE: Ssshhh…

(He kisses her. She breaks it.)

JULIE: It's cold. Are you gonna get yourself a real place to live or not? We can't keep doing like this, and you got a good job now—

RAFE: I'm gonna stay right here as long as I can. It's rugged. But the more money I save, the quicker I can buy that land.

JULIE: The meadow.

RAFE: Yeah. And after that, maybe the long field—

JULIE: "After that?" He wants a hundred thousand for that pukey little meadow! How much is he gonna want for the long field?

RAFE: I can't worry about that yet—

JULIE: For a hundred thousand dollars, you can buy a working farm, right here in this county, with a house and a barn and—

RAFE: I don't want them farms. This is my land. I'm meant to have it, Julie. You gotta back me up on this. We'll…we'll work things out about *us*…

JULIE: I give up, Rafe.

RAFE: …Don't give up…

JULIE: I am. Don't come around. I mean it.

RAFE: *(Beat.)* Up to you. I'll miss you.

> *(Julie slaps him, hard. He stares, amazed, then grabs her arm, anger flying up.)*

RAFE: Don't you never do that again.

JULIE: No, I won't. I won't care enough.

> *(She exits. Slowly, Rafe sits, stares at the fire. Silence. Then noises are heard in the brush.)*

RAFE: *(Rises.)* Julie? *(Waits. No reply.)* JULIE, ANSWER IF THAT'S YOU!… WHO'S OUT THERE? *(No reply; grabs his gun, fires a warning shot.)*

DYLAN: *(Offstage.)* HEY, IT'S DYLAN!

RAFE: *(Lowers the gun.)* COME AHEAD!

> *(Dylan enters, carrying a much-used duffel bag. He's in a shaky state, and the shot didn't help. He stops, looks at Rafe and the gun.)*

RAFE: I'm careful now, is all.

> *(Dylan nods, pulling himself together. Rafe breaks open the gun. Then.)*

RAFE: Ruby back?

DYLAN: …No…no… *(Long beat; with an effort.)* I haven't heard from her.

RAFE: …Huh. *(Beat.)* Want a Coke?

DYLAN: *(Long beat.)* Listen. *(Longer beat.)* I found something.

> *(Dylan squats, opens the duffel bag, takes out a cardboard box. Rafe lays the gun down. Dylan holds the box for a beat, then holds it out to Rafe. Rafe looks at Dylan, takes the box, squats, sets the box down carefully. He opens it gently, looks in for a long moment. He looks at Dylan. Then he lifts out some long bones, holds them up in the firelight.)*

DYLAN: I was digging. Planting trees. Between the farmhouse and the road.

RAFE: *(Examining the bones.)* Don't look like any animal bones I've ever seen. You found 'em by the farmhouse?

DYLAN: *(Nods.)* It's your family's land. I thought…

RAFE: You brung 'em to me. That was right. *(Rafe puts the bones gently back in the box, and closes it, shaken but trying not to show it.)* No way of telling who it is or how they got there.

DYLAN: No way *we* can tell.

RAFE: …I'll bury 'em up here.

> *(Dylan nods. Rafe holds his gaze, then.)*

RAFE: 'Preciate it.

> *(They both rise.)*

DYLAN: I need help from you.

RAFE: You got a right now. But if it's Ruby, I can't side with you.

DYLAN: Brooks is never gonna give you what you want!

RAFE: He don't have to give it to me, I'm earning it—

DYLAN: He doesn't care! About *anybody!* Not even Ruby.

RAFE: We don't know that yet. *(Beat; gently.)* You don't gotta get caught in this. I'd move on if I was you.

DYLAN: I can't…I can't move on.

(Rafe looks at him with empathy. But he makes a helpless gesture like his mother's.)

RAFE: I'll go get the spade.

(Rafe exits. Dylan watches; then in a wild impulse, he grabs Rafe's gun and runs out. Crossfade to the Carrolls' yard. Mom stands in the darkness, gazing toward the farmhouse, thinking of Dylan. Dad enters from the shadows, puts his arms around her. He's a little drunk.)

DAD: …Ceelie…what are you doing out here in the dark? Come on to bed, girl.

MOM: …I'll sit up a while.

DAD: Aw hell, why should them kids have all the fun? *(Nuzzling her.)* "Ceelie, put that flashlight down…"

MOM: You're too drunk, Marlin. Don't waste my time.

DAD: *(Long beat; lets go of her.)* You sure got dried up fast.

(Dad slowly exits. Mom continues gazing out. Crossfade to the farmhouse porch. Darkness. Dylan has Rafe's gun, sits motionless. After a beat, Rafe enters cautiously. He can't see Dylan in the dark, but senses his presence. He stops, squats, ready to flatten himself if Dylan fires.)

RAFE: *(Gently.)* Dylan?

(Dylan jumps. The gun jumps but doesn't fire. Bent low, Rafe keeps moving as he speaks.)

RAFE: Okay, now…I come to get my gun.

(Rafe stops, flattens himself on the ground. He and Dylan are still. Then.)

RAFE: I don't know what you plan to do with it. *(Crouches, moving as he speaks.)* But ain't no harm done yet. You can just give it back to me. *(Rafe flattens himself again. No response.)* Come on, let's talk about it.

(No response. Rafe moves again, flattens. Faint light up on Mom behind the screen, only a few feet from Dylan, hiding inside the house. Scared, very still, she listens.)

RAFE: Dylan, now you know I can't let you do like this. *(Waits. No answer. Moves again.)* Okay, I'm gonna hafta go get help. I don't wanta do that. But I can't let you have that gun.

(Beat; Dylan raises the gun, points it toward Rafe. Rafe rises, bent low, moves

in a crooked route toward offstage. Dylan remains poised to shoot, following the faint sounds Rafe makes, till Rafe is gone. Then Mom speaks from her hiding place.)

MOM: I'm here.

(Dylan swings the gun in her direction, then lowers it, jumps up, very shaken.)

DYLAN: Ruby?

MOM: *(Comes onto the porch.)* Ceelie. I'm here.

DYLAN: Is Ruby back?

MOM: Dylan, she's with *him.*

(Shattered, Dylan just stands there. A still moment; then Mom moves to him, touches his face delicately. Desperate for contact and tenderness, he lets it happen. She's terrified but can't stop—she kisses him, touches him. Still clutching the gun, Dylan feels himself sinking, helpless.)

DYLAN: …I can't do that anymore. Please…go away…go home…

MOM: *(Passion rising.)* No, listen…I got money hid from him…I take it from his pockets when he's drunk…I never knew what I was gonna do with it… but I just had to hide it and count it up…you can have it…

DYLAN: That's not what I want. I've gotta have Ruby and I've gotta stay here in this house—

MOM: I'll get her back for you.

(Dylan is torn, bewildered: can she really do that?)

DYLAN: …You…you better get outa here…I don't know what's gonna happen…

MOM: You gotta do something, Dylan, or she's lost to you. And I know how to do with her…make her think she's losing something…she'll come running back…

(Mom kisses Dylan. He gives in, then pulls away, putting the gun between them.)

DYLAN: Get outa here, I told you!

MOM: But I'll help you, I'll do anything you—

DYLAN: Get away from me!

MOM: Oh, please, please—

DYLAN: Please don't make me hurt you—

MOM: I gotta have *something!*

DYLAN: *(Points the shaking rifle at her.)* Get out! Get out!

(Mom exits. Crossfade to the Carrolls' yard. Ruby and Brooks walk slowly toward the house. Brooks carries Ruby's suitcase. Ruby wears a new, moderately expensive jacket.)

RUBY: I love this jacket.

BROOKS: My pleasure. And we didn't go overboard, so hopefully it won't make your parents nervous.

RUBY: They won't care. I like your car, too.

BROOKS: You do, huh? Not too many of those in your neck of the woods… Looks like your folks are out.

RUBY: Them? They're asleep…I had a real good time.

BROOKS: Well, good. We'll do it again, if you're interested.

RUBY: Oh, I could live like that.

BROOKS: *(Amused.)* Takes money.

RUBY: You've got that part.

BROOKS: *(Laughs, but he's interested.)* Is this a proposal?

> *(Ruby gives a little ambiguous smile. Brooks stops walking, trying to read her. She stops too, but gives nothing away.)*

BROOKS: You'd be shocked if I took you up on it.

RUBY: Why?

BROOKS: …Well, you're seventeen—

RUBY: Eighteen. And you're not that much older.

BROOKS: …Well…there *is* a gap. Your life and mine combined…that's quite an image. I'd have to send you to college, for starters…But you're something, Ruby. I've got to be careful not to spend too much time around you. *(Beat; he gives in, moves to kiss her.)*

RUBY: I wouldn't give up Dylan for all your money.

BROOKS: *(Freezes, pulls back.)* …Really. I didn't see you as a romantic, Ruby. And I can't imagine Dylan will be able to keep you in the style you aspire to. Even with a second income from McDonald's.

RUBY: We're leaving anyway.

BROOKS: He hasn't told me.

RUBY: I just did.

BROOKS: *(Beat.)* I hurt your feelings, didn't I? I'm sorry, that was stupid of me—

RUBY: That's not why. *(Takes her suitcase.)* It was fun. Thanks.

> *(She kisses him, long enough to let him know what he'll be missing, and exits. He watches her. Crossfade to the farmhouse. Rafe and Dad approach very cautiously in the dark, with rifles.)*

DAD: *(Softly.)* Think he's waiting there for Ruby and Brooks?

RAFE: *(Softly.)* I dunno. Maybe not, maybe he won't hurt nobody—

DAD: We gotta make sure of that.

RAFE: You talk to him. Maybe he'll give the gun to you—

DAD: Maybe he'll shoot me too. Don't pull back now. I ain't gonna shoot unless I got to, but I need you to follow my lead here. Will you do that?

RAFE: Yeah.

DAD: That's why you came and got me, ain't it?

(Rafe takes this as a deep cut. Softly, they walk forward a few feet. Then.)

DAD: Stop here. Now stay pretty close. We don't want to fan out too much, might shoot each other.

RAFE: ...Right.

DAD: Wisht it wasn't so goddamn dark. *(Turns head to listen.)* Car coming. Might be them.

(Dad crouches, gun ready. Rafe follows his lead. Faint light maintains on Rafe and Dad. Lights up on Dylan, behind the screen door. Sounds of car arriving. Dylan listens, rifle held at his side. Headlights sweep across the porch, go out. Car sounds out. Dylan waits with every nerve. Faint light up on Ruby in another area, walking through the meadow in the dark. She's coming to Dylan but taking her time, feeling very happy and powerful, and humming the melody of "Mill o' Tifty's Annie." She looks up at the stars, stretches up as if to touch them, and turns slowly, starting to dance. Humming continues till indicated. Dylan speaks aloud the words he's been going over and over in his head for days.)

DYLAN: Mr. Brooks...I just want to ask you respectfully...see, Ruby and I are...Ruby means more to me, and we...we don't have any other place to go...and we belong here, Mr. Brooks...

(Brooks enters, calls from darkness.)

BROOKS: HEY, DYLAN! PUT THE PORCHLIGHT ON!

(Ruby's humming is the only sound. Behind the screen door, Dylan hesitates, then flicks an unseen switch. A pool of light falls on the porch. Dylan is clearly seen behind the door.)

DAD: *(Positioned to fire, mutters.)* There's his mistake, right there. You ready?

RAFE: Maybe he's just got that gun because he's scared.

DAD: Him or you?

(Trembling, Rafe raises his gun, stands ready. Brooks, with his briefcase, enters the porch. He steps into the light, throws a hand up to shield his eyes from the sudden glare.)

DYLAN: Mr. Brooks...where's Ruby?

BROOKS: *(Trying to be amused.)* Well, you won, Dylan.

DYLAN: ...What?

(Ruby hums and dances as Dylan opens the screen door and enters the porch, the rifle dangling in his hand.)

DYLAN: What did you say?

BROOKS: What's with the gun?

(As if he'd forgotten it, Dylan makes a dazed, explaining gesture that sweeps the

*rifle upward. Convulsively, Rafe fires. Dylan jerks backward and falls as Rafe
lets out a shocked cry and drops his gun.)*

DAD: *Goddamnit, you fired too soon!*

*(Blackout on all but Ruby, who has heard the shot, the cries. She stops, fright-
ened, then cries out.)*

RUBY: *Dylan!!*

(Ruby starts to run. Blackout.)

DAD'S VOICE: Well, Christ…for good or ill…you got him, son.

*(Country instrumental music picks up the song. As it fades, Lights up on Dad
and Rafe in one area, and Ruby and Mom in another area. Ruby lies in a heap
on the floor, face in her arms. Mom sits beside her, motionless, knowing that
she must comfort her but too desolate to do it. In the other area, Rafe, in shock,
sits on a kitchen chair. Dad has the shot glass and bottle, pours a hefty shot and
downs it. Spot up on Brooks. To the audience.)*

BROOKS: I wanted to call the troopers. To his credit, so did Rafe. But his father
was convinced that to keep Rafe out of prison, we had to handle it ourselves. And Rafe had saved my life…or meant to, anyway…so I left them
to it. I think they must have buried him where he had been planting
trees…not far from the house…Well, obviously, after that I couldn't even
go there. So I sold the property. I thought Rafe would want to buy the
meadow, and I would have felt compelled to sell it to him…probably…but
I never heard from him. Or Ruby either…Strange people.

(Lights down on Brooks.)

DAD: *(To Rafe.)* Oh, I know I had a part in it. And I gotta carry that. And I will.
I do. But you know, more than that, what I think is, that boy of Ruby's was
disturbed…twisted up inside, like a tree that's windshook. Sometimes you
take and cut a hemlock down that looks beautiful, tall and straight and
fine. But when you cut it open, it just falls apart. 'Cause it's been so twisted
and wrenched around by these winds up here in these mountains that the
grain can't hold together. The other trees can take it, but a windshook
tree…you take and cut it open, and it crumbles in your hands.

*(Dad pours another shot, offers it to Rafe, who doesn't even see it. Dad waits a
beat, drinks it himself. Crossfade slowly down on Ruby and Mom, up on
Darlene in another area.)*

DARLENE: I think I'm the only outside one who knows. Well, Ruby had to have
someone to talk to…acting all crazy like she was…I guess she knew I'd
understand how it coulda happened, 'cause Dale and me…I hate to think
it, 'specially 'cause of Ashley, but *we* could end up some way like that. Shit
happens…but then Ruby's dad give her some money and she left. Taking

the bus across the country, going to Mexico. She sent me a postcard, from some little town out west where they got folks dress up like cowboys and Indians and act out scenes, you know. That was the picture on the post-card. I woulda like to seen that show. But after that, nobody heard nothing… not even her mom and dad… And Rafe, I woulda thought he'd go away too, but he just kept going. Got a good promotion at the prison. Sold off them big old horses and rented that apartment above the hardware store, you know. Julie fixed it up real nice…come summer, they got married.

(Dad pours a third shot, holds it out to Rafe. Rafe doesn't move. Dad waits.)

But pretty soon, every weekend, Rafe'd be back up there at his campsite on that mountainside…trying to clear that land that was mostly rocks and trees. Wanted to build a cabin, somewheres around there where his granddad's cabin used to be.

(Lights down on Darlene. Beat; not looking at his father, Rafe takes and drinks the shot.)

END OF PLAY